Aaron Swartz (1986–2013) was an American computer programmer, a writer, a political organizer, and an Internet hacktivist. He was involved in the development of RSS, Creative Commons, web.py, and Reddit. He helped launch the Progressive Change Campaign Committee in 2009 and founded the online group Demand Progress. He is survived by his parents and two brothers, who live in Chicago.

Lawrence Lessig is Roy L. Furman Professor of Law at Harvard Law School. He was the director of the Edmond J. Safra Center for Ethics at Harvard University and a founding board member of Creative Commons. He lives in Cambridge, Massachusetts.

THE BOY WHO COULD CHANGE THE WORLD

THE WRITINGS OF AARON SWARTZ

AARON SWARTZ

With an introduction by
LAWRENCE LESSIG

THE NEW PRESS

NEW YORK
LONDON

Published in the United States by The New Press, New York, 2015
Distributed by Perseus Distribution

LIBRARY OF CONGRESS CATALOGING-IN-PUBLICATION DATA

Swartz, Aaron, 1986-2013.
   The boy who could change the world : the writings of Aaron Swartz / Aaron Swartz ; with an introduction by Lawrence Lessig ; part introductions by Benjamin Mako Hill, Seth Schoen, David Auerbach, David Segal, Cory Doctorow, James Grimmelmann, and Astra Taylor ; postscript by Henry Farrell.
      pages cm
   Includes bibliographical references and index.
   ISBN 978-1-62097-066-9 (paperback) — ISBN 978-1-62097-076-8 (e-book) 1. Internet—Social aspects. 2. Internet—Political aspects. 3. Intellectual property. 4. Copyright. 5. Computers--Social aspects. 6. Computer architecture. 7. Swartz, Aaron, 1986-2013—Political and social views. 8. Political culture--United States. 9. Popular culture—United States. I. Title.
   HM851.S97 2015
   302.23'1—dc23
                                    2015008414

The New Press publishes books that promote and enrich public discussion and understanding of the issues vital to our democracy and to a more equitable world. These books are made possible by the enthusiasm of our readers; the support of a committed group of donors, large and small; the collaboration of our many partners in the independent media and the not-for-profit sector; booksellers, who often hand-sell New Press books; librarians; and above all by our authors.

www.thenewpress.com

Book design and composition by Bookbright Media
This book was set in Aries and Gill Sans

Printed in the United States of America

10 9 8 7 6 5 4 3 2 1

CONTENTS

Politics

Media

INTRODUCTION

It is a fair question whether it's fair to any of us to gather in one place the writings of a person's life. Writing reflects thinking. Thinking evolves. Who we were at nineteen does not reflect who we were at twenty-five, or who we would have been at fifty. Learning looks like inconsistency. Changes seem unjustified, since they're rarely even acknowledged.

I'm sure Aaron Swartz in particular would have felt this as unfairness. When he was a student at Stanford, he attended a reception at the Stanford Law School, where I was then teaching. After introducing him to some friends, I recounted to them a recent post from his blog.

Afterward, Aaron was upset with me. "That was private," he said.

"But you posted it on your blog," I replied, a bit puzzled by the objection.

"Yes," he responded, "on my blog, for the people who read my blog. Not for the random student at the Stanford Law School."

But Aaron has left us no choice. We have a right to understand the extraordinary influence that this boy had, by understanding his words and thus his thought. And one way to do that is through his words. They are incomplete. They are sometimes inconsistent, as one essay struggles against another. But as I've read the collection gathered here, I recognize the soul who speaks through these writings. I remember these steps, and have learned more as I've walked through them again. There is a reason for us to reflect on these bits from an incomplete life. They teach us something. And they inspire.

From a very young age, Aaron felt a freedom that most of us never really know: the freedom to simply do what you believe is right.

That's not to say that most of us live life in the wrong. But most of us have a way of avoiding the confrontations between right and wrong. We learn early on how to fudge the facts, how to dodge the uncomfortable.

Aaron never quite learned that. Or if he did, he got rid of it when he was young. It isn't as though he was that guy preaching in the corner to the unwilling listener. He wasn't. He spoke through questions, not commands. He inspired by giving others a sense of the best they could be. And he often was super-quiet as he worked out what or whom to believe. A quiet kid among strangers. A deep blue pool, hiding a volcano.

But he was not quiet in his endless writings. And these writings capture well a mind in constant reflection: often aware of his advantage, always working through the politics of a society too mixed in its own advantages, and working endlessly to understand how best to understand and persuade.

In the essays collected here, you can watch a boy working on many problems at the same time. Like the CPU in a computer, different bits are in the foreground at different times. But every theme collected here was being worked on, if differently, at every point in the adult period (from about fourteen on) of this twenty-six-year-old's life.

He was constantly working on Aaron Swartz: on who that was, and how he was constrained. He was constantly working on technology: on how to make it work, and how to make it work better for people. He was constantly working on access: to culture, and particularly access to knowledge especially; to—the stuff that was supposed to be free. He was increasingly working in political philosophy: on how to know what was right, because he certainly had his views of right. He was especially working on progressive politics: the best ways to talk about issues from surveillance to Social Security, how to rally a public. And he read voraciously, fiction as well as nonfiction, reporting at the end of each year on the hundreds of books he had read that year, with a short review of each. And tragically, he was working on what he believed he had to do, the law notwithstanding. He rallied others to cross what he believed to be an unjust line. He crossed it himself.

No one should confuse these writings with revealed truth. Aaron had learned more than many ever will. He had worked out more than most. But there's an incompleteness here, which I know he saw, but which he imagined in the years ahead he would fill out. His technical skills had tripped him into financial freedom; he loved the range to think and act that that freedom gave him, because it gave him the chance to dig deeper, over time. And if there is one thing that I think terrified him the most about the prosecution that brought about the end of his life, it was the slow recognition that even if he had won his case against the government (which his lawyers at the end believed he would), he would be left without that freedom anymore. His fortune wasted, he would have been forced back into a world where he could no longer afford to live a life devoted exclusively to what he believed was right.

In the end, a work like this can only ever be a picture of a life incomplete. Few of us will ever come close to the influence this boy had. That's a puzzle to many. He was never on *The Colbert Report* or *The Daily Show*; *NBC Nightly News* never once covered the thoughts of Aaron Swartz.

Yet his influence weaved itself through the lives of an incredible number of very different souls. He found us, and, wound us up, and set us on the path that he, and maybe we, thought best. There are scores still left in his command. There is an endless amount that we must finish. For this writer, and thinker, and activist, and hacker, and dear friend, we will.

—Lawrence Lessig

FREE CULTURE

Aaron Swartz's life was shaped by an ethical belief that information should be shared freely and openly. Driven by this principle, Aaron worked extensively as a leader in the "free culture" movement, which is where we met him and worked closely with him for nearly a decade. From his earliest writings, included at the beginning of this section, Aaron was transfixed by the fact that a piece of knowledge, unlike a piece of physical property, can be shared by large groups of people without making anybody poorer. For Aaron, the clear implication of this fact was that it was unethical to deprive people of information by creating artificial scarcity in knowledge, culture, or information.

His early writing highlights the diversity of ways in which Aaron approached free culture advocacy. In some situations, he tried to work creatively within the system to reform copyright laws that limited free sharing. For example, Aaron's early writing about compulsory license schemes and his work with Creative Commons reflect attempts to address the injustice caused by "unfree" culture. We met Aaron through the 2003 Supreme Court oral argument in *Eldred v. Ashcroft*. At the time, Aaron was outraged that Congress had given in to industry pressures to make copyright last even longer, and he was thrilled to meet other activists working to limit copyright. With the loss in the Eldred case and other legal changes that increased the scope and power of copyright, Aaron was frustrated by the lack of progress in the free culture movement and increasingly adopted a more transgressive approach.

For example, in 2009 Aaron helped lead a project to download and publish public records about court cases that the federal courts charged substantial sums to access through the PACER system. This project spurred a criminal investigation, although he was never charged in the matter. The government's criminal case against him in the last two years of his life charged that Aaron had similarly downloaded a large number of academic journal articles with the aim of making these articles widely available to the public, regardless of whether they could afford to pay for access. In making its case about Aaron's motives, the government relied on Aaron's long history of writing about issues of free culture and open access and showed a particular interest in "Guerilla Open Access Manifesto," published in this section, which called for the liberation of academic knowledge that was locked up by commercial publishers.

In other work, Aaron's commitment to free culture led him to build and design systems to allow its collaborative production. In particular, he was inspired by the free software movement and its demonstration that commitment to an ethic of information sharing could, in practice, open the door to widespread collaboration with enormously valuable results, such as the GNU/Linux operating system and Wikipedia. In fact, Aaron created his own early predecessor to Wikipedia, called The Info Network, and wrote several essays describing other ideas for mass collaboration around other types of free cultural artifacts. Aaron's start-up Infogami—which merged with Reddit in 2005—was another such platform for collaboration and information sharing. After Aaron's own collaborative encyclopedia failed to gain traction, he became an early and active participant in Wikipedia. This section includes a series of essays that Aaron wrote in 2006 as part of his campaign to be elected a director of the Wikimedia Foundation, the organization that runs Wikipedia.

Aaron was committed to free culture in part because he believed that freely shareable knowledge could transform society for the better. In his earlier writings, he expressed a sense that the mere availability of factual data could be empowering. In 2008, Aaron founded Watchdog.net, an organization that attempted to promote increased government transparency by making government data more widely available. Over time, however, Aaron became skeptical of the power of mere transparency, and he began highlighting the need for activism and journalism. This led to his later focus on politics.

Toward the end of his life, Aaron tried to explicitly distance himself from free culture in order to focus on broader issues of injustice, arguing that copyright issues were merely symptomatic of larger problems of power and corruption and could not usefully be dealt with without addressing these larger political problems. Even in these efforts, however, Aaron repeatedly returned to free culture activism. In the speech that closes this section, Aaron describes being called back into the world of free culture to lead the fight against the Stop Online Piracy Act (SOPA), a proposed U.S. law designed to restrict the Internet in ways that would cut back on the kind of information sharing that Aaron supported. He calls on his listeners to believe that their personal engagement in activism for information freedom is urgently needed and that they can become the "hero of their own story."

—Benjamin Mako Hill and Seth Schoen

Counterpoint: Downloading Isn't Stealing

http://www.aaronsw.com/weblog/001112

January 8, 2004

Age 17

The New York Times *Upfront asked me to contribute a short piece to a point/counterpoint they were having on downloading. (I would defend downloading, of course.) I thought I managed to write a pretty good piece, especially for its size and audience, in a couple days. But then I found out my piece was cut because the* Times *had decided not to tell kids to break the law. So, from the graveyard, here it is.*

Stealing is wrong. But downloading isn't stealing. If I shoplift an album from my local record store, no one else can buy it. But when I download a song, no one loses it and another person gets it. There's no ethical problem.

Music companies blame a fifteen percent drop in sales since 2000 on downloading.* But over the same period, there was a recession, a price hike, a 25% cut in new releases,† and a lack of popular new artists. Factoring all that in, maybe downloading *increases* sales. And

---

*This is from the RIAA's own chart [Dead link—points to year-end marketing data from RIAA for 2002—Ed.]. In 1999, they sold 938.9M CDs, in 2002 they sold 803.3M. (938.9-803.3) ÷ 938.9 =.14 (so it's really closer to 14%, but we'll give them the benefit of the doubt and say 15%).

†It depends on how you count. The RIAA says they released 38,900 new releases in 1999. According to SoundScan the RIAA released 31,734 new releases in 2001, leading to an 18% drop. This isn't really fair, since we're using RIAA numbers for 1999 and SoundScan numbers for 2001, and SoundScan probably doesn't count as many albums as the RIAA does. However, the RIAA said in early 2003 that they released 27,000 new albums the previous year. Apparently embarrassed by this

90% of the catalog of the major labels isn't for sale anymore.* The Internet is the only way to hear this music.

Even if downloading did hurt sales, that doesn't make it unethical. Libraries and video stores (neither of which pay per rental) hurt sales too. Is it unethical to use them?

Downloading may be illegal. But 60 million people used Napster[†] and only 50 million voted for Bush or Gore.[‡] We live in a democracy. If the people want to share files then the law should be changed to let them.

And there's a fair way to change it. A Harvard professor found that a $60/yr. charge for broadband users would make up for all lost revenues.[§] The government would give it to the affected artists and, in return, make downloading legal, sparking easier-to-use systems and more shared music. The artists get more money and you get more music. What's unethical about that?

---

information, they've since removed it from their website. But if you use their numbers, you get a 31% drop. I've split the difference and called it a 25% cut. But I could change this to 30% or 20% if you wanted; I don't think it would change the argument.

*Speech by Ken Hertz [Link inexplicably goes to Xeni Jardin's website—Ed.].

†According to the *New York Times*.

‡According to CNN.

§See Terry Fisher, *Promises to Keep* [Stanford: Stanford University Press, 2004]. "Assuming that the ISPs pass through to consumers the entire amount of the tax, that average fee would rise by $4.88 per month" (p. 31); $4.88 \times 12 \approx 59$, so I say $60/yr.

UTI Interview with Aaron Swartz

https://archive.org/download/AaronSwartz20040123UTIInterview
/Aaron-Swartz-2004-01-23-UTI-interview.html

January 23, 2004

Age 17

Hey. Who are you?

Well, I'm trying to figure that out myself, actually. Broadly, though, I'm a teenage kid who's interested in improving the world (mostly through law, politics, and technology).

This year, I'm going to try to update my weblog daily with interesting thoughts, program some interesting new website software, and work on some website projects that help people better understand what's going on in American politics.

I'm also going to try and learn more about reverse engineering, an important process that there seems to be little published information about, probably because laws like the DMCA are making more and more of it illegal (although the law itself is likely unconstitutional, the threat of losing your house or going to jail is enough to scare away most people).

In previous years, I've worked on the RSS specification for syndicating websites, the RDF specification for sharing databases, and the Creative Commons specification for describing copyright licenses.

From my experience, political discussions on the net almost never convince anyone to switch sides or rethink their position. Do you push your views to change anyone else's or simply to state your view in it?

Well, I'm an optimist about that. I think that most people, when faced with overwhelming facts, will come around. (I know I certainly have.) But it is definitely difficult to overcome people's entrenched beliefs, so I feel that if I only convince people that the other side is a reasonable position to take, even if they themselves don't take it, then I've been a success.

It is sort of a quixotic task in that sense, but it's also useful to me by helping clarify my ideas.

When you say something particularly controversial on the web, you'll get all sorts of people coming at you with arguments. Considering those arguments and seeing if they're right or, if they're wrong, why they're wrong, has been very valuable in clarifying my beliefs (and similarly, I hope my challenges have helped other people clarify *their* beliefs).

Lately, there's been a bit of discussion on piracy, where you once chimed in saying that Nick Bradbury doesn't have any innate right to have people pay for his software. Shouldn't deciding whether you want people to pay for your software be up to the developers? And isn't it a crime to download stuff that should be paid for according to a contract (the user terms) bound to the product itself, even if it "physically" isn't stealing?

Let's take those in reverse order.

First, copyright law is the law, I'm not arguing about that.

Second, whether shrinkwrap or clickthrough contracts that come with products are actually enforceable is still undecided by the courts. Personally, I think enforcing them would be a very bad idea because no one reads those licenses and they put all sorts of absurd things in there.

For example, you have a right *guaranteed* by U.S. copyright law to make a backup copy of software in case the original copy goes bad for some reason. It would be very unfair if they could take those rights away.

When you're forced to follow laws passed by a government of the people, that's one thing, but when you have to follow all sorts of additional restrictions added by some unaccountable corporation, it's quite a different situation. What if they make you promise not to say anything negative about their software, as Google almost tried to do? What if they ask for your firstborn son? No one will actually know they agreed to these provisions, because they didn't read them— they just wanted to use the software they spent their own money to purchase—but they'll be held accountable for violating them.

So, that's still a matter of controversy, but this isn't so unreasonable. Even mainstream organizations like the Association for Computing Machinery (ACM), the oldest association of computing professionals, is against this idea.

Third, as a matter of practice, I think people should pay for software when they can and should donate money to the authors of things they enjoy even when they're not asked to.

If you get these things over the Internet, it's much easier for you to do that, since you don't have to pay all the middlemen—warehouses, distributors, stores, publishers—this large infrastructure that's been built up because of the physical nature of these goods. You may buy a computer book for $50 but the author will be lucky if they see $5 from that. So if you download the book from the author's website and send him $10, then both you and the author will be better off.

However (and this apparently is the controversial part), I agree with Thomas Jefferson: the government has no *duty* to make sure authors get paid.

And even more importantly, I think the government shouldn't be giving authors control over how we express ourselves. The International Olympic Committee should not be able to stop groups from calling themselves the "Gay Olympics," Mattel should not be able to stop people from singing about "Barbie Girl" or taking pictures of "Food Chain Barbie," and Dr. Seuss shouldn't be able to stop people who write in his style.

So we need to be careful in understanding that whenever we expand these intellectual monopoly laws, we inevitably take away people's rights to express themselves.

Even if verbatim copying is illegal, then conceivably you could be sued for quoting Martin Luther King.

There are a range of solutions—some more dramatic, some less. But we cannot discuss any solutions if people continue to insist that authors have an innate all-encompassing moral right to control their works forever. If people believe that, then even the most reasonable of solutions will be decried as theft.

All EULAs aside, there must be something somewhere in the law defining what is a ware and can be bought, and also what is considered "stealing" for this. If a software product qualifies as a ware, shouldn't "stealing" according to this law be applicable to the software too?

The law about what is stealing is very clear. Stealing is taking something away from someone so they cannot use it. There's no way that making a copy of something is stealing under that definition.

If you make a copy of something, you'll be prosecuted for copyright infringement or something similar—not larceny (the legal term for stealing). Stealing, like piracy and intellectual property, is another one of those terms cooked up to make us think of intellectual works the same way we think of physical items. But the two are very different.

You can't just punish people because they took away a "potential sale." Earthquakes take away potential sales, as do libraries and rental stores and negative reviews. Competitors also take away potential sales. One reason people might be buying less CDs is because they're spending their money on DVDs. Or, as Philip Greenspun has argued, they're spending their time on cell phones.

I mean, talking to your girlfriend can often be more enjoyable than listening to music, but I don't think we need to start suing girlfriends.

So the question then becomes what's a reasonable form of taking away sales, and what's an unreasonable one. And that's a tough question, but I think we need to evaluate it by looking at what's best for society. Some people say that getting people to stop copying, whether through threats of lawsuits or technological restraints, is the only way to get people to keep coming up with interesting things.

First, I don't think this is true. Look at weblogs, Homestar Runner, Red vs. Blue, Nothing So Strange, Scott McCloud, etc., etc. There's essentially nothing to stop anyone from copying any of these, yet the authors are all making a good living off their work.

Second, if it is true, I think we're in real trouble, because as a simple matter of technology, it's going to be increasingly difficult to get people to stop copying. We can almost always get around the technical measures and we can find technical ways around most of the social ones. So if we choose this option of stricter and stricter enforcement, we're heading down a very dark path where law enforcement gets more and more heavy-handed and authoritarian, and copying goes farther and farther underground.

At the end of that road, I think copying is going to win out, but either way, the collateral damage to our civil liberties, our computers, and our children is going to be tremendous.

What method would you prefer more for paying creative minds? Optional donations, micropayments, some sort of flat-rate tax/fee that would go to some sort of association which would distribute it accordingly, or something completely different?

Well, compared to that dark path, I'd prefer all of them. :-)

However, I think that easy small donations, perhaps optional, are probably the way to go, along with making money off of ancillary things like T-shirts and CDs and DVDs. For example, Homestar Runner doesn't charge or ask for donations but they've been incredibly successful through selling merchandise. Wikipedia's raised an incredible amount of money, probably $50,000 altogether, simply from donations. So I think we should try all these ways, but I'm optimistic that if you provide something people really like, and you make it easy for them to pay you for it, that you'll do fine.

But if it turns out that doesn't work, I've also been looking into a system called Compulsory Licensing.

The idea is that you pay about $5 more a month on your cable modem bill in exchange for being able to download all the music and movies you want. Then you anonymously submit what you downloaded and the money gets sent to the people who made it. The submission is done all automatically by your computer, so you don't have to do anything.

Now there are a lot of problems with this idea, and there are lots of objections you can come up with to it (privacy! security!), but I think if we solve all of them, we may have a viable system that is a win for everyone. Authors get paid and users save money and get easier access to what they want.

Some people don't take you seriously because you're a lot younger than them. What do you think causes this?

I think there are several reasons. First, people generalize: "Well, most kids I've met are pretty dumb, this guy's a kid, so he's probably pretty dumb too."

Second, one of the (I think, valuable) things about kids is that they don't really know a lot of what you can't say. So when kids say perfectly reasonable things that you're not really supposed to say, they just write it off as "Kids say the darnedest things!" and "He just doesn't know better."

Third, and I should be clear I'm just speculating here, there might be some sort of embarrassment factor.

But one of the great things about the Internet is how it's helped me overcome a lot of these things—first, because your age isn't immediately obvious every time you speak (as it is when someone looks at you), and second, because geeks seem a lot more willing to treat people based on what they can do rather than who they are.

This isn't unique to kids, of course. The Internet has an amazingly liberating aspect for everyone from blacks to the blind. So perhaps that's one reason why I'm especially concerned about draconian proposals for an "Internet Driver's License" or a crackdown on anonymity. Quite aside from the impracticality and ineffectiveness of these proposals, they could have the effect of tagging who people are, and reintroducing those indicators that the Internet has removed.

You've put a tremendous amount of work in, for example, RDF and RSS 1.0 (the latter using the former). People say this is the basis of the "Semantic Web." Could you cue us in on what they hope to achieve with this, how they will make everyone start doing something to achieve it, and what exactly it is we'll start doing? Do you believe this is possible?

So, uh, here's the plan:

1. Collect data
2. ???????
3. PROFIT!!!

Uh, more specifically, the idea is to get everyone sharing their vast databases of information in RDF with each other. Then we can write programs that put this data together to answer questions and take actions to make our lives easier.

The example I always give is a smarter Google. Instead of just being able to ask "What web pages contain these words?" you can ask all sorts of real questions: "What bands that my friends like are playing around here in the next week?" It can then look at who your stated friends are, see what bands they claim to like, get their schedules, find where you are, and see if any of them match, assuming all this data is available in RDF.

It's a very cool idea, but like the original web, it has this chicken-and-egg problem. When Tim Berners-Lee first came up with the web, he could only show people the handful of pages he'd written, so it didn't seem all that interesting, and it was difficult to convince people to provide information in this crazy form for free if no one was going to read it. In the same way, there's not much information out there in RDF now, and, because of that, there aren't a lot of people working on reading it.

The web, of course, eventually took off somehow. This is not to say that the Semantic Web *will* take off, but I think that it could, and if it does, it'll be really cool. Unfortunately, arguing over minor technical details is a lot easier than getting the thing to take off, so right now we're doing a lot more of the former. But I guess we're not in much of a hurry.

You have been very open in sharing at least some personal "real life" data. How do you feel about people that don't want to reveal too much of their identity? (If you've slipped some already by accident, Google remembers forever.) How would they go about protecting their own identities?

I'm of two minds about that. On the one hand, I want to be very open about everything. On the other, I heavily defend people's right to privacy. Of course, as you point out, keeping your privacy is hard because if you slip once, it's out there forever.

I'm not sure what to say to people who want to protect their privacy except be careful when you give out private information and think about where it could end up.

When did you find your way toward the web?

I've been using the web since the days of Mosaic, since I was a little kid. I still wish I had been there since Tim Berners-Lee's World Wide Web, but I guess I was only 4 then, so it's not all that unreasonable that I wasn't. So that was probably '94/'95. I think I wrote my first web page a couple years after that ('97/'98) and probably started programming database-backed websites around 1999. Actually, it must have been a little earlier, since my first db-backed website won an award in 1999. That was an interesting era.

Tell us some things you've seen that made you think "This will be huge one day or another" on the web. Which turned out that way? Which ones are on their way? Which ones failed completely?

Well, weblogs, wikis, wireless were widely well received. Database-backed websites have done well too, although I'm a little surprised there hasn't been as much standardization as I thought.

I guess I thought things like anonymous remailers and other crypto stuff would be more popular than it has, but there's still time for that. File sharing sure came out strong, though. The Semantic Web is probably one to watch. And I think we'll see a lot of interesting stuff with Voice over IP in the next year.

In general, we'll see everything move onto the Internet and, as it does, we'll see it open up room for the little guy to compete. So newspapers moved onto the Internet, but that also gave everyone the chance to start their own newspaper. Directories moved onto the Internet, but with Google even the little guys can be in the directory. Same with encyclopedias (Wikipedia) and ads (AdSense). And, of course, at the same time, you open yourself up to easy copying of your work.

So the same pattern has happened in a more forcible way to music, movies, television. TV companies may not like having their shows on the net, but they're there, and stuff like Red vs. Blue is there to compete right alongside them. So, uh, if you're a company that's in the business of moving information around, I'd watch out. It's one thing to say that copying music is wrong because it hurts the artists, but what will the telephone companies say when Voice over IP drives them out of business, completely legally? How will the *Encyclopedia Britannica* stop Wikipedia? You're next! :-)

One thing I've noticed while using open-source software or other free software is that it usually tends to have a very poor user interface. Since these guys are all out to beat Microsoft and other "bigco"s in their own game, why is no or little attention paid to the most important part of the software, the UI? UI designing standards are standards just as the other standards they embrace, right? Or is it all just laziness; to make the product work is enough?

Well, for most of these programmers UI is hard, because they don't understand it. They see things textually, not visually. The free software culture comes very much from the Unix culture, and Unix is very much expert-oriented. Experts don't need "good UI" they know exactly what to do already and they just want to be able to do it as fast as they can.

This is related to the other problem, which is that free software programmers code mostly for themselves. And since they completely and intuitively understand the software, it doesn't seem like the UI is bad to them—to them, it makes perfect sense. There are certainly attempts to fix this—GNOME has been great about running UI contests and doing usability tests and writing guidelines—but it's an uphill battle because of these cultural things.

What is the worst feature of the web?

Another tough one—I like so much about the web!

I guess I'd prefer if it protected privacy better. Between cookies and IP addresses, it's too easy to track what someone is reading or saying.

Also, I think it's rather disgraceful how browser makers have hobbled the web by making it essentially read-only. Tim Berners-Lee's original plan was to let the web be a collaborative space for people to work together to do great things, and web pages would be the trails left behind by their activities. Web browsers would have an edit button that you could click and modify or annotate any page; it would then upload your changes to the server if you had access, or add them to your personal annotation server if you didn't. Creating a web page would be as easy as using a word processor, and it would all be built in to every web browser.

While wikis have achieved some of this, there's still a lot to be done. Tim calls them the "poor man's" equivalent. For example, wikis aren't WYSIWYG and make it too difficult to use links and other advanced features. And you can't just see a typo and correct it in situ; you have to find the edit link, then find the typo again, then correct it, then find the save button. You can't use images or spreadsheets or any of the things that have been common in word processors forever.

And, as a result, the web is still limited in terms of who can publish their works and who can make a decent-looking and useful site. It doesn't need to be that way.

What would you like to say to all the people out there?

Think deeply about things. Don't just go along because that's the way things are or that's what your friends say. Consider the effects, consider the alternatives, but most importantly, just think.

Jefferson: Nature Wants Information to Be Free

http://www.aaronsw.com/weblog/001115

January 12, 2004

Age 17

Since many have said that my view of copyright and patent law is childish and held merely because I grew up with Napster and do not write for a living, I thought I'd investigate some more respectable views on the subject. And who better than those of our thoughtful third president, Thomas Jefferson?

Judging from his letter to Isaac McPherson, Jefferson's thoughts are thus:

> No one seriously disputes that property is a good idea, but it's bizarre to suggest that *ideas* should be property. Nature clearly wants ideas to be free! While you can keep an idea to yourself, as soon as you share it anyone can have it. And once they do, it's difficult for them to get rid of it, even if they wanted to. Like air, ideas are incapable of being locked up and hoarded.
>
> And no matter how many people share it, the idea is not diminished. When I hear your idea, I gain knowledge without diminishing anything of yours. In the same way, if you use your candle to light mine, I get light without darkening you. Like fire, ideas can encompass the globe without lessening their density.
>
> Thus, inventions cannot be property. Sure, we can give inventors an exclusive right to profit, perhaps to encourage them to invent new useful things, but this is our choice. If we decide not to, nobody can object.

Accordingly, England was the only country with such a law until the United States copied her. In other countries, monopolies may be granted occasionally by special act, but there is no general system. And this doesn't seem to have hurt them any—those countries seem just as inventive as ours.

(I am not directly quoting Jefferson here, I am translating what he said to modern English and omitting a bit, but I have not put any words in his mouth—Jefferson said all these things.)

The first thing to note is that Jefferson may have been the first to say, in essence, "Information wants to be free!" (Jefferson attributed this will to nature, not information, but the sentiment was the same.) Thus, all those people who dismiss this claim as absurd have some explaining to do.

The second is that while Jefferson repeatedly says "idea," his logic applies equally to, say, a catchy tune or phrase and thus pretty much everything we commonly call "intellectual property law" (mostly copyright, trademarks, and patents).

The third is that, surprisingly (especially to me!), Jefferson is just as crazy as I am:

- By their very nature, ideas *cannot* be property.
- The government has no duty to make laws about them.
- The laws we do make aren't all that successful.

If Jefferson wasn't happy with the comparatively modest laws of 1813, can anyone seriously suggest that he wouldn't be furious with the expansionist laws of today? Forget the Free Software Foundation and the Creative Commons; Jefferson would be out there advocating armed resistance and impeaching the justices that voted against *Eldred*! (OK, maybe not, but he'd certainly do more than write copyright licenses.)

It's true that in Jefferson's day there were no movies or networks, but there were certainly books and inventions. People made their livelihoods as writers or inventors. It's difficult to argue that Jefferson would change his mind now on economic grounds—if anything,

I suspect that upon seeing the ease of sharing ideas over the Internet, he would argue for less restrictive laws, not more.

Jefferson thought these laws were contrary to human nature when they only affected people with large workshops or commercial printing presses—imagine how angry he would be when he saw that these laws restricted practically everyone, even doing perfectly unobjectionable things (like teaching your AIBO to dance or making a documentary).

Now perhaps folks will find Jefferson as easy an argument for ad hominem attack as they found me. And just because Jefferson said it doesn't make it true—obviously his views were even the subject of some discussion at the time. But when the suggestions of our third president are called "a ball of self-justification," "bullshit," "the far left," "selfishness," "shallow," those of a "moron," "disgusting," a "misunderstanding" of the law (!), and "immoral", you sort of have to stop and wonder: what in the world is going on?

Guerilla Open Access Manifesto

July 2008, Eremo, Italy

Age 21

The Guerilla Open Access Manifesto was written at a 2008 meeting of librarians in Italy. Aaron published it on his blog but later removed it. The manifesto played an important role in Aaron's prosecution: the government intended to use it at trial to establish Aaron's motive for downloading JSTOR articles, arguing that he had intended to release the articles to the public. Although it was widely attributed to him, Aaron's role in the manifesto's creation—and whether it reflected his later views—was a contentious issue in the course of the legal proceedings. —Benjamin Mako Hill and Seth Schoen

Information is power. But like all power, there are those who want to keep it for themselves. The world's entire scientific and cultural heritage, published over centuries in books and journals, is increasingly being digitized and locked up by a handful of private corporations. Want to read the papers featuring the most famous results of the sciences? You'll need to send enormous amounts to publishers like Reed Elsevier.

There are those struggling to change this. The Open Access Movement has fought valiantly to ensure that scientists do not sign their copyrights away but instead ensure their work is published on the Internet, under terms that allow anyone to access it. But even under the best scenarios, their work will only apply to things published in the future. Everything up until now will have been lost.

That is too high a price to pay. Forcing academics to pay money to read the work of their colleagues? Scanning entire libraries but only allowing the folks at Google to read them? Providing scientific articles to those at elite universities in the First World, but not to children in the Global South? It's outrageous and unacceptable.

"I agree," many say, "but what can we do? The companies hold the copyrights, they make enormous amounts of money by charging for access, and it's perfectly legal—there's nothing we can do to stop them." But there is something we can, something that's already being done: we can fight back.

Those with access to these resources—students, librarians, scientists—you have been given a privilege. You get to feed at this banquet of knowledge while the rest of the world is locked out. But you need not—indeed, morally, you cannot—keep this privilege for yourselves. You have a duty to share it with the world. And you have: trading passwords with colleagues, filling download requests for friends.

Meanwhile, those who have been locked out are not standing idly by. You have been sneaking through holes and climbing over fences, liberating the information locked up by the publishers and sharing them with your friends.

But all of this action goes on in the dark, hidden underground. It's called stealing or piracy, as if sharing a wealth of knowledge were the moral equivalent of plundering a ship and murdering its crew. But sharing isn't immoral—it's a moral imperative. Only those blinded by greed would refuse to let a friend make a copy.

Large corporations, of course, are blinded by greed. The laws under which they operate require it—their shareholders would revolt at anything less. And the politicians they have bought off back them, passing laws giving them the exclusive power to decide who can make copies.

There is no justice in following unjust laws. It's time to come into the light and, in the grand tradition of civil disobedience, declare our opposition to this private theft of public culture.

We need to take information, wherever it is stored, make our copies and share them with the world. We need to take stuff that's out of copyright and add it to the archive. We need to buy secret databases and put them on the web. We need to download scientific journals and upload them to file sharing networks. We need to fight for Guerilla Open Access.

With enough of us, around the world, we'll not just send a strong message opposing the privatization of knowledge—we'll make it a thing of the past. Will you join us?

The Fruits of Mass Collaboration

http://www.aaronsw.com/weblog/masscollab

July 18, 2006

Age 19

I often think that the world needs to be a lot more organized. Lots of people write reviews of television shows, but nobody seems to collect and organize them all. Good introductory guides to subjects are essential for learning, yet I only stumble upon them by chance. The cumulative knowledge of science is one of our most valuable cultural products, yet it can only be found scattered across thousands of short articles in hundreds of different journals.

I suspect the same thoughts occur to many of a similar cast of mind, since there's so much effort put into discouraging them. The arbiters of respectable opinion are frequently found to mock such grand projects or point out deficiencies in them. And a friend of mine explained to me that soon out of school he nearly killed himself by trying to embark on such a grand project and now tries to prevent his friends from making the same mistake.

One can, of course, make the reverse argument: since there is so much need for such organization projects, they must be pretty impossible. But upon closer inspection, that isn't true. Is there a project more grand than an encyclopedia or a dictionary? Who dares to compress all human knowledge or an entire language into a single book? And yet, there's not just one but several brands of each!

It seems that when the audience is large enough (and just about everyone has use for encyclopedias and dictionaries), it is possible to take on grand projects. This suggests that the holdup is not practical, but economic. The funding simply isn't there to do the same for other things.

But all this is only true for the era of the book, where such a project means gathering together a group of experts and having them work full-time to build a reference work which can be published and sold expensively to libraries. I tend to avoid net triumphalism, but the Internet, it would seem, changes that. Wikipedia was created not by dedicated experts but by random strangers, and while we can complain about its deficiencies, all admit that it's a useful service.

The Internet is the first medium to make such projects of mass collaboration possible. Certainly numerous people send quotes to Oxford for compilation in the *Oxford English Dictionary*, but a full-time staff is necessary to sort and edit these notes to build the actual book (not to mention all the other work that must be done). On the Internet, however, the entire job—collection, summarization, organization, and editing—can be done in spare time by mutual strangers.

An even more striking, but less remarked-upon, example is Napster. Within only months, almost as a by-product, the world created the most complete library of music and music catalog data ever seen. The contributors to this project didn't even realize they were doing this! They all thought they were simply grabbing music for their own personal use. Yet the outcome far surpassed anything consciously attempted.

The Internet fundamentally changes the practicalities of large organization projects. Things that previously seemed silly and impossible, like building a detailed guide to every television show, are now being done as a matter of course. It seems like we're in for an explosion of such modern reference works, perhaps with new experiments into tools for making them.

The Techniques of Mass Collaboration: A Third Way Out

http://www.aaronsw.com/weblog/masscollab2

July 19, 2006

Age 19

I'm not the first to suggest that the Internet could be used for bringing users together to build grand databases. The most famous example is the Semantic Web project (where, in full disclosure, I worked for several years). The project, spearheaded by Tim Berners-Lee, inventor of the web, proposed to extend the working model of the web to more structured data, so that instead of simply publishing text web pages, users could publish their own databases, which could be aggregated by search engines like Google into major resources.

The Semantic Web project has received an enormous amount of criticism, much (in my view) rooted in misunderstandings, but much legitimate as well. In the news today is just the most recent example, in which famed computer scientist turned Google executive Peter Norvig challenged Tim Berners-Lee on the subject at a conference.

The confrontation symbolizes the (at least imagined) standard debate on the subject, which Mark Pilgrim termed million-dollar markup versus million-dollar code. Berners-Lee's W3C, the supposed proponent of million-dollar markup, argues that users should publish documents that state in special languages that computers can process exactly what they want to say. Meanwhile Google, the supposed proponent of million-dollar code, thinks this is an impractical fantasy, and that the only way forward is to write more advanced software to try to extract the meaning from the messes that users will inevitably create.*

---

*I say supposed because although this is typically how the debate is seen, I don't think either the W3C or Google actually hold the strict positions on the subject

But yesterday I suggested what might be thought of as a third way out, one Pilgrim might call million-dollar users. Both the code and the markup positions make the assumption that users will be publishing their own work on their own websites and thus we'll need some way of reconciling it. But Wikipedia points to a different model, where all the users come to *one* website, where the interface for inputting data in the proper format is clear and unambiguous, and the users can work together to resolve any conflicts that may come up.

Indeed, this method strikes me as so superior that I'm surprised I don't see it discussed in this context more often. Ignorance doesn't seem plausible; even if Wikipedia was a latecomer, sites like Chef-Moz and MusicBrainz followed this model and were Semantic Web case studies. (Full disclosure: I worked on the Semantic Web portions of MusicBrainz.) Perhaps the reason is simply that both sides—W3C and Google—have the existing web as the foundation for their work, so it's not surprising that they assume future work will follow from the same basic model.

One possible criticism of the million-dollar-users proposal is that it's somehow less free than the individualist approach. One site will end up being in charge of all the data and thus will be able to control its formation. This is perhaps not ideal, certainly, but if the data is made available under a free license it's no worse than things are now with free software. Those angry with the policies can always exercise their right to "fork" the project if they don't like the direction things are going. Not ideal, certainly, but we can try to dampen such problems by making sure the central sites are run as democratically as possible.

Another argument is that innovation will be hampered: under the individualist model, any person can start doing a new thing with their data, and hope that others will pick up the technique. In the centralized model, users are limited by the functionality of the centralized site. This too can be ameliorated by making the centralized site as open to innovation as possible, but even if it's closed, other people can still do new things by downloading the data and

typically ascribed to them. Nonetheless, the question is real and it's convenient to consider the strongest forms of the positions.

building additional services on top of it (as indeed many have done with Wikipedia).

It's been eight years since Tim Berners-Lee published his Semantic Web Roadmap and it's difficult to deny that things aren't exactly going as planned. Actual adoption of Semantic Web technologies has been negligible and nothing that promises to change that appears on the horizon. Meanwhile, the million-dollar-code people have not fared much better. Google has been able to launch a handful of very targeted features, like music search and answers to very specific kinds of questions, but these are mere conveniences, far from changing the way we use the web.

By contrast, Wikipedia has seen explosive growth, Amazon.com has become the premier site for product information, and when people these days talk about user-generated content, they don't even consider the individualized sense that the W3C and Google assume. Perhaps it's time to try the third way out.

Wikimedia at the Crossroads

http://www.aaronsw.com/weblog/wikiroads

August 31, 2006

Age 19

A couple weeks ago I had the great privilege of attending Wikimania, the international Wikimedia conference. Hundreds from all over the world gathered there to discuss the magic that is Wikipedia, thinking hard about what it means and why it works. It was an amazing intellectual and emotional experience.

The main attraction was seeing the vibrant Wikipedia community. There were the hardcore Wikipedians, who spend their days reviewing changes and fixing pages. And there were the elder statesmen, like Larry Lessig and Brewster Kahle, who came to meet the first group and tell them how their work fits into a bigger picture. Spending time with all these people was amazing fun—they're all incredibly bright, enthusiastic, and, most shockingly, completely dedicated to a cause greater than themselves.

At most "technology" conferences I've been to, the participants generally talk about technology for its own sake. If *use* ever gets discussed, it's only about using it to make vast sums of money. But at Wikimania, the primary concern was doing the most good for the world, with technology as the tool to help us get there. It was an incredible gust of fresh air, one that knocked me off my feet.

There was another group attending, however: the people holding up the platform on which this whole community stands. I spent the first few days with the mostly volunteer crew of hackers who keep the websites up and running. In later days, I talked to the site administrators who exercise the power that the software gives them. And I heard much about the Wikimedia Foundation, the not-for-profit that controls and runs the sites.

Much to my surprise, this second group was almost the opposite of the first. With a few notable exceptions, when they were offstage they talked gossip and details: how do we make the code stop doing this, how do we get people to stop complaining about that, how can we get this other group to like us more. Larger goals or grander visions didn't come up in their private conversations; instead they seemed absorbed by the issues of the present.

Of course, they have plenty to be absorbed by. Since January, Wikipedia's traffic has more than doubled and this group is beginning to strain under the load. At the technical level, the software development and server systems are both managed by just one person, Brion Vibber, who appears to have his hands more than full just keeping everything running. The entire system has been cobbled together as the site has grown, a messy mix of different kinds of computers and code, and keeping it all running sounds like a daily nightmare. As a result, actual software development goes rather slowly, which cannot help but affect the development of the larger project.

The small coterie of site administrators, meanwhile, are busy dealing with the ever-increasing stream of complaints from the public. The recent Seigenthaler affair, in which the founding editor of *USA Today* noisily attacked Wikipedia for containing a grievous error in its article on him, has made people very cautious about how Wikipedia treats living people. (Although to judge just from the traffic numbers, one might think more such affairs might be a good idea . . . One administrator told me how he spends his time scrubbing Wikipedia clean of unflattering facts about people who call the head office to complain.

Finally, the Wikimedia Foundation Board seems to have devolved into inaction and infighting. Just four people have been actually hired by the Foundation, and even they seem unsure of their role in a largely volunteer community. Little about this group—which, quite literally, controls Wikipedia—is known by the public. Even when they were talking to dedicated Wikipedians at the conference, they put a public face on things, saying little more than "Don't you folks worry, we'll straighten everything out."

The plain fact is that Wikipedia's gotten too big to be run by just a couple of people. One way or another, it's going to have to become an organization; the question is what kind. Organizational structures are far from neutral: whose input gets included decides what actions get taken, the positions that get filled decide what things get focused on, the vision at the top sets the path that will be followed.

I worry that Wikipedia, as we know it, might not last. That its feisty democracy might ossify into staid bureaucracy, that its innovation might stagnate into conservatism, that its growth might slow to stasis. Were such things to happen, I know I could not just stand by and watch the tragedy. Wikipedia is just too important—both as a resource and as a model—to see fail.

That is why, after much consideration, I've decided to run for a seat on the Wikimedia Foundation's Board. I've been a fairly dedicated Wikipedian since 2003, adding and editing pages whenever I came across them. I've gone to a handful of Wikipedia meetups and even got my photo on the front page of the *Boston Globe* as an example Wikipedian. But I've never gotten particularly involved in Wikipedia politics—I'm not an administrator, I don't get involved in policy debates, I hardly even argue on the "talk pages." Mostly, I just edit.

And, to be honest, I wish I could stay that way. When people at Wikimania suggested I run for a Board seat, I shrugged off the idea. But since then, I've become increasingly convinced that I should run, if only to bring attention to these issues. Nobody else seems to be seriously discussing this challenge.

The election begins today and lasts three weeks. As it rolls on, I plan to regularly publish essays like this one, examining the questions that face Wikipedia in depth. Whether I win or not, I hope we can use this opportunity for a grand discussion about where we should be heading and what we can do to get there. That said, if you're an eligible Wikipedian, I hope that you'll please vote for me.

Who Writes Wikipedia?

http://www.aaronsw.com/weblog/whowriteswikipedia
September 4, 2006
Age 19

I first met Jimbo Wales, the face of Wikipedia, when he came to speak at Stanford. Wales told us about Wikipedia's history, technology, and culture, but one thing he said stands out. "The idea that a lot of people have of Wikipedia," he noted, "is that it's some emergent phenomenon—the wisdom of mobs, swarm intelligence, that sort of thing—thousands and thousands of individual users each adding a little bit of content and out of this emerges a coherent body of work." But, he insisted, the truth was rather different: Wikipedia was actually written by "a community . . . a dedicated group of a few hundred volunteers" where "I know all of them and they all know each other." Really, "it's much like any traditional organization."

The difference, of course, is crucial. Not just for the public, who wants to know how a grand thing like Wikipedia actually gets written, but also for Wales, who wants to know how to run the site. "For me this is really important, because I spend a lot of time listening to those four or five hundred and if . . . those people were just a bunch of people talking . . . maybe I can just safely ignore them when setting policy" and instead worry about "the million people writing a sentence each."

So did the Gang of 500 actually write Wikipedia? Wales decided to run a simple study to find out: he counted who made the most edits to the site. "I expected to find something like an 80-20 rule: 80% of the work being done by 20% of the users, just because that seems to come up a lot. But it's actually much, much tighter than that: it turns out over 50% of all the edits are done by just .7% of the users . . . 524 people. . . . And in fact the most active 2%, which is 1400 people, have done 73.4% of all the edits." The remaining 25% of edits, he said, were from "people who [are] contributing . . . a minor change of a fact or a minor spelling fix . . . or something like that."

Stanford wasn't the only place he's made such a claim; it's part of the standard talk he gives all over the world. "This is the group of around a thousand people who really matter," he told us at Stanford. "There is this tight community that is actually doing the bulk of all the editing," he explained at the Oxford Internet Institute. "It's a group of around a thousand to two thousand people," he informed the crowd at GEL 2005. These are just the three talks I watched, but Wales has given hundreds more like them.

At Stanford the students were skeptical. Wales was just counting the number of edits—the number of times a user changed something and clicked save. Wouldn't things be different if he counted the amount of text each user contributed? Wales said he planned to do that in "the next revision" but was sure "my results are going to be even stronger," because he'd no longer be counting vandalism and other changes that later got removed.

Wales presents these claims as comforting. Don't worry, he tells the world, Wikipedia isn't as shocking as you think. In fact, it's just like any other project: a small group of colleagues working together toward a common goal. But if you think about it, Wales's view of things is actually much *more* shocking: around a thousand people wrote the world's largest encyclopedia in four years for free. Could this really be true?

Curious and skeptical, I decided to investigate. I picked an article at random ("Alan Alda") to see how it was written. Today the Alan Alda page is a pretty standard Wikipedia page: it has a couple photos, several pages of facts and background, and a handful of links. But when it was first created, it was just two sentences: "Alan Alda is a male actor most famous for his role of Hawkeye Pierce in the television series MASH. Or [sic] recent work, he plays sensitive male characters in drama movies." How did it get from there to here?

Edit by edit, I watched the page evolve. The changes I saw largely fell into three groups. A tiny handful—probably around 5 out of nearly 400—were "vandalism": confused or malicious people adding things that simply didn't fit, followed by someone undoing their change. The vast majority, by far, were small changes: people fixing typos, formatting, links, categories, and so on, making the article a little nicer but not adding much in the way of substance. Finally, a much smaller amount were genuine additions: a couple sentences or even paragraphs of new information added to the page.

Wales seems to think that the vast majority of users are just doing the first two (vandalizing or contributing small fixes) while the core group of Wikipedians writes the actual bulk of the article. But that's not at all what I found. Almost every time I saw a substantive edit, I found the user who had contributed it was not an active user of the site. They generally had made less than 50 edits (typically around 10), usually on related pages. Most never even bothered to create an account.

To investigate more formally, I purchased some time on a computer cluster and downloaded a copy of the Wikipedia archives. I wrote a little program to go through each edit and count how much of it remained in the latest version.* Instead of counting edits, as Wales did, I counted the number of letters a user actually contributed to the present article.

If you just count edits, it appears the biggest contributors to the Alan Alda article (7 of the top 10) are registered users who (all but 2) have made thousands of edits to the site. Indeed, #4 has made over 7,000 edits while #7 has over 25,000. In other words, if you use Wales's methods, you get Wales's results: most of the content seems to be written by heavy editors.

But when you count letters, the picture dramatically changes: few of the contributors (2 out of the top 10) are even registered and most (6 out of the top 10) have made less than 25 edits to the entire site. In fact, #9 has made exactly one edit—this one! With the more reason-

---

*The details: I downloaded a copy of the enwiki-20060717-pages-meta-history .xml.bz2 archive, broke it up into pages, iterated over the revisions and recursively applied Python's difflib.SequenceMatcher.find _ longest _ match to each revision and the latest revision. (I used find _ longest _ match instead of get _ matching _ blocks because get _ matching _ blocks didn't properly handle blocks being reordered.) I only counted the characters which hadn't already been matched by an earlier revision.

able metric—indeed, the one Wales himself said he planned to use in the next revision of his study—the result completely reverses.

I don't have the resources to run this calculation across all of Wikipedia (there are over 60 million edits!), but I ran it on several more randomly selected articles and the results were much the same. For example, the largest portion of the "Anaconda" article was written by a user who only made 2 edits to it (and only 100 on the entire site). By contrast, the largest number of edits were made by a user who appears to have contributed no text to the final article (the edits were all deleting things and moving things around).

When you put it all together, the story becomes clear: an outsider makes one edit to add a chunk of information, then insiders make several edits tweaking and reformatting it. In addition, insiders rack up thousands of edits doing things like changing the name of a category across the entire site—the kind of thing only insiders deeply care about. As a result, insiders account for the vast majority of the edits. But it's the outsiders who provide nearly all of the content.

And when you think about it, this makes perfect sense. Writing an encyclopedia is hard. To do anywhere near a decent job you have to know a great deal of information about an incredibly wide variety of subjects. Writing so much text is difficult, but doing all the background research seems impossible.

On the other hand, everyone has a bunch of obscure things that, for one reason or another, they've come to know well. So they share them, clicking the edit link and adding a paragraph or two to Wikipedia. At the same time, a small number of people have become particularly involved in Wikipedia itself, learning its policies and special syntax, and spending their time tweaking the contributions of everybody else.

Other encyclopedias work similarly, just on a much smaller scale: a large group of people write articles on topics they know well, while a small staff formats them into a single work. This second group is clearly very important—it's thanks to them encyclopedias have a consistent look and tone—but it's a severe exaggeration to say that they wrote the encyclopedia. One imagines the people running *Britannica* worry more about their contributors than their formatters.

And Wikipedia should too. Even if all the formatters quit the project tomorrow, Wikipedia would still be immensely valuable. For the most part, people read Wikipedia because it has the information they need, not because it has a consistent look. It certainly wouldn't be as nice without one, but the people who (like me) care about such things would probably step up to take the place of those who had left. The formatters aid the contributors, not the other way around.

Wales is right about one thing, though. This fact does have enormous policy implications. If Wikipedia is written by occasional contributors, then growing it requires making it easier and more rewarding to contribute occasionally. Instead of trying to squeeze more work out of those who spend their life on Wikipedia, we need to broaden the base of those who contribute just a little bit.

Unfortunately, precisely because such people are only occasional contributors, their opinions aren't heard by the current Wikipedia process. They don't get involved in policy debates, they don't go to meetups, and they don't hang out with Jimbo Wales. And so things that might help them get pushed on the back burner, assuming they're even proposed.

Out of sight is out of mind, so it's a short hop to thinking these invisible people aren't particularly important. Thus Wales's belief that 500 people wrote half an encyclopedia. Thus his assumption that outsiders contribute mostly vandalism and nonsense. And thus the comments you sometimes hear that making it hard to edit the site might be a good thing.

"I'm not a wiki person who happened to go into encyclopedias," Wales told the crowd at Oxford. "I'm an encyclopedia person who happened to use a wiki." So perhaps his belief that Wikipedia was written in the traditional way isn't surprising. Unfortunately, it is dangerous. If Wikipedia continues down this path of focusing on the encyclopedia at the expense of the wiki, it might end up not being much of either.

Who Runs Wikipedia?

http://www.aaronsw.com/weblog/whorunswikipedia

September 7, 2006

Age 19

During Wikimania, I gave a short talk proposing some new features for Wikipedia. The audience, which consisted mostly of programmers and other high-level Wikipedians, immediately began suggesting problems with the idea. "Won't bad thing X happen?" "How will you prevent Y?" "Do you really think people are going to do Z?" For a while I tried to answer them, explaining technical ways to fix the problem, but after a couple rounds I finally said:

> Stop.
>
> If I had come here five years ago and told you I was going to make an entire encyclopedia by putting up a bunch of web pages that anyone could edit, you would have been able to raise a thousand objections: It will get filled with vandalism! The content will be unreliable! No one will do that work for free!
>
> And you would have been right to. These were completely reasonable expectations at the time. But here's the funny thing: it worked anyway.

At the time, I was just happy this quieted them down. But later I started thinking more about it. Why did Wikipedia work anyway?

It wasn't because its programmers were so farsighted that the software solved all the problems. And it wasn't because the people running it put clear rules in place to prevent misbehavior. We know this because when Wikipedia started it didn't have any programmers (it used off-the-shelf wiki software) and it didn't have clear rules (one of the first major rules was apparently "Ignore all rules").

No, the reason Wikipedia works is because of the community, a group of people that took the project as their own and threw themselves into making it succeed.

People are constantly trying to vandalize Wikipedia, replacing articles with random text. It doesn't work; their edits are undone within minutes, even seconds. But why? It's not magic—it's a bunch of incredibly dedicated people who sit at their computers watching every change that gets made. These days they call themselves the "recent changes patrol" and have special software that makes it easy to undo bad changes and block malicious users with a couple clicks.

Why does anyone do such a thing? It's not particularly fascinating work, they're not being paid to do it, and nobody in charge asked them to volunteer. They do it because they care about the site enough to feel responsible. They get upset when someone tries to mess it up.

It's hard to imagine anyone feeling this way about *Britannica*. There are people who love that encyclopedia, but have any of them shown up at their offices offering to help out? It's hard even to imagine. Average people just don't feel responsible for *Britannica*; there are professionals to do that.

Everybody knows Wikipedia as the site anyone can edit. The article about tree frogs wasn't written because someone in charge decided they needed one and assigned it to someone; it was written because someone, somewhere, just went ahead and started writing it. And a chorus of others decided to help out.

But what's less well known is that it's also the site that anyone can run. The vandals aren't stopped because someone is in charge of stopping them; it was simply something people started doing. And it's not just vandalism: a "welcoming committee" says hi to every new user, a "cleanup taskforce" goes around doing fact-checking. The site's rules are made by rough consensus. Even the servers are largely run this way—a group of volunteer sysadmins hang out on IRC, keeping an eye on things. Until quite recently, the Foundation that supposedly runs Wikipedia had no actual employees.

This is so unusual, we don't even have a word for it. It's tempting to say "democracy," but that's woefully inadequate. Wikipedia doesn't hold a vote and elect someone to be in charge of vandal fighting. Indeed, "Wikipedia" doesn't do anything at all. Someone simply sees that there are vandals to be fought and steps up to do the job.

This is so radically different that it's tempting to see it as a mistake. Sure, perhaps things have worked so far on this model, but when the real problems hit, things are going to have to change: certain people must have clear authority, important tasks must be carefully assigned, everyone else must understand that they are simply volunteers.

But Wikipedia's openness isn't a mistake; it's the source of its success. A dedicated community solves problems that official leaders wouldn't even know were there. Meanwhile, their volunteerism largely eliminates infighting about who gets to be what. Instead, tasks get done by the people who genuinely want to do them, who just happen to be the people who care enough to do them right.

Wikipedia's biggest problems have come when it's strayed from this path, when it's given some people official titles and specified tasks. Whenever that happens, real work slows down and squabbling speeds up. But it's an easy mistake to make, so it gets made again and again.

Of course, that's not the only reason this mistake is made; it's just the most polite. The more frightening problem is that people love to get power and hate to give it up. Especially with a project as big and important as Wikipedia, with the constant swarm of praise and attention, it takes tremendous strength to turn down the opportunity to be its official X, to say instead, "It's a community project, I'm just another community member."

Indeed, the opposite is far more common. People who have poured vast amounts of time into the project begin to feel they should be getting something in return. They insist that, with all their work, they *deserve* an official job or a special title. After all, won't clearly assigning tasks be better for everyone?

And so, the trend is clear: more power, more people, more problems. It's not just a series of mistakes, it's the tendency of the system.

It would be absurd for me to say that I'm immune to such pressures. After all, I'm currently running for a seat on the Wikimedia Board. But I also lie awake at night worrying that I might abuse my power.

A systemic tendency like this is not going to be solved by electing the right person to the right place and then going to back to sleep while they solve the problem. If the community wants to remain in charge, it's going to have to fight for it. I'm writing these essays to help people understand that this is something worth fighting for. And if I'm elected to the Board, I plan to keep on writing.

Just as Wikipedia's success as an encyclopedia requires a world of volunteers to write it, Wikipedia's success as an organization requires the community of volunteers to run it. On the one hand, this means opening up the Board's inner workings for the community to see and get involved in. But it also means opening up the actions of the community so the wider world can get involved. Whoever wins this next election, I hope we all take on this task.

Making More Wikipedians

http://www.aaronsw.com/weblog/morewikipedians

September 11, 2006

Age 19

Wikipedia, the vice president of the *World Book* told us, is now recognized by ten percent of Americans. He presented this in a tone of congratulation: with no marketing budget or formal organization, a free online-only encyclopedia written by volunteers had achieved a vast amount of attention. But I took it a different way. "Only ten percent?" I thought. "That means we have ninety percent to go!"

Wikipedia is one of the few things that pretty much everyone finds useful. So how do we get all of them to use it? The first task, it appears, is telling them it exists. An ad campaign or PR blitz doesn't quite seem appropriate for the job, though. Instead, our promotion should work the same way the rest of Wikipedia works: let the community do it.

Wikipedia's users come from all over society: different cultures, different countries, different places, different fields of study. The physics grad students who contribute heavily to physics articles are in a much better position to promote it to physicists than a promotional flack from the head office. The Pokemon fan maintaining the Pokemon articles probably knows how to reach other Pokemaniacs [better] than any marketing expert.

Sure, you might say, but isn't the whole question of marketing Wikipedia somewhat silly? After all, you obviously know about Wikipedia, and your friends probably all seem to as well. But things are a lot thinner than you might expect: as noted above, only one in ten Americans even knows what Wikipedia is, and most of those don't truly understand it.

It's shocking to discover how even smart, technically minded people can't figure out how to actually edit Wikipedia. Dave Winer wrote some of the first software to have an "Edit This Page" button (indeed, he operated EditThisPage.com for many years) and yet he at first complained that he couldn't figure out how to edit a page on Wikipedia. Michael Arrington reviews advanced Web 2.0 websites daily, yet he noted that "many people don't realize how easy it is for anyone to add content to Wikipedia (I've done it several times)." If prominent technologists have trouble, imagine the rest of the world.

Obviously, this has implications for the software side: we need to work hard on making Wikipedia's interface clearer and more usable. But there's also a task here for the community: giving talks and tutorials to groups that you know about, explaining the core ideas behind Wikipedia, and giving demonstrations of how to get involved in it. The best interface in the world is no substitute for real instruction, and even the clearest document explaining our principles will be ignored in a way that a personal presentation won't.

But beyond simply giving people the ability to contribute, we need to work to make contributing more rewarding. As I previously noted, many people decide to dive into writing for Wikipedia, only to watch their contributions be summarily reverted. Many people create a new article, only to see it get deleted after an AfD discussion where random Wikipedians try to think up negative things to say about it. For someone who thought they were donating their time to help the project, neither response is particularly encouraging.

I'm not saying that we should change our policies or automatically keep everything a newcomer decides to add so we don't hurt their feelings. But we do need to think more about how to enforce policies without turning valuable newcomers away, how we can educate them instead of alienating them.

At Wikimania, no less an authority than Richard Stallman (who himself long ago suggested the idea of a free online encyclopedia) wandered around the conference complaining about a problem he'd discovered with a particular Wikipedia article. He could try to fix it himself, he noted, but it would take an enormous amount of his time and the word would probably just get reverted. He's not the only one—I constantly hear tales from experts about problems they encounter on Wikipedia, but [which] are too complicated for them to fix alone. What if we could collect these complaints on the site, instead of having these people make them at parties?

One way to do that would be to have some sort of complaint-tracking system for articles, like the discussion system of talk pages. Instead of simply complaining about an article in public, Stallman could follow a link from it to file a complaint. The complaint would be tracked and stored with the article. More dedicated Wikipedians would go through the list of complaints, trying to address them and letting the submitter know when they were done. Things like POV allegations could be handled in a similar way: a notice saying neutrality was disputed could appear on the top of the page until the complaint was properly closed.

This is just one idea, of course, but it's an example of the kinds of things we need to think about. Wikipedia is visited by millions each day; how do get them to contribute back their thoughts on the article instead of muttering them under their breath or airing them to their friends?

Making More Wikipedias

http://www.aaronsw.com/weblog/morewikipedias

September 14, 2006

Age 19

Maybe it's just me, but it seems like everywhere you look people are trying to get a piece of Wikipedia. Wiki sites have been started in every field from the Muppets to the law. The domain Wiki.com recently was sold for 3 million dollars. Professor Cass Sunstein, previously seen arguing the Internet could tear apart the republic, just published a new book arguing tools like wikis will lead us to "Infotopia." So is it possible to replicate Wikipedia's success? What's the key that made it work?

Unfortunately, this question hasn't gotten the attention it deserves. For the most part, people have simply assumed that Wikipedia is as simple as the name suggests: install some wiki software, say that it's for writing an encyclopedia, and *voila!*—problem solved. But as pretty much everyone who has tried has discovered, it isn't as simple as that.

Technology industry people tend to reduce websites down to their technology: Wikipedia is simply an instance of wiki software, DailyKos just blog software, and Reddit just voting software. But these sites aren't just installations of software, they're also communities of people.

Building a community is pretty tough; it requires just the right combination of technology and rules and people. And while it's been clear that communities are at the core of many of the most interesting things on the Internet, we're still at the very early stages of understanding what it is that makes them work.

But Wikipedia isn't even a typical community. Usually Internet communities are groups of people who come together to discuss something, like cryptography or the writing of a technical specification. Perhaps they meet in an IRC channel, a web forum, a newsgroup, or on a mailing list, but the focus is always something "out there," something outside the discussion itself.

But with Wikipedia, the goal is building Wikipedia. It's not a community set up to make some other thing, it's a community set up to make itself. And since Wikipedia was one of the first sites to do it, we know hardly anything about building communities like that.

Indeed, we know hardly anything about building software for that. Wiki software has been around for years—the first wiki was launched in 1995; Wikipedia wasn't started until 2001—but it was always used like any other community, for discussing something else. It wasn't generally used for building wikis in themselves; indeed, it wasn't very good at doing that.

Wikipedia's real innovation was much more than simply starting a community to build an encyclopedia or using wiki software to do it. Wikipedia's real innovation was the idea of radical collaboration. Instead of having a small group of people work together, it invited the entire world to take part. Instead of assigning tasks, it let anyone work on whatever they wanted, whenever they felt like it. Instead of having someone be in charge, it let people sort things out for themselves. And yet it did all this towards creating a very specific product.

Even now, it's hard to think of anything else quite like it. Books have been co-authored, but usually only by two people. Large groups have written encyclopedias, but usually only by being assigned tasks. Software has been written by communities, but typically someone is in charge.

But if we take this definition, rather than wiki software, as the core of Wikipedia, then we see that other types of software are also forms of radical collaboration. Reddit, for example, is radical collaboration to build a news site: anyone can add or edit, nobody is in charge, and yet an interesting news site results. Freed from the notion that Wikipedia is simply about wiki software, one can even imagine new kinds of sites. What about a "debate wiki," where people argue about a question, but the outcome is a carefully constructed discussion for others to read later, rather than a morass of bickering messages?

If we take radical collaboration as our core, then it becomes clear that extending Wikipedia's success doesn't simply mean installing more copies of wiki software for different tasks. It means figuring out the key principles that make radical collaboration work. What kinds of projects is it good for? How do you get them started? How do you keep them growing? What rules do you put in place? What software do you use?

These questions can't be answered from the armchair, of course. They require experimentation and study. And that, in turn, requires building a community around strong collaboration itself. It doesn't help us much if each person goes off and tries to start a wiki on their own. To learn what works and what doesn't, we need to share our experiences and be willing to test new things—new goals, new social structures, new software.

Code, and Other Laws of Wikipedia

http://www.aaronsw.com/weblog/wikicodeislaw

September 18, 2006

Age 19

Code is law, Lawrence Lessig famously said years ago, and time has not robbed the idea of any of its force. The point, so eloquently defended in his book *Code, and Other Laws of Cyberspace*, is that in the worlds created by software, the design of the software regulates behavior just as strongly as any formal law does; more effectively, in fact.

The point is obvious in some contexts. In the online 3-D universe of Second Life, if the software prevents you from typing a certain word, that's a far more effective restraint on speech in that world than any U.S. law could ever be in ours. But the point is far more subtle than that; it applies with equal force to the world of Wikipedia, the thriving community and culture that our wiki software creates.

For one thing, the software decides who gets to be part of the community. If using it is clear and simple, then lots of people can use it. But if it's complicated, then only those who take the time to learn it are able to take part. And, as we've seen, lots of intelligent people don't even understand how to edit Wikipedia, let alone do any of the other things on the site.

For another, the software decides how the community operates. Features like administrative controls privilege some users over others. Support for things like stable revisions decides what sorts of things get published. The structure of talk pages helps decide what and how things get discussed.

The page design the site uses encourages specific actions by making some links clear and prominent. Software functions like categories make certain kinds of features possible. The formatting codes used for things like info boxes and links determine how easy it is for newcomers to edit those pieces of the site.

All of these things are political choices, not technical ones. It's not like there's a right answer that's obvious to any intelligent programmer. And these choices can have huge effects on the community. That's why it's essential the community be involved in making these decisions.

The current team of Wikipedia programmers is a volunteer group (although a couple of them were recently hired by the Wikimedia Foundation so they could live a little more comfortably) working much like a standard free software community, discussing things on mailing lists and IRC channels. They got together in person in the days before Wikimania to discuss some of the current hot topics in the software.

One presentation was by a usability expert who told us about a study done on how hard people found it to add a photo to a Wikipedia page. The discussion after the presentation turned into a debate over *whether* Wikipedia should be easy to use. Some suggested that confused users should just add their contributions in the wrong way and more experienced users would come along to clean their contributions up. Others questioned whether confused users should be allowed to edit the site at all—were their contributions even valuable?

As a programmer, I have a great deal of respect for the members of my trade. But with all due respect, are these really decisions that the programmers should be making?

Meanwhile, Jimbo Wales also has a for-profit company, Wikia, which recently received $4 million in venture capital funding. Wales has said, including in his keynote speech at Wikimania, that one of the things he hopes to spend it on is hiring programmers to improve the Wikipedia software.

This is the kind of thing that seems like a thoughtful gesture if you think of the software as neutral—after all, improvements are improvements—but becomes rather more problematic if technical choices have political effects. Should executives and venture capitalists be calling the shots on some of these issues?

The Wikipedia community is enormously vibrant and I have no

doubt that the site will manage to survive many software changes. But if we're concerned about more than mere survival, about how to make Wikipedia the best that it can be, we need to start thinking about software design as much as we think about the rest of our policy choices.

False Outliers

http://www.aaronsw.com/weblog/writefp

September 5, 2006

Age 19

So far my Wikipedia script has churned through about 200 articles, calculating who wrote what in each. This morning I looked through them to see if there were any that didn't match my theory. It printed out a couple and I decided to investigate.

The first it found was "Alkane," a long technical article about acyclic saturated hydrocarbons that it said was largely written by Physchim62. Yesterday a good friend was telling me that he thought long technical articles were likely written by a single person, so I immediately thought that here was the proof that he was right. But, just to check, I decided to look in the edit history to make sure my script hadn't made an error.

It hadn't, I found, but once again simply looking at the numbers missed the larger point. Physchim62 had indeed contributed most of the article, but according to the edit comments, it was by translating the German version! I don't have the German data, but presumably it was written in the same incremental way as most of the articles in my study.

The next serious case was "Characters in Atlas Shrugged," which the script said was written by CatherineMunro. Again, it seemed plausible that one person could have written all those character bios. But again, an investigation into the actual edit history found that Munro hadn't written them; instead she'd copied them from a bunch of subpages, merging them into one bigger page.

The final serious example was "Anchorage, Alaska," which appeared to have been written by JeffreyAllen1975. Here the contributions seemed quite genuine; JeffreyAllen1975 made tons of edits, each contributing a paragraph at a time. The work seemed to take quite a toll on him; at his user page he noted, "I just got burned-out and tired of the online encyclopedia. My time is being taken away from me by being with Wikipedia." He lasted about four months.

Still, something seemed fishy about JeffreyAllen1975, so I decided to investigate further. Currently, the "Anchorage" page has a tag noting that "The current version of the article or section reads like an advertisement." A bit of Googling revealed why: JeffreyAllen1975's contributions had been copied and pasted from other websites, like the Anchorage Chamber of Commerce ("Anchorage's public school system is ranked among the best in the nation. . . . The district's average SAT and ACT College entrance exam scores are consistently above the national average and Advanced Placement courses are offered at each of the district's larger high schools").

I suspect JeffreyAllen1975 didn't know what he was doing. His writing style suggests he's just a kid: "In my free time, I am very proud of my self by how much I've learned by making good edits on Wikipedia articles." I'm pretty sure he just thought he was helping the project: "Wikipedia is like the real encyclopedia books (A through Z) that you see in the library, but better." But his plagiarism will still have to be removed.

When I started, just looking at the numbers these seemed to be several cases that strongly contradicted my theory. And had I just stuck to looking at the numbers, I would have believed that to be the case as well. But, once again, investigation shows the picture to be far more interesting: translation, reorganization, and plagiarism. Exciting stuff!

(The Dandy Warhols) Come Down

http://www.aaronsw.com/weblog/comedown

September 22, 2006

Age 19

Well, the Wikipedia election has finally ended. The good news is that I can now talk about other things again. (For example, did you know that Erik Möller eats babies?) I have a backlog of about 20 posts that I built up over the course of the election. But instead of springing them on you all at once, I'll try to do daily posting again starting Monday. (Oooh.)

The actual results haven't been announced yet (and probably won't be for another couple days, while they check the list of voters for people who voted twice) but my impression is that I probably lost. Many wags have commented on how my campaign was almost destined to lose: I argued that the hard-core Wikipedia contributors weren't very important, but those were precisely the people who could vote for me—in other words, I alienated my only constituency.

"Aaron Swartz: Why is he getting so much attention?" wrote fellow candidate Kelly Martin. "The community has long known that edit count is a poor measure of contributions." Others, meanwhile, insisted my claims were so obviously wrong as to not be even worth discussing.

Jimbo Wales, on the other hand, finally sent me a nice message the other day letting me know that he'd removed the offending section from his talk and looked forward to sitting down with me and investigating the topic more carefully.

And for my part, I hope to be able to take up some of the offers I've received for computer time and run my algorithm across all of Wikipedia and publish the results in more detailed form. (I'd also like to use the results to put up a little website where you can type in the name of a page and see who wrote what, color-coded or something like that.)

As for the election itself, it's much harder to draw firm conclusions. It's difficult in any election, this one even more so because we have so little data—no exit polls or phone surveys or even TV pundits to rely upon. Still, I'm fairly content seeing the kind words of all the incredible people I respect. Their support means a great deal to me.

The same is true of the old friends who wrote in during my essays along with all the new people who encouraged me to keep on writing. Writing the essays on a regular schedule was hard work—at one point, after sleeping overnight at my mother's bedside in the hospital, I trundled down at seven in the morning to find an Internet connection so I could write and post one—but your support made it worth the effort.

I hope that whoever wins takes what I've written into consideration. I'm not sure who that is yet, but there are some hints. I was reading an irreverent site critical of Wikipedia when I came across its claim that Jimbo Wales had sent an email to the Wikipedia community telling them who they should vote for. I assumed the site had simply made it up to attack Jimbo, but when I searched I found it really was genuine:

I personally strongly strongly support the candidacies of Oscar and Mindspillage.

[. . .]

There are other candidates, some good, but at least some of them are entirely unacceptable because they have proven themselves repeatedly unable to work well with the community.

For those reading the tea leaves, this suggests that the results will be something like: Eloquence, Oscar, Mindspillage. But we'll see.

The letdown after the election is probably not the best time to make plans, but if I had to, I'd probably decide to stay out of Wikipedia business for a while. It's a great and important project, but not the one for me.

Anyway, now everyone can go back to vandalizing my Wikipedia page. Laters.

Up with Facts: Finding the Truth in WikiCourt

http://www.aaronsw.com/weblog/001175

February 19, 2004

Age 17

I'm an optimist. I believe that statements like "Bush went AWOL" or "Gore claims to have invented the Internet" can be evaluated and decided pretty much true or false. (The conclusion can be a little more nuanced, but the important thing is that there's a definitive conclusion.)

And even crazier, I believe that if there was a fair and accurate system for determining which of these things were lies, people would stop repeating the lies. I would certainly try to. No matter how much I wanted to believe "Dean's state record sealing was normal" or "global warming does exist," if a fair system had decided against it, I would stop.

And perhaps most crazy of all, I want to stop repeating falsehoods. I believe the truth is more important than particular political goals, so I want to build a system I can trust. I want to know that when I make claims, I'm not speaking out of political distortion but out of honest truth. And I want to be able to evaluate the claims of others too.

So how would such a system work? First, large claims ("Gore is a serial liar," "Ronald Reagan was a great president") would be broken down into smaller component parts ("Gore claimed to have invented the Internet," "Ronald Reagan's economic plan created jobs"). On each small claim, we'd run The Process. Let's take "Gore falsely claimed to have invented the Internet."

First, some ground rules. Everything is open. Anyone can submit anything, and all the records are put on a public website.

We'd begin with collecting evidence. Anyone could submit help-ful factual evidence. We'd get videotape from CNN of what exactly Gore said. We'd get congressional records about Gore's funding of the Arpanet. We'd get testimony from people involved. And so on. If someone challenged a piece of evidence's validity (e.g., "that photo is doctored," "that testimony is forged"), a Mini-Process could be started to resolve the issue.

Then there'd be the argument phase. A wiki page would be cre-ated where each side would try to take facts from the evidence and use them to build an argument for their case. But then the other side could modify the page to provide their own evidence, expand selec-tive quotations, and otherwise modify the page to make it more ac-curate and less partisan. Each side would continue bashing the other side's work until the page gave the best arguments from each side, presented in such a way that nobody could object. (You may think that this is impossible, but Wikipedia has ably proven that it can work.)

Finally, there'd be the adjudication phase. This is the hard part. A group of twelve fair-minded intelligent people (experts in the field, if necessary) would agree to put aside their partisanship and come to a conclusion based on the argument. Hopefully, most of the time this conclusion would be (after a little wiki-rewriting from both sides) unanimous. For example, "While Gore's phrasing was a little misleading, it is clear Gore was claiming to have led the fight for providing funding for research that was later developed into the Internet—a claim that is mostly true. Gore was one of the research's major backers, although others were involved."

The panel would be assembled by selecting people widely seen as fair-minded and intelligent, but coming from different sides of the political spectrum. It is likely many would accept—all they'd need to do was read a page and spend a little time agreeing to summarize it. And in doing so, they'd provide a great contribution to political debate (as well as getting their side represented).

All of these phases would be going on essentially simultaneously—the argument could be updated as new evidence came to light, new evidence could be added to fill holes in the argument, and the adju-dicating jury could keep tabs on the page as updated.

And once a decision on an issue was made, it could be cited as evidence in the argument for a related issue ("Gore is a serial liar").

Everything would be very fluid and wiki-like. We'd make up the rules as we went along, seeing what was necessary. And when we learned from our mistakes, we could go back and fix them.

This seems like an awful lot of effort for just coming to a decision on a couple of silly issues, but I think it's far more than that. The result would be a vast collection of trustable arguments for many of the hot topics of the day, a collection that could be relied on through time to give you the fair truth—because everybody had essentially signed off on it (it is publicly modifiable, after all). And if you look at the effort expended on these claims and political fights, spending a little time getting the facts right seems like a small price to pay.

Welcome, Watchdog.net

http://www.aaronsw.com/weblog/watchdog

April 14, 2008

Age 21

As you've probably noticed, it's political insanity season in the U.S. I can hardly go outside these days without running into someone complaining about the latest piece of campaign gossip. I've mostly tried to keep it off this blog, but it's hard to not get swept up in the fever. As someone who wants to make a difference in the world, I've long wondered whether there was an effective way for a programmer to get involved in politics, but I've never been able to quite figure it out.

Well, recent events and Larry Lessig got me thinking about it again and I've spent the past few months working with and talking to some amazing people about the problem. I've learned a lot and must have gone through a dozen different project ideas, but I finally think I've found something. It's not so much a finished solution as a direction, where I hope to figure more of it out along the way.

So the site is called Watchdog.net and the plan has three parts. First, pull in data sources from all over—district demographics, votes, lobbying records, campaign finance reports, etc.—and let people explore them in one elegant, unified interface. I want this to be one of the most powerful, compelling interfaces for exploring a large data set out there.

But just giving people information isn't enough; unless you give them an opportunity to do something about it, it will just make them more apathetic. So the second part of the site is building tools to let people take action: write or call your representative, send a note to local papers, post a story about something interesting you've found, generate a scorecard for the next election.

And tying these two pieces together will be a collaborative database of political causes. So on the page about global warming, you'll be able to learn more about the problem and proposed solutions, research the donors and votes on the issue, and see or start a letter-writing campaign.

All of it, of course, is free software and free data. And it's all got a dozen different APIs to make it easy for others to build on what we've done in their own work. The goal is to be a hub, connecting citizens, activists, organizations, politicians, programmers, and everybody else who's interested in politics.

The hope is to make it as interesting and easy as possible to pull people into politics. It's an ambitious goal with many pieces and possibilities, but with all the excitement right now we want to get something up as fast as possible. So we'll be developing live on Watchdog .net, releasing pieces as soon as we finish them. Our first goal is to put up data about every representative and a way to write them.

I've managed to find an amazing group of people willing to help out with building it so far. And the Sunlight Network has encouraged me and graciously agreed to fund it. But we still need many more hands, especially programmers. If you're interested in working on it, whether as a volunteer or for pay, please email me, telling me what you'd like to help with.

A Database of Folly

http://crookedtimber.org/2012/07/03/a-database-of-folly/

July 3, 2012

Age 26

The open data movement is a hammer which has gathered the support of many nails. There are the curious taxpayers, who feel their annual checks mean they deserve a peek at the interesting facts the government has collected. There are the ambitious business owners, who see an opportunity to privatize profits from work with socialized costs. And there are the self-styled activists, who believe that if we reveal the data on what the government is really doing, we will arrest corruption by exposing it to sunlight.

The coalition is a confusing mix of these very different motivations (as Tom Slee observes), and the benefits of such a tactical alliance has come with the cost of some confusion. So let's be clear about what open data can and cannot do.

If the St. Louis Fed publishes reams of economic data, it can certainly make it easier for Mr. Yglesias to make his fantastic charts. If the MTA makes real-time subway information public, it can certainly let Mr. Ernst improve his fantastic app. And, as the talented Mr. Lee pointed out to me, his careful collection of data about members of Congress and the bills they're passing can be an invaluable resource for professional activists.

So, if I got to choose whether the government should share the data it's collected, I'd happily vote yes. In fact, I spent several years of my life using the FOIA laws to force it to do just that. I can't claim my work had any particular impact, but as a curious taxpayer, it was a weirdly enjoyable hobby.

But the open data movement often claims to be much more than that. They insist open data will not just help a few people with their jobs or a few kids with their hobbies but, as the Sunlight Foundation puts it, "make government transparent and accountable." And that I just don't see.

I've outlined my theory why elsewhere, but the short version is pretty simple: people hide their crimes. Imagine you learn lots of bribes are exchanged at top of the Capitol Reflecting Pool. So you lobby Congress hard to set up bright lights and a camera to catch the perpetrators. The video would be live-streamed to the Internet so dedicated watchdogs can name and shame the bribe-taking politicians. Your lobbying succeeds and, on January 1st, the lights go up and the cameras switch on.

But as an engaged citizenry tunes in, there is nothing but disappointment. Nobody seems to be taking bribes; just a couple pieces of litter blowing by the pool.

Was Congress really squeaky clean after all? Of course not—the bribes just moved to the other end at the pool, out of the spotlights.

When you have time to prepare, it's pretty easy to disguise the data. And this is exactly the pattern we've seen. It's always been investigative journalism, not data mining, that's revealed the big scandals about politicians. I, more than anyone, would love to believe that the next great Watergate is just lying in plain sight to be uncovered by a swashbuckling econometrician, but the sad fact is, it simply isn't so.

But it's also worth pausing to ask: what was any of this *supposed* to achieve? Imagine, for some strange reason, members of Congress didn't bother avoiding the spotlight. Every day, we saw them, in full HD video, taking money from prominent businessmen. Do we really think even this (far-fetched) instance of transparency would change much? After all, most Americans already think Congress is corrupt. Most Americans think money actually buys politicians' votes. Seeing it happen in video might be striking, and maybe make for some good segments on the evening news (or, these days, some viral YouTube videos), but would it really change anything?

After a couple weeks of chatter, and perhaps a few grandstanding legislative proposals, I suspect it'd just fade into the background. More dramatic examples are not exactly what's most missing from the reform debate—Lessig's recent book has enough to last us a couple decades. Structural reforms have failed because of the incompetence of reformers, not because there's a lack of evidence that there's a problem. (Free tip to structural reformers: get state legislators to sign on to your constitutional amendment. They're very susceptible to public pressure, there's a lot of them [so you'll have a constant narrative of progress], and they're the ones you'll ultimately need to actually pass the amendment.)

But maybe open data was supposed to improve politics in other ways. Structural reform is an ambitious goal—maybe the open data proponents wanted something much more modest. But all the more modest stories suffer from a similar excess of naïveté. Whenever geeks turn their eyes to politics, they always have the same reaction: There's so much inefficiency! And they naturally propose the obvious ideas for reducing it—for example: If only it was easier for citizens to read bills, citizens with relevant expertise could assist Congress by sharing their hard-earned wisdom!

The fact is, Congress isn't interested in availing itself of your wisdom any more than the sausagemaker needs your help tidying the floor. Lawmaking is *The Wire*, not *Schoolhouse Rock*. It's about blood and war and power, not evidence and argument and policy. (I have one friend who was startled to learn that when members of Congress debate an issue on C-SPAN, they're speaking not to each other but to cameras in a largely empty room.)

I don't want this to sound overly harsh. The truth is, it's really hard to do effective philanthropy. With a little work, you could mount a similar critique of the vast majority of our bumbling efforts to do good. Most ideas for helping people that seem reasonable in the abstract turn out to fall apart upon close confrontation with reality. The real question is what happens then. There's no shame in admitting your mistakes, learning from them, and trying again. Indeed, as my old professor Carol Dweck has shown, that's the only real route to success. But most of us are too vain or too proud to take that route. We insist that the purity of our intentions reduces the need for careful scrutiny of our effects. Or we try to make ourselves feel better by grasping at any factoid that suggests we had an impact.

I have no particular interest in correcting people's pride or vanity.

This movement is populated by my friends and I respect them enormously and wish them well. Throwing darts at their day jobs has only made my life worse. But this stuff matters—funders and volunteers face tough choices about which causes to pursue. It's important that they know the case for opening up data to hold government accountable simply isn't there. (And that they should invest in metaresearch, including open scientific data, instead.) It's nothing personal—just trying to help everyone do their best. I dearly hope that if anyone ever has a similar critique of the causes I pursue, they will be even more blunt in pointing out my folly.

When Is Transparency Useful?

http://www.aaronsw.com/weblog/usefultransparency

June 2009

Age 22

The following essay appears in the new O'Reilly book Open Government *and attempts to combine and clarify some of the points I made in previous essays. It was written in June 2009.*

Transparency is a slippery word; the kind of word that, like *reform*, sounds good and so ends up getting attached to any random political thing that someone wants to promote. But just as it's silly to talk about whether "reform" is useful (it depends on the reform), talking about transparency in general won't get us very far. Everything from holding public hearings to requiring police to videotape interrogations can be called "transparency"—there's not much that's useful to say about such a large category.

In general, you should be skeptical whenever someone tries to sell you on something like "reform" or "transparency." In general, you should be skeptical. But in particular, reactionary political movements have long had a history of cloaking themselves in nice words. Take the Good Government (goo-goo) movement early in the twentieth century. Funded by prominent major foundations, it claimed that it was going to clean up the corruption and political machines that were hindering city democracy. Instead, the reforms ended up choking democracy itself, a response to the left-wing candidates who were starting to get elected.

The goo-goo reformers moved elections to off-years. They claimed this was to keep city politics distinct from national politics, but the real effect was just to reduce turnout. They stopped paying politicians a salary. This was supposed to reduce corruption, but it just made sure that only the wealthy could run for office. They made the elections nonpartisan. Supposedly this was because city elections were about local issues, not national politics, but the effect was to increase the power of name recognition and make it harder for voters to tell which candidate was on their side. And they replaced mayors with unelected city managers, so winning elections was no longer enough to effect change.

Of course, the modern transparency movement is very different from the Good Government movement of old. But the story illustrates that we should be wary of kind nonprofits promising to help. I want to focus on one particular strain of transparency thinking and show how it can go awry. It starts with something that's hard to disagree with.

Sharing Documents with the Public

Modern society is made of bureaucracies and modern bureaucracies run on paper: memos, reports, forms, filings. Sharing these internal documents with the public seems obviously good, and indeed, much good has come out of publishing these documents, whether it's the National Security Archive, whose Freedom of Information Act (FOIA) requests have revealed decades of government wrongdoing around the globe, or the indefatigable Carl Malamud and his scanning, which has put terabytes of useful government documents, from laws to movies, online for everyone to access freely.

I suspect few people would put "publishing government documents on the web" high on their list of political priorities, but it's a fairly cheap project (just throw piles of stuff into scanners) and doesn't seem to have much downside. The biggest concern—privacy—seems mostly taken care of. In the United States, FOIA and the Privacy Act (PA) provide fairly clear guidelines for how to ensure disclosure while protecting people's privacy.

Perhaps even more useful than putting government documents online would be providing access to corporate and nonprofit records. A lot of political action takes place outside the formal government, and thus outside the scope of the existing FOIA laws. But such things seem totally off the radar of most transparency activists; instead, giant corporations that receive billions of dollars from the government are kept impenetrably secret.

Generating Databases for the Public

Many policy questions are a battle of competing interests—drivers don't want cars that roll over and kill them when they make a turn, but car companies want to keep selling such cars. If you're a member of Congress, choosing between them is difficult. On the one hand are your constituents, who vote for you. But on the other hand are big corporations, which fund your reelection campaigns. You really can't afford to offend either one too badly.

So, there's a tendency for Congress to try a compromise. That's what happened with, for example, the Transportation Recall Enhancement, Accountability, and Documentation (TREAD) Act. Instead of requiring safer cars, Congress simply required car companies to report how likely their cars were to roll over. Transparency wins again!

Or, for a more famous example: after Watergate, people were upset about politicians receiving millions of dollars from large corporations. But, on the other hand, corporations seem to like paying off politicians. So instead of banning the practice, Congress simply required that politicians keep track of everyone who gives them money and file a report on it for public inspection.

I find such practices ridiculous. When you create a regulatory agency, you put together a group of people whose job is to solve some problem. They're given the power to investigate who's breaking the law and the authority to punish them. Transparency, on the other hand, simply shifts the work from the government to the average citizen, who has neither the time nor the ability to investigate these questions in any detail, let alone do anything about it. It's a farce: a way for Congress to look like it has done something on some pressing issue without actually endangering its corporate sponsors.

Interpreting Databases for the Public

Here's where the technologists step in. "Something is too hard for people?" they hear. "We know how to fix that." So they download a copy of the database and pretty it up for public consumption—generating summary statistics, putting nice pictures around it, and giving it a snazzy search feature and some visualizations. Now inquiring citizens can find out who's funding their politicians and how dangerous their cars are just by going online.

The wonks love this. Still stinging from recent bouts of deregulation and antigovernment zealotry, many are now skeptical about government. "We can't trust the regulators," they say. "We need to be able to investigate the data for ourselves." Technology seems to provide the perfect solution. Just put it all online—people can go through the data while trusting no one.

There's just one problem: if you can't trust the regulators, what makes you think you can trust the data?

The problem with generating databases isn't that they're too hard to read; it's the lack of investigation and enforcement power, and websites do nothing to help with that. Since no one's in charge of verifying them, most of the things reported in transparency databases are simply lies. Sometimes they're blatant lies, like how some factories keep two sets of books on workplace injuries: one accurate one, reporting every injury, and one to show the government, reporting just 10% of them. But they can easily be subtler: forms are misfiled or filled with typos, or the malfeasance is changed in such a way that it no longer appears on the form. Making these databases easier to read results only in easier-to-read lies.

Three examples:

- Congress's operations are supposedly open to the public, but if you visit the House floor (or if you follow what they're up to on one of these transparency sites) you find that they appear to spend all their time naming post offices. All the real work is passed using emergency provisions and is tucked into subsections of innocuous bills. (The bank bailouts were put in the Paul Wellstone Mental Health Act.) Matt Taibbi's *The Great Derangement* tells the story.

- Many of these sites tell you who your elected official is, but what impact does your elected official really have? For 40 years, people in New York thought they were governed by their elected officials—their city council, their mayor, their governor. But as Robert Caro revealed in *The Power Broker*, they were all wrong. Power in New York was controlled by one man, a man who had consistently lost every time he'd tried to run for office, a man nobody thought of as being in charge at all: Parks Commissioner Robert Moses.

- Plenty of sites on the Internet will tell you who your representative receives money from, but disclosed contributions are just the tip of the iceberg. As Ken Silverstein points out in his series of pieces for *Harper's* (some of which he covers in his book *Turkmeniscam*), being a member of Congress provides for endless ways to get perks and cash while hiding where it comes from.

Fans of transparency try to skirt around this. "OK," they say, "but surely *some* of the data will be accurate. And even if it isn't, won't we learn something from how people lie?" Perhaps that's true, although it's hard to think of any good examples. (In fact, it's hard to think of any good examples of transparency work accomplishing anything, except perhaps for more transparency.) But everything has a cost.

Hundreds of millions of dollars have been spent funding transparency projects around the globe. That money doesn't come from the sky. The question isn't whether some transparency is better than none; it's whether transparency is really the best way to spend these resources, whether they would have a bigger impact if spent someplace else.

I tend to think they would. All this money has been spent with the goal of getting a straight answer, not of doing anything about it. Without enforcement power, the most readable database in the world won't accomplish much—even if it's perfectly accurate. So people go online and see that all cars are dangerous and that all politicians are corrupt. What are they supposed to do then?

Sure, perhaps they can make small changes—this politician gets slightly less oil money than that one, so I'll vote for her (on the other hand, maybe she's just a better liar and gets her oil money funneled through PACs or foundations or lobbyists)—but unlike the government, they can't solve the bigger issue: a bunch of people reading a website can't force car companies to make a safe car. You've done nothing to solve the real problem; you've only made it seem more hopeless: all politicians are corrupt, all cars are dangerous. What can you do?

An Alternative

What's ironic is that the Internet does provide something you can do. It has made it vastly easier, easier than ever before, to form groups with people and work together on common tasks. And it's through people coming together—not websites analyzing data—that real political progress can be made.

So far we've seen baby steps—people copying what they see elsewhere and trying to apply it to politics. Wikis seem to work well, so you build a political wiki. Everyone loves social networks, so you build a political social network. But these tools worked in their original setting because they were trying to solve particular problems, not because they're magic. To make progress in politics, we need to think best about how to solve its problems, not simply copy technologies that have worked in other fields. Data analysis can be part of it, but it's part of a bigger picture. Imagine a team of people coming together to tackle some issue they care about—food safety, say. You can have technologists poring through safety records, investigative reporters making phone calls and sneaking into buildings, lawyers subpoenaing documents and filing lawsuits, political organizers building support for the project and coordinating volunteers, members of Congress pushing for hearings on your issues and passing laws to address the problems you uncover, and, of course, bloggers and writers to tell your stories as they unfold.

Imagine it: an investigative strike team, taking on an issue, uncovering the truth, and pushing for reform. They'd use technology, of course, but also politics and the law. At best, a transparency law gets you one more database you can look at. But a lawsuit (or congressional investigation)? You get to subpoena all the databases, as well as the source records behind them, then interview people under oath about what it all means. You get to ask for what you need, instead of trying to predict what you may someday want.

This is where data analysis can be really useful. Not in providing definitive answers over the web to random surfers, but in finding anomalies and patterns and questions that can be seized upon and investigated by others. Not in building finished products, but by engaging in a process of discovery. But this can be done only when members of this investigative strike team work in association with others. They would do what it takes to accomplish their goals, not be hamstrung by arbitrary divisions between "technology" and "journalism" and "politics."

Right now, technologists insist that they're building neutral platforms for anyone to find data on any issue. Journalists insist that they're objective observers of the facts. And political types assume they already know the answers and don't need to investigate further questions. They're each in their own silo, unable to see the bigger picture.

I certainly was. I care passionately about these issues—I don't want politicians to be corrupt; I don't want cars to kill people—and as a technologist I'd love to be able to solve them. That's why I got swept up in the promise of transparency. It seemed like just by doing the things I knew how to do best—write code, sift through databases—I could change the world.

But it just doesn't work. Putting databases online isn't a silver bullet, as nice as the word *transparency* may sound. But it was easy to delude myself. All I had to do was keep putting things online and someone somewhere would find a use for them. After all, that's what technologists do, right? The World Wide Web wasn't designed for publishing the news—it was designed as a neutral platform that could support anything from scientific publications to pornography.

Politics doesn't work like that. Perhaps at some point putting things on the front page of the *New York Times* guaranteed that they would be fixed, but that day is long past. The pipeline of leak to investigation to revelation to report to reform has broken down. Technologists can't depend on journalists to use their stuff; journalists can't depend on political activists to fix the problems they uncover.

Change doesn't come from thousands of people, all going their separate ways. Change requires bringing people together to work on a common goal. That's hard for technologists to do by themselves.

But if they do take that as their goal, they can apply all their talent and ingenuity to the problem. They can measure their success by the number of lives that have been improved by the changes they fought for, rather than the number of people who have visited their website. They can learn which technologies actually make a difference and which ones are merely indulgences. And they can iterate, improve, and scale.

Transparency can be a powerful thing, but not in isolation. So, let's stop passing the buck by saying our job is just to get the data out there and it's other people's job to figure out how to use it. Let's decide that our job is to fight for good in the world. I'd love to see all these amazing resources go to work on *that*.

How We Stopped SOPA

https://www.youtube.com/watch?v=Fgh2dFngFsg

May 2012

Age 25

For me, it all started with a phone call. It was September—not last year, but the year before that, September 2010. And I got a phone call from my friend Peter. "Aaron," he said, "there's an amazing bill that you have to take a look at." "What is it?" I said. "It's called COICA, the Combating Online Infringement and Counterfeiting Act." "But, Peter," I said, "I don't care about copyright law. Maybe you're right. Maybe Hollywood is right. But either way, what's the big deal? I'm not going to waste my life fighting over a little issue like copyright. Health care, financial reform—those are the issues that I work on, not something obscure like copyright law." I could hear Peter grumbling in the background. "Look, I don't have time to argue with you," he said, "but it doesn't matter for right now, because this isn't a bill about copyright." "It's not?" "No," he said. "It's a bill about the freedom to connect." Now I was listening.

Peter explained what you've all probably long since learned, that this bill would let the government devise a list of websites that Americans weren't allowed to visit. On the next day, I came up with lots of ways to try to explain this to people. I said it was a great firewall of America. I said it was an Internet blacklist. I said it was online censorship. But I think it's worth taking a step back, putting aside all the rhetoric, and just thinking for a moment about how radical this bill really was. Sure, there are lots of times when the government makes rules about speech. If you slander a private figure, if you buy a television ad that lies to people, if you have a wild party that plays booming music all night, in all these cases, the government can come stop you. But this was something radically different. It wasn't that the government went to people and asked them to take down particular material that was illegal; it shut down whole websites. Essentially, it stopped Americans from communicating entirely with certain groups. There's nothing really like it in U.S. law. If you play loud music all night, the government doesn't slap you with an order requiring you be mute for the next couple weeks. They don't say nobody can make any more noise inside your house. There's a specific complaint, which they ask you to specifically remedy, and then your life goes on.

The closest example I could find was a case where the government was at war with an adult bookstore. The place kept selling pornography; the government kept getting the porn declared illegal. And then, frustrated, they decided to shut the whole bookstore down. But even that was eventually declared unconstitutional, a violation of the First Amendment.

So, you might say, surely COICA would get declared unconstitutional as well. But I knew that the Supreme Court had a blind spot around the First Amendment, more than anything else, more than slander or libel, more than pornography, more even than child pornography. Their blind spot was copyright. When it came to copyright, it was like the part of the justices' brains shut off, and they just totally forgot about the First Amendment. You got the sense that, deep down, they didn't even think the First Amendment applied when copyright was at issue, which means that if you did want to censor the Internet, if you wanted to come up with some way that the government could shut down access to particular websites, this bill might be the only way to do it. If it was about pornography, it probably would get overturned by courts, just like the adult bookstore case. But if you claimed it was about copyright, it might just sneak through.

And that was especially terrifying, because, as you know, because copyright is everywhere. If you want to shut down WikiLeaks, it's a bit of a stretch to claim that you're doing it because they have too much pornography, but it's not hard at all to claim that WikiLeaks is violating copyright, because everything is copyrighted. This speech, you know, the thing I'm giving right now, these words are copyrighted. And it's so easy to accidentally copy something, so easy, in fact, that the leading Republican supporter of COICA, Orrin Hatch, had illegally copied a bunch of code into his own Senate website. So if even Orrin Hatch's Senate website was found to be violating copyright law, what's the chance that they wouldn't find something they could pin on any of us?

There's a battle going on right now, a battle to define everything that happens on the Internet in terms of traditional things that the law understands. Is sharing a video on BitTorrent like shoplifting from a movie store? Or is it like loaning a videotape to a friend? Is reloading a webpage over and over again like a peaceful virtual sit-in or a violent smashing of shop windows? Is the freedom to connect like freedom of speech or like the freedom to murder?

This bill would be a huge, potentially permanent, loss. If we lost the ability to communicate with each other over the Internet, it would be a change to the Bill of Rights. The freedoms guaranteed in our Constitution, the freedoms our country had been built on, would be suddenly deleted. New technology, instead of bringing us greater freedom, would have snuffed out fundamental rights we had always taken for granted. And I realized that day, talking to Peter, that I couldn't let that happen.

But it was going to happen. The bill, COICA, was introduced on September 20th, 2010, a Monday, and in the press release heralding the introduction of this bill, way at the bottom, it was scheduled for a vote on September 23rd, just three days later. And while, of course, there had to be a vote—you can't pass a bill without a vote—the results of that vote were already a foregone conclusion, because if you looked at the introduction of the law, it wasn't just introduced by one rogue eccentric member of Congress; it was introduced by the chair of the Judiciary Committee and co-sponsored by nearly all the other members, Republicans and Democrats. So, yes, there'd be a vote, but it wouldn't be much of a surprise, because nearly everyone who was voting had signed their name to the bill before it was even introduced.

Now, I can't stress how unusual this is. This is emphatically not how Congress works. I'm not talking about how Congress should work, the way you see on *Schoolhouse Rock*. I mean, this is not the way

Congress actually works. I mean, I think we all know Congress is a
dead zone of deadlock and dysfunction. There are months of debates
and horse trading and hearings and stall tactics. I mean, you know,
first you're supposed to announce that you're going to hold hearings
on a problem, and then days of experts talking about the issue, and
then you propose a possible solution, you bring the experts back
for their thoughts on that, and then other members have different
solutions, and they propose those, and you spend a bunch of time
debating, and there's a bunch of trading, they get members over to
your cause. And finally, you spend hours talking one-on-one with
the different people in the debate, try and come back with some sort
of compromise, which you hash out in endless backroom meetings.
And then, when that's all done, you take that, and you go through
it line by line in public to see if anyone has any objections or wants
to make any changes. And then you have the vote. It's a painful, ar-
duous process. You don't just introduce a bill on Monday and then
pass it unanimously a couple days later. That just doesn't happen in
Congress.

But this time, it was going to happen. And it wasn't because there
were no disagreements on the issue. There are always disagreements.
Some senators thought the bill was much too weak and needed to be
stronger; as it was introduced, the bill only allowed the government
to shut down websites, and these senators, they wanted any company in the world to have the power to get a website shut down.
Other senators thought it was a drop too strong. But somehow, in
the kind of thing you never see in Washington, they had all managed
to put their personal differences aside to come together and support one bill they were persuaded they could all live with: a bill that
would censor the Internet. And when I saw this, I realized: whoever
was behind this was good.

Now, the typical way you make good things happen in Washington is you find a bunch of wealthy companies who agree with you.
Social Security didn't get passed because some brave politicians decided their good conscience couldn't possibly let old people die
starving in the streets. I mean, are you kidding me? Social Security
got passed because John D. Rockefeller was sick of having to take
money out of his profits to pay for his workers' pension funds. Why

do that, when you can just let the government take money from the workers? Now, my point is not that Social Security is a bad thing—I think it's fantastic. It's just that the way you get the government to do fantastic things is you find a big company willing to back them. The problem is, of course, that big companies aren't really huge fans of civil liberties. You know, it's not that they're against them; it's just there's not much money in it.

Now, if you've been reading the press, you probably didn't hear this part of the story. As Hollywood has been telling it, the great, good copyright bill they were pushing was stopped by the evil Internet companies who make millions of dollars off of copyright infringement. But it just—it really wasn't true. I was in there, in the meetings with the Internet companies—actually probably all here today. And, you know, if all their profits depended on copyright infringement, they would have put a lot more money into changing copyright law. The fact is, the big Internet companies, they would do just fine if this bill passed. They wouldn't be thrilled about it, but I doubt they would even have a noticeable dip in their stock price. So they were against it, but they were against it, like the rest of us, on grounds primarily of principle. And principle doesn't have a lot of money in the budget to spend on lobbyists. So they were practical about it. "Look," they said, "this bill is going to pass. In fact, it's probably going to pass unanimously. As much as we try, this is not a train we're going to be able to stop. So, we're not going to support it—we couldn't support it. But in opposition, let's just try and make it better." So that was the strategy: lobby to make the bill better. They had lists of changes that would make the bill less obnoxious or less expensive for them, or whatever. But the fact remained at the end of the day, it was going to be a bill that was going to censor the Internet, and there was nothing we could do to stop it.

So I did what you always do when you're a little guy facing a terrible future with long odds and little hope of success: I started an online petition. I called all my friends, and we stayed up all night setting up a website for this new group, Demand Progress, with an online petition opposing this noxious bill, and I sent it to a few friends. Now, I've done a few online petitions before. I've worked at some of the biggest groups in the world that do online petitions.

I've written a ton of them and read even more. But I've never seen anything like this. Starting from literally nothing, we went to 10,000 signers, then 100,000 signers, and then 200,000 signers and 300,000 signers, in just a couple of weeks. And it wasn't just signing a name. We asked those people to call Congress, to call urgently. There was a vote coming up this week, in just a couple days, and we had to stop it. And at the same time, we told the press about it, about this incredible online petition that was taking off. And we met with the staff of members of Congress and pleaded with them to withdraw their support for the bill. I mean, it was amazing. It was huge. The power of the Internet rose up in force against this bill. And then it passed unanimously.

Now, to be fair, several of the members gave nice speeches before casting their vote, and in their speeches they said their office had been overwhelmed with comments about the First Amendment concerns behind this bill, comments that had them very worried, so worried, in fact, they weren't sure that they still supported the bill. But even though they didn't support it, they were going to vote for it anyway, they said, because they needed to keep the process moving, and they were sure any problems that were had with it could be fixed later. So, I'm going to ask you, does this sound like Washington, D.C., to you? Since when do members of Congress vote for things that they oppose just to keep the process moving? I mean, whoever was behind this was good.

And then, suddenly, the process stopped. Senator Ron Wyden, the Democrat from Oregon, put a hold on the bill. Giving a speech in which he called it a nuclear bunker-buster bomb aimed at the Internet, he announced he would not allow it to pass without changes. And as you may know, a single senator can't actually stop a bill by themselves, but they can delay it. By objecting to a bill, they can demand Congress spend a bunch of time debating it before getting it passed. And Senator Wyden did. He bought us time—a lot of time, as it turned out. His delay held all the way through the end of that session of Congress, so that when the bill came back, it had to start all over again. And since they were starting all over again, they figured, why not give it a new name? And that's when it began being called PIPA, and eventually SOPA.

So there was probably a year or two of delay there. And in retrospect, we used that time to lay the groundwork for what came later. But that's not what it felt like at the time. At the time, it felt like we were going around telling people that these bills were awful, and in return, they told us that they thought we were crazy. I mean, we were kids wandering around waving our arms about how the government was going to censor the Internet. It does sound a little crazy. You can ask Larry tomorrow. I was constantly telling him what was going on, trying to get him involved, and I'm pretty sure he just thought I was exaggerating. Even I began to doubt myself. It was a rough period. But when the bill came back and started moving again, suddenly all the work we had done started coming together. All the folks we talked to about it suddenly began getting really involved and getting others involved. Everything started snowballing. It happened so fast.

I remember there was one week where I was having dinner with a friend in the technology industry, and he asked what I worked on, and I told him about this bill. And he said, "Wow! You need to tell people about that." And I just groaned. And then, just a few weeks later, I remember I was chatting with this cute girl on the subway, and she wasn't in technology at all, but when she heard that I was, she turned to me very seriously and said, "You know, we have to stop 'SOAP.'" So, progress, right?

But, you know, I think that story illustrates what happened during those couple weeks, because the reason we won wasn't because I was working on it or Reddit was working on it or Google was working on it or Tumblr or any other particular person. It was because there was this enormous mental shift in our industry. Everyone was thinking of ways they could help, often really clever, ingenious ways. People made videos. They made infographics. They started PACs. They designed ads. They bought billboards. They wrote news stories. They held meetings. Everybody saw it as their responsibility to help. I remember at one point during this period I held a meeting with a bunch of start-ups in New York, trying to encourage everyone to get involved, and I felt a bit like I was hosting one of these Clinton Global Initiative meetings, where I got to turn to every start-up in the—every start-up founder in the room and be like, "What are you going to do? And what are you going to do?" And everyone was trying to one-up each other.

If there was one day the shift crystallized, I think it was the day of the hearings on SOPA in the House, the day we got that phrase, "It's no longer OK not to understand how the Internet works." There was just something about watching those clueless members of Congress debate the bill, watching them insist they could regulate the Internet and a bunch of nerds couldn't possibly stop them. They really brought it home for people that this was happening, that Congress was going to break the Internet, and it just didn't care.

I remember when this moment first hit me. I was at an event, and I was talking, and I got introduced to a U.S. senator, one of the strongest proponents of the original COICA bill, in fact. And I asked him why, despite being such a progressive, despite giving a speech in favor of civil liberties, why he was supporting a bill that would censor the Internet. And, you know, that typical politician smile he had suddenly faded from his face, and his eyes started burning this fiery red. And he started shouting at me, said, "Those people on the Internet, they think they can get away with anything! They think they can just put anything up there, and there's nothing we can do to stop them! They put up everything! They put up our nuclear missiles, and they just laugh at us! Well, we're going to show them! There's got to be laws on the Internet! It's got to be under control!"

Now, as far as I know, nobody has ever put up the U.S.'s nuclear missiles on the Internet. I mean, it's not something I've heard about. But that's sort of the point. He wasn't having a rational concern, right? It was this irrational fear that things were out of control. Here was this man, a United States senator, and those people on the Internet, they were just mocking him. They had to be brought under control. Things had to be under control. And I think that was the attitude of Congress. And just as seeing that fire in that senator's eyes scared me, I think those hearings scared a lot of people. They saw this wasn't the attitude of a thoughtful government trying to resolve trade-offs in order to best represent its citizens. This was more like the attitude of a tyrant. And so the citizens fought back.

The wheels came off the bus pretty quickly after that hearing. First the Republican senators pulled out, and then the White House issued a statement opposing the bill, and then the Democrats, left all alone out there, announced they were putting the bill on hold so they could have a few further discussions before the official vote. And that was when, as hard as it was for me to believe, after all this, we had won. The thing that everyone said was impossible, that some of the biggest companies in the world had written off as kind of a pipe dream, had happened. We did it. We won.

And then we started rubbing it in. You all know what happened next. Wikipedia went black. Reddit went black. Craigslist went black. The phone lines on Capitol Hill flat-out melted. Members of Congress started rushing to issue statements retracting their support for the bill that they were promoting just a couple days ago. And it was just ridiculous. I mean, there's a chart from the time that captures it pretty well. It says something like "January 14th" on one side and has this big, long list of names supporting the bill, and then just a few lonely people opposing it; and on the other side, it says "January 15th," and now it's totally reversed—everyone is opposing it, just a few lonely names still hanging on in support.

I mean, this really was unprecedented. Don't take my word for it, but ask former senator Chris Dodd, now the chief lobbyist for Hollywood. He admitted, after he lost, that he had masterminded the whole evil plan. And he told the *New York Times* he had never seen anything like it during his many years in Congress. And everyone I've spoken to agrees. The people rose up, and they caused a sea change in Washington—not the press, which refused to cover the story—just coincidentally, their parent companies all happened to be lobbying for the bill; not the politicians, who were pretty much unanimously in favor of it; and not the companies, who had all but given up trying to stop it and decided it was inevitable. It was really stopped by the people, the people themselves. They killed the bill dead; so dead that when members of Congress propose something now that even touches the Internet, they have to give a long speech beforehand about how it is definitely not like SOPA; so dead that when you ask congressional staffers about it, they groan and shake their heads like it's all a bad dream they're trying really hard to forget; so dead that it's kind of hard to believe this story, hard to remember how close it all came to actually passing, hard to remember how this could have gone any other way. But it wasn't a dream or a nightmare; it was all very real.

And it will happen again. Sure, it will have yet another name, and maybe a different excuse, and probably do its damage in a different way. But make no mistake: The enemies of the freedom to connect have not disappeared. The fire in those politicians' eyes hasn't been put out. There are a lot of people, a lot of powerful people, who want to clamp down on the Internet. And to be honest, there aren't a whole lot who have a vested interest in protecting it from all of that. Even some of the biggest companies, some of the biggest Internet companies, to put it frankly, would benefit from a world in which their little competitors could get censored. We can't let that happen.

Now, I've told this as a personal story, partly because I think big stories like this one are just more interesting at human scale. The director J. D. Walsh says good stories should be like the poster for *Transformers*. There's a huge evil robot on the left side of the poster and a huge, big army on the right side of the poster. And in the middle, at the bottom, there's just a small family trapped in the middle. Big stories need human stakes. But mostly, it's a personal story, because I didn't have time to research any of the other part of it. But that's kind of the point. We won this fight because everyone made themselves the hero of their own story. Everyone took it as their job to save this crucial freedom. They threw themselves into it. They did whatever they could think of to do. They didn't stop to ask anyone for permission. You remember how Hacker News readers spontaneously organized this boycott of GoDaddy over their support of SOPA? Nobody told them they could do that. A few people even thought it was a bad idea. It didn't matter. The senators were right: The Internet really is out of control. But if we forget that, if we let Hollywood rewrite the story so it was just big company Google who stopped the bill, if we let them persuade us we didn't actually make a difference, if we start seeing it as someone else's responsibility to do this work and it's our job just to go home and pop some popcorn and curl up on the couch to watch *Transformers*, well, then next time they might just win. Let's not let that happen.

COMPUTERS

In 2000, at the age of thirteen, Aaron Swartz coauthored the RDF Site Summary (RSS), 1.0 specification, which became the first major standard for syndicating website and blog content through feeds. It was published a few days after he turned fourteen. It is no easy task to work out a technical standard with nearly a dozen other people—something many adults lack both the patience and maturity to do. I call attention to it because Swartz's technical achievements show that he practiced what he preached—a very rare quality. He wanted openness, debate, rationality, and critical thinking, and he refused to cut corners—even at the age of thirteen.

RSS itself was fundamentally about sharing, taking the content out of its presented form on a website and allowing it to be redistributed and aggregated by other individuals and entities. Another of Swartz's projects, the webpage authoring tool Markdown (2004, co-designed with John Gruber), was a lightweight tool to easily generate webpages and blogposts by turning marked-up text into HTML. Both point to one of Swartz's central driving passions: making the creation, distribution, and freedom of information as easy and frictionless as possible.

Swartz's technical skills were obviously superior, but what differentiated him from most programmers, even some of the greatest open-source gurus, was the *way* he went about his technical projects. Rather than retreating into a "cathedral" of elite programmers, he wanted to keep things simple, include people, and welcome them in by making things as accessible as he could. The technical projects he chose perfectly mirrored this instinct. They all point to his later, more explicitly political work, where two projects stand out: first, the tor2web proxy project, intended to make hidden deep websites accessible to everyday web users and not just techies; and second, the anonymous leak platform SecureDrop, now known as Strongbox and currently deployed at the *New Yorker, The Guardian,* and elsewhere. Swartz saw the deep web as a good platform for sharing information anonymously, and told *Wired*, "the idea was to kind of produce this hybrid where people could publish stuff using Tor and make it so that anyone on the Internet could view it." That, in essence, was his technical philosophy: to build things for *anyone on the Internet*, not just hackers.

Swartz's remarkable achievement was that he managed to merge political activism and technical knowhow to a degree managed by few before—perhaps Edward Felten's analysis of DRM methods and advocacy against them come closest. His technical efforts to ease and democratize the creation and flow of information aligned perfectly with his political ideals of openness, transparency, and reform. That the Internet is growing farther from his ideals rather than closer signals just how much we lost with him.

—David Auerbach

Excerpt: A Programmable Web

http://www.morganclaypool.com/doi/pdf/10.2200/S00481EDIV01Y
201302WBE005

November 2009

Age 22

The following is an excerpt from Aaron Swartz's A Programmable Web:
An Unfinished Work *published in 2013 by Morgan & Claypool. Excerpted
by permission of Morgan & Claypool Publishers.—Ed.*

If you are like most people I know (and, since you're reading this
book, you probably are—at least in this respect), you use the Web. A
lot. In fact, in my own personal case, the vast majority of my days are
spent reading or scanning web pages—a scroll through my webmail
client to talk with friends and colleagues, a weblog or two to catch
up on the news of the day, a dozen short articles, a flotilla of Google
queries, and the constant turn to Wikipedia for a stray fact to answer
a nagging question.

All fine and good, of course; indeed, nigh indispensable. And yet,
it is sobering to think that little over a decade ago none of this existed. Email had its own specialized applications, weblogs had yet to
be invented, articles were found on paper, Google was yet unborn,
and Wikipedia not even a distant twinkle in Larry Sanger's eye.

And so, it is striking to consider—almost shocking, in fact—what
the world might be like when our software turns to the Web just as
frequently and casually as we do. Today, of course, we can see the
faint, future glimmers of such a world. There is software that phones
home to find out if there's an update. There is software where part
of its content—the help pages, perhaps, or some kind of catalog—
is streamed over the Web. There is software that sends a copy of
all your work to be stored on the Web. There is software specially

designed to help you navigate a certain kind of web page. There is software that consists of *nothing but* a certain kind of web page. There is software—the so-called "mashups"—that consists of a web page combining information from two other web pages. And there is software that, using "APIs," treats other web sites as just another part of the software infrastructure, another function it can call to get things done.

Our computers are so small and the Web so great and vast that this last scenario seems like part of an inescapable trend. Why *wouldn't* you depend on other web sites whenever you could, making their endless information and bountiful abilities a seamless part of yours? And so, I suspect, such uses will become increasingly common until, one day, your computer is as tethered to the Web as you yourself are now.

It is sometimes suggested that such a future is impossible, that making a Web that other computers could use is the fantasy of some (rather unimaginative, I would think) sci-fi novelist. That it would only happen in a world of lumbering robots and artificial intelligence and machines that follow you around, barking orders while intermittently unsuccessfully attempting to persuade you to purchase a new pair of shoes.

So it is perhaps unsurprising that one of the critics who has expressed something like this view, Cory Doctorow, is in fact a rather imaginative sci-fi novelist (amongst much else). Doctorow's complaint is expressed in his essay "Metacrap: Putting the torch to seven straw-men of the meta-utopia." It is also reprinted in his book of essays *Content: Selected Essays on Technology, Creativity, Copyright, and the Future of the Future* (2008, Tachyon Publications) which is likewise available online at http://craphound.com/content/download/.

Doctorow argues that any system that collects accurate "metadata"—the kind of machine-processable data that will be needed to make this dream of computers using-the-Web come true—will run into seven inescapable problems: people lie, people are lazy, people are stupid, people don't know themselves, schemas aren't neutral, metrics influence results, and there's more than one way to describe something. Instead, Doctorow proposes that instead of trying to get people to provide data, we should instead look at the data they produce incidentally while doing other things (like how Google looks at the links people make when they write web pages) and use that instead.

Doctorow is, of course, attacking a strawman. Utopian fantasies of honest, complete, unbiased data about everything are obviously impossible. But who was trying for that anyway? The Web is rarely perfectly honest, complete, and unbiased—but it's still pretty damn useful. There's no reason making a Web for computers to use can't be the same way.

I have to say, however, the idea's proponents do not escape culpability for these utopian perceptions. Many of them have gone around talking about the "Semantic Web" in which our computers would finally be capable of "machine understanding." Such a framing (among other factors) has attracted refugees from the struggling world of artificial intelligence, who have taken it as another opportunity to promote their life's work.

Instead of the "let's just build something that works" attitude that made the Web (and the Internet) such a roaring success, they brought the formalizing mindset of mathematicians and the institutional structures of academics and defense contractors. They formed committees to form working groups to write drafts of ontologies that carefully listed (in 100-page Word documents) all possible things in the universe and the various properties they could have, and they spent hours in Talmudic debates over whether a washing machine was a kitchen appliance or a household cleaning device.

With them has come academic research and government grants and corporate R&D and the whole apparatus of people and institutions that scream "pipedream." And instead of spending time building things, they've convinced people interested in these ideas that the first thing we need to do is write *standards*. (To engineers, this is absurd from the start—standards are things you write *after* you've got something working, not before!)

And so the "Semantic Web Activity" at the Worldwide Web Consortium (W3C) has spent its time writing standard upon standard: the Extensible Markup Language (XML), the Resource Description Framework (RDF), the Web Ontology Language (OWL), tools for Gleaning Resource Descriptions from Dialects of Languages

(GRDDL), the Simple Protocol And RDF Query Language (SPARQL) (as created by the RDF Data Access Working Group (DAWG)).

Few have received any widespread use and those that have (XML) are uniformly scourges on the planet, offenses against hardworking programmers that have pushed out sensible formats (like JSON) in favor of overly complicated hairballs with no basis in reality (I'm not done yet!—more on this in chapter 5).

Instead of getting existing systems to talk to each other and writing up the best practices, these self-appointed guarantors of the Semantic Web have spent their time creating their own little universe, complete with Semantic Web databases and programming languages. But databases and programming languages, while far from perfect, are largely solved problems. People already have their favorites, which have been tested and hacked to work in all sorts of unusual environments, and folks are not particularly inclined to learn a new one, especially for no good reason. It's hard enough getting people to share data as it is, harder to get them to share it in a particular format, and completely impossible to get them to store it and manage it in a completely new system.

And yet this is what Semantic Webheads are spending their time on. It's as if to get people to use the Web, they started writing a new operating system that had the Web built-in right at the core. Sure, we might end up there someday, but insisting that people do that from the start would have doomed the Web to obscurity from the beginning.

All of which has led "web engineers" (as this series' title so cutely calls them) to tune out and go back to doing real work, not wanting to waste their time with things that don't exist and, in all likelihood, never will. And it's led many who have been working on the Semantic Web, in the vain hope of actually building a world where software can communicate, to burn out and tune out and find more productive avenues for their attentions.

For an example, look at Sean B. Palmer. In his influential piece, "Ditching the Semantic Web?," he proclaims "It's not prudent, perhaps even not moral (if that doesn't sound too melodramatic), to work on RDF, OWL, SPARQL, RIF, the broken ideas of distributed trust, CWM, Tabulator, Dublin Core, FOAF, SIOC, and any of these kinds of things" and says not only will he "stop working on the Semantic Web" but "I will, moreover, actively dissuade anyone from working on the Semantic Web where it distracts them from working on" more practical projects.

It would be only fair here to point out that I am not exactly an unbiased observer. For one thing, Sean, like just about everyone else I cite in the book, is a friend. We met through working on these things together but since have kept in touch and share emails about what we're working on and are just generally nice to each other. And the same goes for almost all the other people I cite and criticize.

Moreover, the reason we were working together is that I too did my time in the Semantic Web salt mines. My first web application was a collaboratively written encyclopedia, but my second, aggregated news headlines from sites around the Web, led me into a downward spiral that ended with many years spent on RDF Core Working Groups and an ultimate decision to get out of the world of computers altogether.

Obviously, that didn't work out quite as planned. Jim Hendler, another friend and one of the AI transplants I've just spend so much time taking a swing at, asked me if I'd write a bit on the subject to kick off a new series of electronic books he's putting together. I'll do just about anything for a little cash (just kidding; I just wanted to get published (just kidding; I've been published plenty of times (just kidding; not that many times (just kidding; I've never been published (just kidding; I have, but I just wanted more practice (just kidding; I practice plenty (just kidding; I never practice (just kidding; I just wanted to publish a book (just kidding; I just wanted to write a book (just kidding; it's easy to write a book (just kidding; it's a death march (just kidding; it's not so bad (just kidding; my girlfriend left me (just kidding; I left her (just kidding, just kidding, just kidding)))))))))))))))) and so here I am again, rehashing all the old ground and finally getting my chance to complain about what a mistake all the Semantic Web folks have made.

Yet, as my little thought experiment above has hopefully made clear, the programmable web is anything but a pipe dream—it is today's reality and tomorrow's banality. No software developer will remain content to limit themselves only to things on the user's own computer. And no web site developer will be content to limit their site only to users who act with it directly.

Just as the interlinking power of the World Wide Web sucked all available documents into its maw—encouraging people to digitize them, convert them into HTML, give them a URL, and put them on the Internet (hell, as we speak, Google is even doing this to entire libraries)—the programmable Web will pull all applications within its grasp. The benefits that come from being connected are just too powerful to ultimately resist.

They will, of course, be granted challenges to business models—as new technologies always are—especially for those who make their money off of gating up and charging access to data. But such practices simply aren't tenable in the long term, legally or practically (let alone morally). Under US law, facts aren't copyrightable (thanks to the landmark Supreme Court decision in *Feist v. Rural Telephone Service*) and databases are just collections of facts. (Some European countries have special database rights, but such extensions have been fervently opposed in the US.)

But even if the law didn't get in the way, there's so much value in sharing data that most data providers will eventually come around. Sure, providing a website where people can look things up can be plenty valuable, but it's nothing compared to what you can do when you combine that information with others.

To take an example from my own career, look at the website OpenSecrets.org. It collects information about who's contributing money to US political candidates and displays nice charts and tables about the industries that have funded the campaigns of presidential candidates and members of Congress.

Similarly, the website Taxpayer.net provides a wealth of information about Congressional earmarks—the funding requests that members of Congress slip into bills, requiring a couple million dollars be given to someone for a particular pet project. (The $398 million "Bridge to Nowhere" being the most famous example.)

Both are fantastic sites and are frequently used by observers of American politics, to good effect. But imagine how much better they would be if you put them together—you could search for major campaign contributors who had received large earmarks.

Note that this isn't the kind of "mashup" that can be achieved with today's APIs. APIs only let you look at the data in a particular way, typically the way that the hosting site looks at it. So with OpenSecrets' API you can get a list of the top contributors to a candidate. But this isn't enough for the kind of question we're interested in—you'd need to compare each earmark against each donor to see if they match. It requires real access to the data.

Note also that the end result is ultimately in everyone's best interest. OpenSecrets.org wants people to find out about the problematic influence of money in politics.Taxpayer.net wants to draw attention to this wasteful spending. The public wants to know how money in politics causes wasteful spending and a site that helps them do so would further each organization's goals. But they can only get there if they're willing to share their data.

Fortunately for us, the Web was designed with this future in mind. The protocols that underpin it are not designed simply to provide pages for human consumption, but also to easily accommodate the menagerie of spiders, bots, and scripts that explore its fertile soil. And the original developers of the Web, the men and women who invented the tools that made it the life-consuming pastime that it is today, have long since turned their sights towards making the Web safe, even inviting, for applications.

Unfortunately, far too few are aware of this fact, leading many to reinvent—sloppily—the work that they have already done. (It hasn't helped that the few who are aware have spent their time working on the Semantic Web nonsense that I criticized above.) So we will begin by trying to understand the architecture of the Web—what it got right and, occasionally, what it got wrong, but most importantly why it is the way it is. We will learn how it allows both users and search engines to co-exist peacefully while supporting everything from photo-sharing to financial transactions.

We will continue by considering what it means to build a program on top of the Web—how to write software that both fairly serves its immediate users as well as the developers who want to build on top of it. Too often, an API is bolted on top of an existing application, as an afterthought or a completely separate piece. But, as we'll see, when a web application is designed properly, APIs naturally grow out of it and require little effort to maintain.

Then we'll look into what it means for your application to be not just another tool for people and software to use, but part of the ecology—a section of the programmable web. This means exposing your data to be queried and copied and integrated, even without explicit permission, into the larger software ecosystem, while protecting users' freedom.

Finally, we'll close with a discussion of that much-maligned phrase, "the Semantic Web," and try to understand what it would really mean.

Let's begin.

Privacy, Accuracy, Security: Pick Two

http://www.aaronsw.com/weblog/001016

July 29, 2003

Age 16

The Problems with Compulsory Licensing

Millions of people want to download music for, essentially, free. The record companies don't want them to do this, and claim that they're losing money and threaten to sue you into oblivion. How do we reconcile these two? One proposal is compulsory licensing.

The basic idea is that a large portion of the population pays a relatively small tax to the government, who then gives it to the artists whose work is downloaded. Terry Fisher says that a small tax on CD burners, DVD burners, DSL, and cable modems (costing the average family $50, less than they spend on DVDs and CDs) could pay for all the music and movies plus a 20% bureaucratic overhead.

Assuming this could be made to work, people could be convinced to accept it, and Congress could pass it, there are still three problems which can't all be solved.

Privacy

Some proposals suggest that we simply monitor everyone's Internet connection (or, usually, get the ISPs to do it) and send the results to the government. I think this is an unacceptable invasion of privacy. It's bad enough we have to have Carnivore watching our packets and describing our emails when law enforcement gets a warrant, but now you want the government to keep track of all the music and movies we download, all the time? I don't think that's going to fly.

Accuracy

OK, they say, *we won't watch everyone's computers. We'll just use sampling.* This has worked well in other media. TV networks, for example, make money off of advertising. They charge for ads based on how many people watch the shows. They figure out how many people watch the shows using Nielsen ratings. Nielsen ratings are calculated by getting a small percentage of the population to install a set-top box which monitors what they watch and when and sends the results back to Nielsen.

(This has some interesting effects, among which is the fact that boycotts of shows only have a real effect insofar as the boycotters are Nielsen homes. This means that as long as you're not a Nielsen home, you can boycott a show and still watch it.)

("Sweeps week" is a similar phenomenon but on a somewhat smaller scale. Each individual TV station [like our local NBC affiliate, WMAQ] sells advertising also, so they need to know how many people locally watch the shows. But each little station can't afford to do the Nielsen thing, so they do something similar with paper diaries that they send out one week of the year. But they all do it on the same week [sweeps week], so the networks purposely introduce big guest stars and major cliffhangers that week to get more people to watch the show.)

This sounds good, and it works reasonably well for TV, but it won't work on the Internet. Popularity on the Internet doesn't follow the old rules; it follows something called a power law. [. . .] There are hundreds of thousands of sites with tens of users and tens of sites with hundreds of thousands of users. And there are tens of thousands of sites with hundreds of users, and thousands of sites with thousands of users and so on.

Sampling can't cope with this kind of disparity. It can deal when there are a small number of known groups who make up a very small amount of the population (just seek out those groups specifically). But it can't deal when there's a large number of unknown groups who each make up a very small amount of the population (like the tons of small websites, each with a small but loyal fan base).

Who cares about these people? you may say. But while each of these groups have small fan bases individually, collectively they make up a significant portion, if not a majority, of the overall system. In other words, if you count these guys out you'll be doubling the amount of money folks like Britney Spears get over what they deserve.

Britney Spears seems to be doing just fine with the current system. If all we're doing is helping her, why are we going to all this trouble? And furthermore, if you're going to tax me to pay the artists I listen to, it's a little unfair if none of that money goes to the ones I actually care about.

Security

Fine, fine, they say, if they read this far. *How about we just have people submit the songs they listen to anonymously? People want their favorite artists to be paid, so they'll be happy to.*

Yeah, but that's exactly the problem. People want their favorite artists to be paid, especially when those artists are *themselves.* What stops me from anonymously submitting that 1M people listened to my band and waiting for the money to roll in? Small things like that will get lost in the noise.

Even if the system isn't anonymous (so we're forgetting about privacy) you still have this problem. An enterprising MIT student, taking advantage of the fact that MIT has 16.5M IP addresses to themselves, writes a little program to pretend to be a whole bunch of MIT students who all have decided that his band is their new favorite. Again, it'll get lost in the noise of MIT and the money will roll in.

It doesn't seem right to tax Americans and give their money to fraudsters, no matter how clever the fraudsters are. It'll be really hard to eliminate fraud, and when it's so easy and anonymous, it'll be more widespread than anything we've seen before.

Conclusion

I've gone through all the compulsory licensing scenarios, and I always seem to get stuck on one (or more) of these issues. If anyone's found a way to eliminate all of them, please let me know!

Fixing Compulsory Licensing

http://www.aaronsw.com/weblog/001036

September 15, 2003

Age 16

In a previous post I dashed the world's hopes for a viable compulsory licensing system, no matter how attractive one might seem. Luckily for the world, I'm back to explain how to make a compulsory licensing system that doesn't run into any of those problems using . . . *cryptography*!

(To review, the idea for our compulsory licensing system is this: we tax Internet connections and CD/DVD burners a small amount and send the money to the artists. In exchange, they let us download their songs and movies off the Internet. The problem is how to decide which artists should get the money without losing privacy, accuracy, or security.)

Here's the key to my proposal: when you pay the tax you get a vote.

So when you buy a CD or DVD burner, it comes with a short string (a random-looking series of letters and numbers) to type into your computer. (The strings are given to the manufacturers by the government when they pay the tax.) When you pay the bill for your Internet connection, you're emailed another such string. (The string from your email can be handled automatically, and the one in the CD burner box could be made relatively easy to type in.)

The string is a digital gift certificate, worth however much the tax you paid was, but only spendable on donations to artists. Once your computer has the string, it looks at all the songs you've listened to and decides what songs to spend your gift certificate money on. (It knows what you listen to because it's built in to your MP3 player.) If you've listened to one Britney Spears song day and night for the past month and nothing else, it will give all your money to Britney. If you listen to a variety of independent bands, it will split your money among them. (Advanced users can of course customize how their money will be spent, but it's simpler to have the computer choose automatically by default.)

The result is sent anonymously to the government using the string. (The strings will be unique enough that it will be nearly impossible to guess a correct one.) The government checks this against the list of strings they gave out and the list of strings that have already been used to make sure that it's legitimate, and then credits the appropriate accounts.

Does this solve all the problems?

Yes, it's private. The strings are received and sent anonymously. ("But wait," you say, "the Internet providers know who gets what string." OK, if you're really paranoid a solution to this is explained below.) The government can't connect you with your vote.

Yes, it's accurate. The money goes to the artists that the people like and want to support, as chosen by the people themselves. There are a few edge cases. For example, if everyone listens to but hates Jerry Falwell, they might choose not to give him any money, even though they've taken advantage of his work. I think this is an acceptable problem—the majority of people won't bother to change the defaults and even if they do, hey, it's their money.

Yes, it's secure. The amount of money you have control over is equal to the amount of money you paid in taxes, so the worst-case scenario is that you get your tax money back. There is a chance that everyone will give all their money to themselves, but this can be prevented by only paying out to accounts that meet some higher threshold of cash.

Won't artists offer to buy people's gift certificates for cash? The artist can spend the gift certificate on themselves and recover their money. (Seth Schoen)

The government could make such behavior against the terms of service for having an artist account. To be successful, any such operation would have to be publicized. The government could keep an eye out for such things, send the operator a known gift certificate, see whose account it went into, and shut down the account.

Can't operators use this to shut down the account of someone they don't like?

The government gift certificate would be indistinguishable from a normal one, so they'd have to be giving lots of gift certificates to that person, in which case they'd be losing lots of money. To be extra sure, the government could trace the source of the payment for the gift certificate. Or they could just bankrupt whoever was running the scam by feeding them lots of bogus gift certificates that appeared to go through, but are never credited to the artist's account.

Hey, where's the crypto?

OK, here's the fun part. The money can be securely distributed to you using digital cash techniques. Here's how that system works, by physical analogy:

1. You send "the bank" (probably the government or your ISP) a gift certificate with a random string on it and a piece of carbon paper in a sealed envelope.
2. They sign the outside of the envelope and their signature goes through the carbon paper onto the gift certificate.
3. You open the envelope, take out the signed gift certificate, and use this as described above. (The government uses the random string to make sure you don't use it twice and they verify the signature to make sure it's legitimate.)
4. Each signed gift certificate is worth a set amount ($1?) so you repeat as necessary to get the amount you're owed.

Since the government can't open the envelope (we use crypto to ensure this), they have no idea of knowing which gift certificate they signed, so they can't associate you with it when you spend it later.

Now, to anonymously submit the gift certificates to the government, you reuse the peer-to-peer network you downloaded the songs from as a remailer network. You encrypt your gift certificate so only the government can read it, then you pass it to a friend on the peer-to-peer network, who passes it to a friend, etc., until someone gives it to the government. The government publishes the list of identifiers for gift certificates they've received, so you can make sure it got through and resend it if it didn't.

Conclusion

This proposal isn't the simplest, and probably not the most elegant, but unlike the others it will work without cheating the public. I hope the people building these compulsory licensing systems see the value in that.

Postel's Law Has No Exceptions

http://www.aaronsw.com/weblog/001025

August 18, 2003

Age 16

As Mark Pilgrim is fond of saying, "There are no exceptions to Postel's Law." (Postel's Law is generally quoted as "be liberal in what you accept and conservative in what you put out" or something to that effect.) The message of the law is that interoperability is the primary concern, and that programs should accept things, even things that are against the spec, if necessary to achieve interoperability.

HTML, as you may know, is a mess. It's contorted in a hundred different ways with tons of bugs and their work-arounds encrusted into the web, and browsers are expected to make sense of all of it. The XML people saw this and said, "We have to fix this." Their solution was to break Postel's Law.

With XML you are supposed to die and never look back if the document you come across violates the spec. The idea was that if everything died on invalid feeds, no one would ever write them. This is wrong for three reasons:

1. Even with the rule, there will be invalid documents. Someone will write some code, test it, see that it works and move on. One day the code will be given data that trips one of XML's exceptions (AT&T is a common example—XML requires it be written AT&T) and an invalid document will be created.

2. XML apps compete for users. Users want to read these documents, even if they're broken. Users will switch to apps that read these documents and the rule will be useless, since folks will likely test with those apps. The only way we can keep

the rule in effect is by getting *everyone* who writes an app to act against the wishes of their users, which seems like a bad idea.

3. Essentially the same effect can be achieved by having a validation display (like iCab or Straw's smiley face that frowns on invalid documents) and an easy-to-use validator.

This is not to say that all apps should have to process invalid documents, or that they should work hard to guess what the author meant, or that we should encourage or tolerate invalid documents. We should still try to get rid of invalid documents, but taking things out on the users is the wrong way to do it.

The creators of XML were wrong. Postel's Law has no exceptions.

Squaring the Triangle: Secure, Decentralized, Human-Readable Names

http://www.aaronsw.com/weblog/squarezooko

January 6, 2011

Age 24

When using computers, we like to refer to things with names. For example, this website is known as "www.aaronsw.com." You can type that into your browser and read these words. There are three big properties we might want from such names:

- *secure*: that when you type the name in you actually get my website and not the website of an imposter
- *decentralized*: that no central authority controls all the names
- *human-readable*: that the name is something you can actually remember instead of some long string of randomness

In a classic paper, my friend Zooko argued that you can get at most two of these properties at any one time.

Recently, DNS legend Dan Kaminsky used this to argue that since electronic cash was pretty much the same as naming, Zooko's triangle applied to it as well. He used this to argue that Bitcoin, the secure, decentralized, human-meaningful electronic cash system was impossible. I have my problems with Bitcoin, but it's manifestly not impossible, so I just assumed Kaminsky had gone wrong somewhere.

But tonight I realized that you can indeed use Bitcoin to square Zooko's triangle. Here's how it works:

Let there be a document called the scroll. The scroll consists of a series of lines and each line consists of a tuple (name, key, nonce) such that the first N bits of the hash of the scroll from the beginning to the end of a line are all zero. As a result, to add a line to the scroll, you need to do enough computation to discover an appropriate nonce that causes the bits of the hash to be zero.

To look up a name, you ask everyone you know for the scroll, trust whichever scroll is the longest, and then start from the beginning and take the key for the first line with the name you're looking up. To publish a name, you find an appropriate nonce and then send the new line to everyone you know.

OK, let's pause there for a second. How do you steal names in such a system? First, you need to calculate a new nonce for the line you want to steal and every subsequent line. Second, you need to get your replacement scroll to the user. The first is difficult, but perhaps not impossible, depending on how many lines ago the name you want to steal is. It requires having some large multiple of the rest of the network's combined CPU power. This seems like a fairly strong constraint to me, but apparently not to Dan. Luckily, we're saved by the second question.

Let there be a group of machines called the network. Each remembers the last scroll it trusted. When a new valid line is created it's sent to everyone in the network and they add it to their scroll.* Now stealing an old name is impossible, since machines in the network only add new names, they don't accept replacements for old ones.

That's fine for machines already in the network, but how do you join? Well, as a physical law, to join a network you need the identity of at least one machine already in the network. Now when you join, that machine can give you a fabricated scroll where they've stolen all the names. I don't think there's any way to avoid this—if you don't know anyone willing to tell you the correct answer, you can't will the correct answer out of thin air. Even a centralized system depends on knowing at least one honest root.

You can ameliorate this problem by knowing several nodes when you connect and asking each of them for their scroll. It seems like the best theoretically possible case would be requiring only one node to

---

*What happens if two people create a new line at the same time? The debate should be resolved by the creation of the next new line—whichever line is previous in its scroll is the one to trust.

be honest. That would correspond to trusting whichever node had the longest scroll. But this would leave you vulnerable to an attacker who (a) has enough CPU power to fabricate the longest scroll, and (b) can co-opt at least one of your initial nodes. The alternative is to trust only scrolls you receive from a majority of your list of nodes. This leaves you vulnerable to an attacker who can co-opt a majority of your initial nodes. Which trade-off you pick presumably depends on how much you trust your initial nodes.

Publishing a false scroll is equivalent to fragmenting the namespace and starting a separate network. (We can enforce this by requiring nodes to sign each latest scroll and publish their signature to be considered members in good standing of the network. Any node that attempts to sign two contradictory scrolls is obviously duplicitous and can be discounted.) So another way of describing scenario (b) is to say that to join a network, you need a list of nodes where at least a majority are actually nodes in the network. This doesn't seem like an overly strenuous requirement.

And we're actually slightly safer than that, since the majority needs a fair amount of CPU to stay plausible. If we assume that you hear new names from some out-of-band source, for them to work on the attacker's network the attacker must have enough CPU to generate lines for each name you might use. Otherwise you realize that the names you type in on your computer are returning 404s while they work on other people's computers, and begin to realize you've been had by an attacker.

So there you have it. The names are secure: they're identifiable by a key of arbitrary length and cannot be stolen. They're human-meaningful: the name can be whatever string you like. And they're decentralized: no centralized authority determines who gets what name and yet they're available to everyone in the network.

Zooko's triangle has been squared.

Release Late, Release Rarely

http://www.aaronsw.com/weblog/rlrr

July 5, 2006

Age 19

When you look at something you're working on, no matter what it is, you can't help but see past the actual thing to the ideas that inspired it, your plans for extending it, the emotions you've tied to it. But when others look at it, all they see is a piece of junk.

You only get one chance to make a first impression; why have it be "junk"? Once that's associated with your name or project, it's tough to scrape off. Even people who didn't see it themselves may have heard about it secondhand. And once they hear about it, they're not likely to see for themselves. Life's too short to waste it on junk.

But when you release late, after everything has been carefully polished, you can share something of genuine quality. Apple, for example, sometimes releases stupid stuff, but it always looks good. Even when they flub, people give them the benefit of the doubt. "Well, it looks great but I don't really like it" is a lot better then "It's a piece of junk."

Still, you can do better. Releasing means showing it to the world. There's nothing wrong with showing it to friends or experts or even random people in a coffee shop. The friends will give you the emotional support you would have gotten from actual users, without the stress. The experts will point out most of the errors the world would have found, without the insults. And random people will not only give you most of the complaints the public would, they'll also tell you why the public gave up even before bothering to complain.

This is why "release early, release often" works in open source: you're releasing to a community of insiders. Programmers know what it's like to write programs and they don't mind using things that are unpolished. They can see what you're going to do next and maybe help you get there.

The public isn't like that. Don't treat them like they are.

Bake, Don't Fry

http://www.aaronsw.com/weblog/000404

July 9, 2002

Age 15

I really got started with this whole web mess with the ArsDigita Prize where I learned how to build database-backed websites by building one myself. However, it was always assumed that these sites would be built by having a bunch of code on the server which generated pages for the user on demand by calling the database. That was simply how such sites were built, I never questioned it.

Now, a number of tools are challenging that assumption. Movable Type, the program that runs this weblog, has a series of Perl scripts which are used to build your webpage, but the end result is a bunch of static pages which are served to the public. All the content here is plain old web pages, served up by Apache. Tinderbox uses a similar system, drawing from your database of notes to produce a bunch of static pages. My book collection pages are done this way. Radio UserLand statically generates the pages on your local computer and then "upstreams" them to your website.

Finally, while researching Webmake, the Perl CMS that generates pages like Jmason's Weblog and SpamAssassin, I found a good bit of terminology for this. Some websites, the documentation explains, are fried up for the user every time. But others are baked once and served up again and again.

Why bake your pages instead of frying? Well, as you might guess, it's healthier, but at the expense of not tasting quite as good. Baked pages are easy to serve. You can almost always switch servers and software and they'll still work. Plus, you get to take advantage of the great features built into your web server, like content negotiation, caching, ETags, etc. You don't get the bells and whistles like providing a personalized greeting on every page, but those are things that aren't very good for you anyway.

The one problem with the "bake" philosophy is dependencies. It's difficult to keep track of which pages depend on which others and regenerate them correctly when they change. Movable Type handles this in the obvious cases, but when you do anything other than creating or editing an entry, it makes you manually rebuild the corrector portions of the site. Tinderbox, a speedy C++ program, seems to regenerate the whole site every time. It seems that for this philosophy of database-backed static pages to take off, we'd need a really good dependency system to back it. Has anyone built such a system?

Let me know.

Update: Some people seem to think that I want to bake because of performance. Honestly, I don't care about performance. I don't care about performance! I care about not having to maintain cranky AOLserver, Postgres, and Oracle installs. I care about being able to back things up with scp. I care about not having to do any installation or configuration to move my site to a new server. I care about being platform and server independent. I care about full-featured HTTP implementations, including ETags, content negotiation, and If-Modified-Since. (And I know that nobody else will care about it enough to actually implement it in a frying solution.) I hope that clarifies things.

If you liked this article, also check out the sequel, Building Baked Sites.

Building Baked Sites

http://www.aaronsw.com/weblog/000406

July 10, 2002

Age 15

Bake, Don't Fry has been one of my more successful blog entries. I wonder if this was because of style or content (or both?). Anyway, since people seem interested in it, I thought I'd sketch out my views on how to make baked sites work.

First, let me clarify that using static web pages for your site does not preclude things that people generally associate with dynamic sites (like templates, newsboxes, stock tickers, etc.). Nor does it mean that your site can't have any interaction or collaboration (comments, boards, polls). While these things obviously won't work if you move platforms or server software, at least the content already on your site won't die. The key is to keep a strict separation between input (which needs dynamic code to be processed) and output (which can usually be baked).

So how would this work? You'd need a dependency tracking system (good old GNU Make might even do the job) that would allow you to add new content to the system (something tricky with Make alone—is this what Automake does?) or modify old content and would then rebuild the dependent pages or create new ones as necessary. As an example, a new blog entry should create a new page for the entry, rebuild the previous entry page, rebuild the day/week/month's pages, and rebuild the home page. It would also have to add all the dependencies for the new page (to the template, to the previous entry, to that entry, to the category name) and add a dependency to the previous entry page.

Current systems (like OpenACS) could even be hoodwinked into doing this with little or no modification. The dependency information could be layered on top and then the system could simply call the dynamic scripts when that page needed to be regenerated. Of course, a purebred system would probably be better since it would give a chance for URL structure to be designed more sensibly.

Baking doesn't do everything, though. Input systems, like the code that accepts comments, would still need to be dynamic. This is a limitation of web servers which I doubt will ever be solved in a standard way. Dynamic tools (like homepage generators and search software) will either have to be fried, or use client-side technologies like SVG, Java(Script), Flash (ick!). There's no way around that.

If you're interested in helping build a system to help with baking sites, please let me know.

A Brief History of Ajax

http://www.aaronsw.com/weblog/ajaxhistory

December 22, 2005

Age 19

New technology quickly becomes so pervasive that it's sometimes hard to remember what things were like before it. The latest example of this in miniature is the technique known as Ajax, which has become so widespread that it's often thought that the technique has been around practically forever.

In some ways it has. During the first big stretch of browser innovation, Netscape added a feature known as LiveScript, which allowed people to put small scripts in web pages so that they could continue to do things after you'd downloaded them. One early example was the Netscape form system, which would tell you if you'd entered an invalid value for a field as soon as you entered it, instead of after you tried to submit the form to the server.

LiveScript became JavaScript and grew more powerful, leading to a technique known as Dynamic HTML, which was typically used to make things fly around the screen and change around in response to user input. Doing anything serious with Dynamic HTML was painful, however, because all the major browsers implemented its pieces slightly differently.

Shortly before web development died out, in early versions of Mozilla, Netscape showed a new kind of technique. I don't think it ever had a name, but we could call it Dynamic XML. The most vivid example I remember seeing was a mockup of an Amazon.com search result. The web page looked just like a typical Amazon.com search result page, but instead of being written in HTML, it was a piece of XML data which was then rendered for the user by a piece of

JavaScript. The cool part was that this meant the rendering could be changed on the fly—there were a bunch of buttons that would allow you to sort the books in different ways and have them display using different schemes.

Shortly thereafter the bubble burst and web development crashed. Not, however, before Microsoft added a little-known function call named XMLHttpRequest to IE5. Mozilla quickly followed suit and, while nobody I know used it, the function stayed there, just waiting to be taken advantage of.

XMLHttpRequest allowed the JavaScript inside web pages to do something they could never really do before: get more data.* Before, all the data had to be sent with the web page. If you wanted more data or new data, you had to grab another web page. The JavaScript inside web pages couldn't talk to the outside world. XMLHttpRequest changed that, allowing web pages to get more data from the server whenever they pleased.

Google was apparently the first to realize what a sea change this was. With Gmail and Google Maps, they built applications that took advantage of this to provide a user interface that was much more like a web application. (The start-up Oddpost, bought by Yahoo, actually predated this, but their software was for-pay and so they didn't receive as much attention.)

With Gmail, for example, the application is continually asking the server if there's new email. If there is, then it live updates the page; it doesn't make you download a new one. And Google Maps lets you drag a map around and, as you do so, automatically downloads the parts of it you want to look at inline, without making you wait for a whole new page to download.

Jesse James Garrett of Adaptive Path described this new tactic as Ajax (Asynchronous Javascript And XML) in an essay, and the term immediately took off. Everyone began using the technique in their

---

*As my commenters point out—and as I well knew, but momentarily forgot—this isn't really true. Before XMLHttpRequest, people used a trick of not closing the connection to the server. The server would keep adding more and more to the page, never saying it had finished downloading. Ka-Ping Yee used this technique to make a real-time chat system based on an animated GIF. And the ill-fated start-up KnowNow used a similar technique with JavaScript to allow for live-updating pages.

own software and JavaScript tool kits sprung up to make doing so even easier.

And the rest is future history.

Both systems were relatively ill-supported by browsers in my experience. They were, after all, hacks. So while they both seemed extremely cool (KnowNow, in particular, had an awesome demo that allowed for a WYSIWYG SubEthaEdit-style live collaboration session in a browser), they never really took off.

Now apparently there is another technique, which I was unaware of, that involved changing the URL of an iframe to load new JavaScript. I'm not sure why this technique didn't quite take off. While Google Maps apparently used it (and Oddpost probably did as well), I don't know of any other major users.

djb

http://www.aaronsw.com/weblog/djb

October 19, 2009

Age 22

I think it's time to remind people that D. J. Bernstein is the greatest programmer in the history of the world.

First, look only at the objective facts. djb has written two major pieces of system software: a mail server and a DNS server. Both are run by millions of Internet domains. They accomplish all sorts of complicated functions, work under incredibly high loads, and confront no end of unusual situations. And they both run pretty much exactly as Bernstein first wrote them. One bug—one bug!—was found in qmail. A second bug was recently found in djbdns, but you can get a sense of how important it is by the fact that it took people nearly a decade to find it.

No other programmer has this kind of track record. Donald Knuth probably comes closest, but his diary about writing TeX (printed in *Literate Programming*) shows how he kept finding bugs for years and never expected to be finished, only to get closer and closer (thus the odd version numbering scheme). Not only does no one else have djb's track record, no one else even comes close.

But far more important are the subjective factors. djb's programs are some of the greatest works of beauty to be comprehended by the human mind. As with great art, the outline of the code is somehow visually pleasing—there is balance and rhythm and meter that rivals even the best typography. As with great poetry, every character counts—every single one is there because it needs to be. But these programs are not just for being seen or read—like a graceful dancer, they move! And not just as a single dancer either, but a whole choreographed number—processes splitting and moving and recombining at great speeds, around and around again.

But, unlike a dance, this movement has a purpose. They accomplish things that need accomplishing—they find your websites, they ferry your email from place to place. In the most fantastic movies, the routing and sorting of the post office is imagined as a giant endless choreographed dance number. (Imagine, perhaps, "The Office" from Brazil.) But this is no one-time fantasy, this is how your email gets sorted every day.

And the dance is not just there to please human eyes—it is a dance with a purpose. Each of its inner mechanisms is perfectly crafted, using the fewest number of moving parts, accomplishing its task with the most minimal energy. The way jobs are divided and assigned is nothing short of brilliant. The brilliance is not merely linguistic, although it is that too, but contains a kind of elegant mathematical effectiveness, backed by a stream of numbers and equations that show, through pure reason alone, that the movements are provably perfect, a better solution is guaranteed not to exist.

But even all this does not capture his software's incredible beauty. For djb's programs are not great machines to be admired from a distance, vast powerhouses of elegant accomplishment. They are also tools meant to be used by man, perfectly fitted to one's hand. Like a great piece of industrial design, they bring joy to the user every time they are used.

What other field combines all these arts? Language, math, art, design, function. Programming is clearly in a class of its own. And, when it comes to programmers, who even competes with djb? Who else has worked to realize these amazing possibilities? Who else even knows they are there?

Oddly, there are many people who profess to hate djb. Some of this is just the general distaste of genius: djb clearly has a forceful, uncompromising vision, which many misinterpret as arrogance and rudeness. And some of it is the practical man's disregard for great design: djb's programs do not work like most programs, for the simple reason that the way most programs work is wrong. But the animosity goes much deeper than that. I do not profess to understand it, but I do honestly suspect at some level it's people without taste angry and frustrated at the plaudits showered on what they cannot see. Great art always generates its share of mocking detractors.

This is not to say that djb's work is perfect. There are the bugs, as mentioned before, and the log files, which are nothing if not inelegant, and no doubt djb would make numerous changes were he to write the software again today. But who else is even trying? Who else even knows this is possible? I did not realize what great art in software could be until I read djb. And now I feel dirty reading anything else.

A Non-Programmer's Apology

http://www.aaronsw.com/weblog/nonapology

May 27, 2006

Age 19

In his classic *A Mathematician's Apology*, published 65 years ago, the great mathematician G. H. Hardy wrote that "A man who sets out to justify his existence and his activities" has only one real defense, namely that "I do what I do because it is the one and only thing that I can do at all well." "I am not suggesting," he added,

> that this is a defence which can be made by most people, since most people can do nothing at all well. But it is impregnable when it can be made without absurdity. . . . If a man has any genuine talent he should be ready to make almost any sacrifice in order to cultivate it to the full.

Reading such comments one cannot help but apply them to oneself, and so I did. Let us eschew humility for the sake of argument and suppose that I am a great programmer. By Hardy's suggestion, the responsible thing for me to do would be to cultivate and use my talents in that field, to spend my life being a great programmer. And that, I have to say, is a prospect I look upon with no small amount of dread.

It was not always quite this way. For quite a while programming was basically my life. And then, somehow, I drifted away. At first it was small steps—discussing programming instead of doing it, then discussing things for programmers, and then discussing other topics altogether. By the time I reached the end of my first year in college, when people were asking me to program for them over the summer, I hadn't programmed in so long that I wasn't even sure I really could. I certainly did not think of myself as a particularly good programmer.

Ironic, considering Hardy writes that

> Good work is not done by "humble" men. It is one of the first duties of a professor, for example, in any subject, to exaggerate a little both the importance of his subject and his own importance in it. A man who is always asking "Is what I do worthwhile?" and "Am I the right person to do it?" will always be ineffective himself and a discouragement to others. He must shut his eyes a little and think a little more of his subject and himself than they deserve. This is not too difficult: it is harder not to make his subject and himself ridiculous by shutting his eyes too tightly.

Perhaps, after spending so much time not programming, the blinders had worn off. Or perhaps it was the reverse: that I had to convince myself that I was good at what I was doing now, and, since that thing was not programming, by extension, that I was not very good at programming.

Whatever the reason, I looked upon the task of actually having to program for three months with uncertainty and trepidation. For days, if I recall correctly, I dithered. Thinking myself incapable of serious programming, I thought to wait until my partner arrived and instead spend my time assisting him. But days passed and I realized it would be weeks before he would appear, and I finally decided to try to program something in the meantime.

To my shock, it went amazingly well and I have since become convinced that I'm a pretty good programmer, if lacking in most other areas. But now I find myself faced with this dilemma: it is those other areas I would much prefer to work in.

The summer before college I learned something that struck me as incredibly important and yet known by very few. It seemed clear to me that the only responsible way to live my life would be to do something that would only be done by someone who knew this thing—after all, there were few who did and many who didn't, so it seemed logical to leave most other tasks to the majority.

I concluded that the best thing to do would be to attempt to explain this thing I'd learned to others. Any specific task I could do with the knowledge would be far outweighed by the tasks done by those I'd explained the knowledge to.* It was only after I'd decided on this course of action (and perhaps this is the blinders once again) that it struck me that explaining complicated ideas was actually something I'd always loved doing and was really pretty good at.

That aside, having spent the morning reading David Foster Wallace, it is plain that I am no great writer. And so, reading Hardy, I am left wondering whether my decision is somehow irresponsible.

I am saved, I think, because it appears that Hardy's logic to some extent parallels mine. Why is it important for the man who "can bat unusually well" to become "a professional cricketer"? It is, presumably, because those who can bat unusually well are in short supply and so the few who are gifted with that talent should do us all the favor of making use of it. If those whose "judgment of the markets is quick and sound" become cricketers, while the good batters become stockbrokers, we will end up with mediocre cricketers and mediocre stockbrokers. Better for all of us if the reverse is the case.

But this, of course, is awfully similar to the logic I myself employed. It is important for me to spend my life explaining what I'd learned because people who had learned it are in short supply—much shorter supply, in fact (or so it appears), than people who can bat well.

However, there is also an assumption hidden in that statement. It only makes sense to decide what to become based on what you can presently do if you believe that abilities are somehow granted innately and can merely be cultivated, not created in themselves. This is a fairly common view, although rarely consciously articulated (as indeed Hardy takes it for granted), but not one that I subscribe to.

---

*Explaining what that knowledge is, naturally, a larger project and must wait for another time.

†You can probably see DFW's influence on this piece, not least of which in these footnotes.

Instead, it seems plausible that talent is made through practice, that those who are good batters are that way after spending enormous quantities of time batting as a kid.* Mozart, for example, was the son of "one of Europe's leading musical teachers"† and said teacher began music instruction at age three. While I am plainly no Mozart, several similarities do seem apparent. My father had a computer programming company and he began showing me how to use the computer as far back as I can remember.

The extreme conclusion from the theory that there is no innate talent is that there is no difference between people and thus, as much as possible, we should get people to do the most important tasks (writing, as opposed to cricket, let's say). But in fact this does not follow.

Learning is like compound interest. A little bit of knowledge makes it easier to pick up more. Knowing what addition is and how to do it, you can then read a wide variety of things that use addition, thus knowing even more and being able to use that knowledge in a similar manner.‡ And so, the growth in knowledge accelerates.§ This is why children who get started on something at a young age, as Mozart did, grow up to have such an advantage.

And even if (highly implausibly) we were able to control the cir-

---

*Indeed, this apparently parallels the views of the psychologists who have studied the question. Anders Ericsson, a psychology professor who studies "expert performance," told the New York Times Magazine that "the most general claim" in his work "is that a lot of people believe there are some inherent limits they were born with. But there is surprisingly little hard evidence. . . ." The conclusion that follows, the NYTM notes, is that "when it comes to choosing a life path, you should do what you love—because if you don't love it, you are unlikely to work hard enough to get very good. Most people naturally don't like to do things they aren't 'good' at. So they often give up, telling themselves they simply don't possess the talent for math or skiing or the violin. But what they really lack is the desire to be good and to undertake the deliberate practice that would make them better."

†The quote is from Wikipedia where, indeed, the other facts are drawn from as well, the idea having been suggested by Stephen Jay Gould's essay "Mozart and Modularity," collected in his book Eight Little Piggies.

‡I've always thought that this was the reason kids (or maybe just me) especially disliked history. Every other field—biology, math, art—had at least some connection to the present and thus kids had some foundational knowledge to build on. But history? We simply weren't there and thus know absolutely nothing of it.

§It was tempting to write that "the rate of growth" accelerates, but that would mean something rather different.

cumstances in which all children grew up so as to maximize their ability to perform the most important tasks, that still would not be enough, since in addition to aptitude there is also interest.

Imagine the three sons of a famous football player. All three are raised similarly, with athletic activity from their earliest days, and thus have an equal aptitude for playing football. Two of them pick up this task excitedly, while one, despite being good at it, is uninterested* and prefers to read books.† It would not only be unfair to force him to use his aptitude and play football, it would also be unwise. Someone whose heart isn't in it is unlikely to spend the time necessary to excel.

And this, in short,‡ is the position I find myself in. I don't want to be a programmer. When I look at programming books, I am more tempted to mock them than to read them. When I go to programmer conferences, I'd rather skip out and talk politics than programming. And writing code, although it can be enjoyable, is hardly something I want to spend my life doing.

Perhaps, I fear, this decision deprives society of one great programmer in favor of one mediocre writer. And let's not hide behind the cloak of uncertainty; let's say we know that it does. Even so, I would make it. The writing is too important, the programming too unenjoyable.

And for that, I apologize.

*Many people, of course, are uninterested in such things precisely because they aren't very good at them. There's nothing like repeated failures to turn you away from an activity. Perhaps this is another reason to start young—young children might be less stung by failure, as little is expected from them.
†I apologize for the clichédness of this example.
‡Well, shorter than most DFW.

POLITICS

Aaron's politics are easiest to define, particularly in the context of his renown as a programmer and an Internet and information freedom activist, by what they were not: Aaron was decidedly not a cyber-utopian.

He did, of course, believe in the right of ready access to information (a pursuit that in some sense cost him his life), and he told me that he was a "free speech fundamentalist." Yet Aaron's highest goal was to help build a society defined by social justice, and he understood that this would not automatically flow smoothly from the right, and the means, to know about political and corporate corruption.

No, transparency and paper rights wouldn't suffice. Aaron knew that to create a more just world, one must employ knowledge, civil liberties, and civil rights as tools in the hard work of organizing against entrenched power.

Justice, defined how, exactly? How, exactly, did he define justice? Though Aaron eschewed labels, his ideals seemed essentially libertarian socialist: he sought to minimize coercion (governmental, corporate, and economic) and maximize utility, while understanding the importance of equity and solidarity in achieving these ends. But he was willing to engage within the system to get there.

During the time I knew him well, he thought a lot about monetary policy, believing that in order to resolve the immediate economic downturn, and eventually achieve full employment by mobilizing people and capital in ways that improve lives, "the Fed should be printing money that we then give to poor people (or everyone if that's easier)." His final tweet, composed when yet another contentious fight over the debt limit loomed, urged the minting of a trillion-dollar coin to fund government operations.

These are the policy prescriptions of the post-Keynesian. But he wouldn't call himself one; rather, he told me, "I generally like the post-Keynesians." And when a friend announced that he self-identified as a socialist, Aaron replied, "Good—we need more of those."

Though he worked hard to elect Democrats, even volunteering to assist the Democratic National Committee's tech team during the crunch before Election Day, he was an ideologue in pursuit of utility maximization rather than a partisan. He would have preferred a more pluralistic democracy that accurately mapped the varied political impulses of the American populace onto the Congress, and he was willing to ally with Republicans. He would be heartened by the increasing left-right solidarity we see in spaces such as the antiwar, civil libertarian, and criminal justice reform movements today.

Aaron strived to ensure that his efforts, no matter the cause, were as strategic as possible. He believed that one must dissect structures and learn how they tick, develop the tools, tactics, and strategies that are most likely to manipulate them for good, and organize people to implement those approaches.

His poignant deconstruction of the processes of running for office and legislating illuminates the incentives, sample biases, filters, and veto points that determine what does and doesn't get accomplished in Washington. His proposed solutions can be read as a retrospective blueprint for the workings of groups he co-founded, including Demand Progress and the Progressive Change Campaign Committee, and his thinking on these matters informed his friend Lawrence Lessig's Mayday PAC. Each of these organizations still bears the stamp of Aaron's ideals and is better for it, whether or not we always succeed at living up to those principles.

—David Segal

How Congress Works

Age 24

Given as a seminar at the Safra Center at Harvard University in the spring of 2011—Ed.

A Note from Professor Rebecca Sandefur:

Aaron took my course on social stratification during the year he was at Stanford. Our conversations after class and in office hours centered on three themes that animate this essay: whether stable organization is necessary to accomplish complex tasks that benefit society, why people are so often quiescent in the face of acts and organization that go against their interests, and whether democratizing access to information can on its own spur their mobilization. Aaron's notes on this essay to his seminar colleagues ask for suggestions about style. If I were given the gift of speaking with him again, I would say: Keep it as it is, your own: supremely confident, unpretentiously brilliant, sincerely engaged. And thank you for this, and for everything.

for Becky Sandefur

Part One: Elections

You'll probably never run for Congress. For starters, I bet you've never even considered it. Isn't running for Congress a job for celebrities, larger-than-life figures, people with big egos and an unquenchable thirst for power? But that's just the problem: the sort of people who want to run for office tend to be terrible officeholders. As Gore Vidal put it, "Any American who is prepared to run for president should automatically, by definition, be disqualified from ever doing so."[*]

One theory of the ideal politician is of some kind of selfless public servant. Such a representative would fairly represent local interests, listening to their constituents and faithfully fighting for their views in the Capitol. They use their judgment and shared values to decide what's best for the people they represent.

But such a man can only exist in a world devoid of conflict. If there are no deep policy disputes, then legislating is easy. But in most modern American communities, this is pure fancy. There are rich and poor, corporations and unions, left and right. Their demands are serious—and typically irreconcilable. No representative can faithfully represent their common interests because on the biggest questions of public concern there simply is no common interest.

As a result, the notion of "a national interest" is inevitably hijacked by the dominant group in society. Reagan, for example, claimed his opponents represented the special interests: women, poor people, workers, young people, old people, ethnic minorities—in short, most of the population. ("This confusion allows Reagan to treat the exploited as exploiters by contrasting the people with the 'special interests.'")[†] As a result, the people who claim to be simply representing their district end up playing something like the role Domhoff ascribes to the town newspaper:

> Competing [business] interests often regard newspaper executives as general community leaders, as ombudsmen and arbiters of internal bickering, and at times, as enlightened third parties who can restrain the short-term profiteers in the interest of a more stable, long-term, and properly planned growth. The newspaper becomes the reformist influence, the "voice of the community," re-

---

[*]Metcalf, Fred. February 5, 2002. *The Penguin Dictionary of Modern Humorous Quotations* (Penguin). ISBN 0141009217.

[†]Chomsky, Noam. October 24, 1986. "Political Discourse and the Propaganda System." in Carlos P. Otero, ed. 2004. *Language and Politics* (AK Press). ISBN 1902593820, 541.

straining the competing subunits, especially the small-scale arriviste "fast-buck artists" among them.[*]

The "rational choice" interpretation of this character explains this by treating the representative as a sly and cynical operator. Instead of fighting for a shared objective, the "rational" politician is driven by incentives. He does not vote the way he thinks is best for his constituents, but simply the way he thinks is most likely to get him reelected. If there's something he believes is right, but is unpopular, he will drop it. Given a difficult decision, he'll conduct a poll. And as his electorate changes, so do his views. He'll tack to an extreme for the primary, then back to center for the general election.

The rational choice politician is an easy fellow to corrupt. If a special interest can help him win reelection, he'll work for the benefit of that interest. But even beyond such blatant corruption, his whole view of his constituency is warped by his quest for victory. He doesn't care about the people who live in his district, he cares merely about the ones that vote. And in the U.S., that means the wealthy: in a typical election, about 35% of the poorest quintile turns out; that number is 71% for the richest quintile.[†]

Those numbers are even more exaggerated when you look at other forms of voter engagement. It's obviously the wealthy who make the biggest campaign contributions, but they also are the ones who write letters to the editor and volunteer their time to political campaigns. As a result, any "rational" politician is going to skew their opinions toward the wealthy.

And this in fact is what we see. Bartels found a regression coefficient of 4.15 when measuring a member of Congress's responsiveness to the views of their wealthiest constituents; compare this to a score of -0.11 for the poorest. As Bartels summarizes: "Senators' roll call votes were quite responsive to the ideological views of their middle-

---

[*]Domhoff, G. William. April 2005. "Power at the Local Level: Growth Coalition Theory."

[†]Cervantes, Esther and Amy Gluckman. January/February 2004. "Who Votes, and How?" *Dollars & Sense.* http://www.dollarsandsense.org/archives/2004/0104cervan tes.html; Linz, Juan, Alfred Stephan, and Yogendra Yadav. 2007. *Democracy and Diversity* (Oxford University Press). ISBN 0195683684, 99.

and high-income constituents. In contrast, the views of low-income constituents had *no* discernable impact on the voting behavior of their senators."[*]

But just as focusing obsessively on profit-making turns out to be a poor way to make a profit, focusing obsessively on vote-getting turns out to be a poor way to get votes. Voters don't like a "flip-flopper." Voters want a representative with strong beliefs that won't waver, even in the face their own opposing views. Sen. Paul Wellstone (D-MN) had a record of "controversial" votes, like opposing Bush's invasion of Iraq or Clinton's welfare reform. But even when they disagreed, his constituents appreciated these stands. As his campaign manager recounts: "In countless conversations with Minnesota voters, Wellstone heard comments like: 'I don't always agree with you, but I like it that I know where you stand.'"[†]

And thus the third type of politician: the ideologue. A person with strong beliefs who sees elected office as a way to enact their beliefs into law for the greater good. They fight for ends and not for means. If their district opposes their decision, it is irrelevant except insofar as it will prevent them from getting reelected and thus pushing through more policies (that their constituents might also oppose).

Ideologues are constrained by the other two factors. Even as ideologues, most are hesitant to make decisions that go strongly against the interests of their district. And they often make "rational" compromises to get the support that will allow them to continue to serve.

Not only do ideologues want to run for office more than most people, there are groups dedicated toward helping and encouraging them. For example, Progressive Majority looks for young progressive activists in key states, trains them, finds a race for them, and helps them run and win. Perhaps you start off just running the school board, but if you succeed and learn the craft, they help you move up to higher office.

But there's not much of an apparatus for encouraging selfless public servants to run for office. And they're precisely the type least

[*]Bartels, Larry M. 2010. *Unequal Democracy: The Political Economy of the New Gilded Age* (Princeton University Press). ISBN 0691146233.

[†]Blodget, Jeff. May 4, 2006. "Populism, Organization, and Conviction."

likely to run. As normal people they have normal ambitions and a normal level of interest in politics, they don't burn with the desire to make the laws for their countrymen.

When communities were smaller and more homogenous, they could be pushed into the job. Sam Ealy Johnson, Jr. (Lyndon Johnson's father) was just such a representative. A well-liked lawyer in town, he had repeatedly gone above and beyond the call of duty to help his friends and neighbors. He was encouraged to run for the Democratic nomination and won the vote unanimously.[*] But that was 1905. It's hard to imagine many towns with enough of a functioning social system to make a collective decision like that, and even if they do exist, they're surely too small to make up a whole congressional district.

The first Congress had one representative for every 600 voters. If we imagine only half of them voted in the primary, and only half of those in the Democratic primary, you're left with 150 voters—the number Dunbar famously proposed as the number of people one can maintain stable social relationships with.[†] You could imagine Sam Ealy Johnson, Jr. personally knowing each one of the voters who unanimously elected him.

Today we have one representative for every 208,000 voters. Even if we again assume only a quarter will vote in the primary, that's still 50,000 people. Just to have a three-minute conversation with each of them would be a year's worth of work—and that's assuming that they were all lined up to talk to you, with no downtime in between conversations.

So instead of talking with voters, you talk at them: through TV ads and postal mailers and signs along the street. And all those things cost money. Instead of finding your friends and neighbors electing you to run, you throw fund-raisers for the wealthy and try to prove to them you have the right stuff.

Just as with candidates, we can imagine three different types of

---

[*]Caro, Robert. 1982. *The Path to Power* (*The Years of Lyndon Johnson, vol. 1*) (Alfred A. Knopf). ISBN 0394499735, 43.

[†]Dunbar, R. I. M. June 1992. "Neocortex size as a constraint on group size in primates." *Journal of Human Evolution* 22 (6): 469–493. <doi:10.1016/0047-2484(92)900 81-J>

wealthy people involved in politics: the self-described public servant, who wants to support candidates that will actually help out the
community; the cynical operator, who gives money to those who
give him profitable laws in return; and the ideologue, who supports
the candidates who believe in the same strong values they do.

But just as the candidates are drawn mostly from the ranks of the
self-aggrandizing and ambitious, the campaign donors are drawn
from the wealthy. Even our selfless public servant donor spends most
of his time at the cocktail parties of the fellow rich. He may care
about the poor beggars on the street, but it's difficult to imagine he
spends much time talking to them and considering their views. No,
instead he supports sensible, moderate candidates who care about
things like reducing the deficit and the other things he's read about
in the *New York Times*. ("We're facing a fiscal crisis!" he insists, while
millions are out of work, on the street.)

Similarly, the wealthy ideologue may fancy herself an activist,
but she is not the sort of activist who chains herself to power plants
and sleeps in abandoned buildings. No, she is an activist because
she goes to fund-raisers for noble causes and serves on the board
of worthy organizations. Like the "public servant," even when her
heart is in the right place it's only natural that she'll do a better job
representing herself and the others like her. Protecting abortion may
be a litmus test for her, but ending homelessness rarely is.

All types of donors see themselves, quite genuinely, as playing
a role. They do not lavish money on anyone who wants to run for
office because they have some deep beliefs in democracy per se. Instead, they support the candidates they agree with and snub the ones
they don't. This seems to them entirely natural—indeed, the opposite would seem bizarre. Would you give money to every shop that
opens just because you support capitalism?

But just as the businesses that don't receive patronage go out of
business, the candidates that don't flatter the wealthy don't raise
enough money to run a serious campaign. Perhaps you persuade the
"public servants" that you're the sober-minded serious type who can
do this district some good. Or maybe you convince the local business executives that in exchange for their checks and those of their
subordinates, they'll get a representative who will earmark money

to support their local business and loosen the insane regulations that hamper their growth (but perhaps not the ones hampering their competitors). Or maybe you convince the ideologue that you, too, care passionately about abortion and will be a strong voice in Congress to make sure that right is never weakened. And if you're really good, you'll do all three.

Republicans have an easier time of this, of course. It's a lot easier to appear to be on the same side as both the anti-government ideologue and the local businessman choked by regulation, since both appear to want the same thing. (No surprise, since it's businessmen who are funding the anti-government talk shows.) It's a lot harder to be both a left-wing activist and friend of local business. And so the right-wing ideologues make out better than the left-wing ones.

The same is true all the way back. There are many more institutions dedicated to persuading fresh-faced college students that government regulation is the root of all evil than there are those that argue the unconstrained free market tramples on the rights of average citizens. That's because the former can obtain grants from the "charitable giving" of wealthy businessmen, while the latter depend on the support of the odd old foundation or activist billionaire. And while the businessman may believe that extremism in the defense of liberty is no vice, billionaires and foundations have a strong aversion to extremism.

When you say "corruption in Congress," people think of sleazy members of Congress in suits, making shady deals with lobbyists behind closed doors. But the real corruption starts earlier than that— much earlier than that. It starts at those fund-raisers, where the wealthy take the measure of the man, and decide whether he agrees with them enough to deserve their funds for his campaign. (I don't think it's quite fair to describe some people deciding not to run as corruption, although its effect is undoubtedly important.)

It is this—the filter—that is crucial. Everyone in Congress, everyone running for Congress could be a total saint, the perfect public servant, voting only in accordance with their genuine beliefs about what was best for their constituents, and the place would *still* be hopelessly corrupt. Because the issue is not just that the politicians skew their votes toward the whims of the wealthy once they're in office, but that politicians who do not share the wealthy's views never make it that far.

Imagine if they tried. First, they wouldn't know any wealthy people to invite to the fund-raiser. Second, even if they some-how got some wealthy people to attend, they would seem odd and distasteful—perhaps even unelectable. These fund-raisers are as diffi-cult a gauntlet as any social filter—you have to know how to properly sample hors d'oeuvres and sip cocktails, while at the same time giv-ing the "right" answer to every political question you're confronted with. You have to persuade these people that you are *one of them*, that you share their vision, their worldview. That as a congressman you will make the same decisions they will. But, remember, they are not your actual constituents, they are the wealthy. Your average anti-poverty activist doesn't stand a chance.

So let's say you've done it. You've persuaded your wealthy friends to entrust you with the seed money necessary to kick off your cam-paign. What now? You've never run for serious office before, you have no clue about running a campaign. You're the candidate, not the campaign manager. You don't know even the first place to start.

Enter the political consultant.

Wherever there are unworldly people with pockets full of cash, there are unscrupulous professionals eager to lighten the load. Poli-tics is no different. Like piranhas smelling blood, the candidate is quickly surrounded by consultants eager to help.

The typical campaign, in fact, is not run by a campaign manager, but a council of consultants, each hired for some particular job but justifying their exorbitant fees with claims of great expertise in "campaign strategy." The campaign manager's job then is to assemble these big shots on weekly strategy calls and carry out their expensive advice.

So the average campaign hires a mail consultant to advise on what they should send prospective voters, a television consultant to help create and purchase TV ads, a targeting consultant who uses "ad-vanced models" to decide which voters to contact, and a pollster who conducts polls and then attempts to interpret their results. Now, with the Internet revolution, there's also usually an online strategist who advises on using the website and email list. (There's never anyone advising how to attract and use campaign volunteers, because volunteers are not a profitable business.) The campaign's backers also join in on these calls—perhaps there will be a representative from the unions (for the left) or the Chamber of Commerce (for the right), particular political groups (like EMILY's List or the Club for Growth), and sometimes the national political party (D or R).

The consultants are not paid directly for their advice; instead they charge hefty markups for their normal services to cover the cost of their time. Thus while conducting a scientific poll costs under $1,000 in the average congressional district, a pollster will charge you $15,000 for a poll. And $15,000 is actually a special deal just for you, because they really believe in you and what you stand for—normally they'd charge $20,000 or even $30,000. "I'm doing this practically at cost," they'll claim. (This might even be true, if the "costs" include their inflated salaries.)

The candidate, like most people, has never purchased a poll before and so has no idea what they actually cost. And the pollster never discloses the actual amount of their markup. If they're ever questioned about a discrepancy in price, they point to all sorts of difficult-to-measure factors. "Oh, our polls cost more because they're conducted by specially trained operators—because we work with you to develop the most scientific questions—because we put a lot of effort into properly interpreting the results." These claims never stand up to even basic scrutiny (the operators are poorly paid temps, the question wording violates basic principles of professional practice, the results are incorrectly calculated through spreadsheets so bad the pollsters must be borderline innumerate), but in the rush of a campaign who has time for this kind of investigation? And who's going to look a gift horse in the mouth—they're doing this at cost, remember?

The mail and TV and other consultants play exactly the same game, each with slightly different lies and gimmicks, but the pollster has special influence because of their control over "the evidence." Their supposed expertise is not in any particular aspect of campaign tactics, but in that most basic question: what it is *the people* actually want. And by controlling that, they can come to control a great deal of campaign strategy. As a result, the pollster is usually first among equals in these strategic councils.

Observers of the political scene often complain about the high-tech calculations and incredible brainpower that goes into properly packaging a candidate.* But in reality it's difficult to overstate the general level of incompetence. Political consultants are largely shielded from market competition by the tribal instincts of politicos. If you were to buy mailers for a commercial company, you'd talk to different print shops and compare their rates and reviews. But if you're a left-wing political candidate, you cannot go to a standard print shop—you have to go to a political print shop. And certainly not a Republican print shop or even the standard Democratic print shop, but one subdivided to cater to your specific political grouping (left-wing vs. centrist, moderate Republican vs. Tea Party). After all, who wants to support the enemy?

Of course the market for left-wing Democratic political candidates is pretty small, so there're not many prospective competitors eager to home in on the business. And even if they do, these firms' marketing departments largely consist of going to the right cocktail parties. Particular cliques (e.g., left-wing Democratic electoral activists) all tend to know and recommend each other, in that way that loose social circles do, where genuine good feeling towards acquaintances merges with good business sense.

But the biggest problem is that the scientific basis for their vaunted and expensive expertise is practically zero. Psychologists have long recognized that to become an expert at some skill, you need a great deal of practice with rapid feedback.[†] There are lots of expert basketball shooters, because when you miss a basket you know right away and can adjust your shot next time. There are very few expert long-term economic forecasters because your forecast comes true months

---

*Chomsky, Noam. March 12/13, 2005. "The Toothpaste Election." *Counterpunch*. <http://www.counterpunch.org/chomsky03122005.html>http://www.webcitation.org/5wBAuAiau; Wallace, David Foster. 2004. "Mister Squishy" in *Oblivion: Stories* (Little, Brown). ISBN 0316919810. Wallace, David Foster. 2005 [written February 2000].

"Up, Simba!" in *Consider the Lobster: And Other Essays* (Little, Brown). ISBN 0316156116.

†Ericsson, K. Anders, Neil Charness, Paul J. Feltovich, Robert R. Hoffman. June 26, 2006. *The Cambridge Handbook of Expertise and Expert Performance* (Cambridge University Press). ISBN 0521600812.

or years after you make it, when you've long forgotten what it was you did right or wrong.

Expertise in politics is much more like prediction than basketball. At the end of an election, you get basically just one bit of information: you either won or lost. And it's easy for everyone involved to (rightly!) point to circumstances outside of their control. The candidate didn't take their advice, the strategy was derailed by a late-breaking scandal, the campaign didn't have enough money to fully execute on the plan, etc.

When you suggest a candidate emphasize a particular issue or put a particular photo on their mailer, you'll simply never know whether you were right or wrong. The candidate will succeed or fail months after you make a decision, there's no way to measure how much an individual decision affected the results, and even if you were somehow the only one responsible for a candidate's entire campaign, the results could always have been skewed by some surprise in the news or some fluke of your opponent's.

But the end result is that nobody ever learns from their mistakes, and without learning there can be no real expertise in politics. So, in the absence of real knowledge, practitioners naturally tend to believe in themselves and their products. The TV consultant insists what's needed is more and different TV commercials, the mail consultant argues late-campaign mail has a proven effect, the targeting consultant says we need to spend more money on targeting to make sure our other dollars aren't being wasted, and so on. The result is that campaigns get very expensive very fast.

But most expensive of all is the fund-raising consultant. Because fund-raising directly involves money, fund-raising consultants are able to set incredible prices—rates like 1/3 of all money they raise. In part, this is because fund-raising consultants are in more demand than any of the other consultants—the thing you do on day one of a campaign is not buy TV ads or conduct polls, but raise money, so even campaigns that never get off the ground need fund-raising consultants. But also, these rates seem to be justified by improperly specified hypotheticals. The candidate thinks, "If I didn't hire a fund-raising candidate, I'd have no money—so what's wrong with giving up a third of money I don't even have?" instead of "How much of that money could I raise without a consultant?"

It's true that the best fund-raising consultants have connections to networks of wealthy donors. In the same way that television consultants and pollsters advise on how to market the candidate to the public, these fund-raising consultants advise on how to market a candidate to the donor scene. They know what issues different wealthy people especially care about, how to talk to them, and they can often set up meetings to pitch a candidate to wealth.

The wealthiest don't meet with candidates directly, of course, but have full-time professionals who advise them on their giving. These professionals typically advise an entire wealthy family or support a wealthy person who acts as a kingmaker themselves. Some wealthy people have more interest in politics than others: they like to vet candidates themselves and recommend them to their circle of less politically engaged wealthy friends.

And there are the classic fund-raisers, as mentioned above, where you persuade a circle of existing donors to invite their own social networks to a party at one of their houses so you have a chance to woo their friends.

But the vast majority of fund-raising is much simpler than any of this, almost ridiculous in its simplicity. It is: call time. The fund-raising consultant uses public records about campaign contributions to pull the names of people who have donated to similar candidates (or, even better, if you have a good relationship with a similar candidate, you can get explicit permission to use their donor list). Phoning people straight off public records is illegal, but if you find their phone number some other way, it's OK to research their donation history. The fund-raising consultant looks up their phone number in the phonebook or on Google, along with any other basic info they can find or glean about the donor, and prints it out on a piece of paper (a call sheet). This is called "prospecting."

A stack of such sheets is always kept in a binder and whenever a candidate gets a free moment, they are dragged to a closet with a phone and forced to do their call time. This is the real substance of the fund-raising consultant's job: forcing the candidate to do the most humiliating and degrading and torturous work of the campaign—to become a telemarketer.

The closet is typically kept far away from campaign headquarters and contains nothing besides the binder and the phone (step one: no distractions). Then the fund-raising consultant uses every psychological tactic in the book to sit there and force the candidate to make calls. And, eventually, they do—with all the results you'd expect. ("How did you get this number?" people demand. "I don't know," the candidate lies, "my fund-raising consultant gave it to me.")

But because these are people with a history of donating, the calls are not always so overtly angry. Sometimes you reach practiced professionals who know just the questions to ask to determine if you're the kind of candidate they'll support. They'll angrily quiz you on their pet issue, sound out your support for business in general, or even begin deal making right over the phone.

I've heard of countless candidates who abhor call time. Running for office seems like a glamorous and important profession; it's difficult to lower yourself from that image to the reality that it consists mostly of begging strangers for money. Like children who hate doing homework, candidates devise all sorts of excuses and devices to avoid having to do it. But it is inescapable, and never-ending—even winning is no escape.

After the consultants comes the world of political staffers. These are the people you actually employ, as opposed to the consultants you just rent. Being a political staffer is a dark life. You spend one year out of every two working 90-hour weeks, rarely leaving the office, sleeping only with the other staffers who work on the campaign, and giving up any semblance of an outside life. Then you typically spend the other year unemployed.

Occasionally your candidate succeeds and you manage to get a job in their administration, but this is rare and limited. Most campaign skills don't translate well into office and even when they do, an office employs far fewer people than the campaign. So you try to pick up work on "issue campaigns," organizations that try to use campaign tactics to get particular legislation passed. But without a strong model and a clear deadline, issue campaigns are a pretty demoralizing experience on their own.

So the job attracts a specific kind of person, an odd type of person, who would give up a steady job to throw themselves into semiannual fits of obsession over a random person. (Every two years the staffer claims, "*This* guy is really special, he's the real deal," without even a hint of self-consciousness.)

But the campaign staffers play little causal role in the campaigns, other than through the difficulty of hiring reliable people for such an unreliable job. So let us dwell no longer on their plight.

We have our team and their squabbling semblance of a strategy. But what does the actual campaign look like?

First, obviously, you raise money. A healthy war chest scares off potential opponents, gets you taken seriously by the press (before any actual votes are cast or polls are taken, the press usually judges candidates by their success in the "money primary"), and supplies you with the resources to run the rest of your campaign. This means the ability to raise money is crucial in its own right—before even a single dollar gets spent, the race is biased toward those who can fund-raise.

Then there is the "inside game" of collecting endorsements from local public officials, unions, interest groups, and the rest. These endorsements sometimes come with practical benefits—like lists of donors and volunteers that can be tapped—but mostly, like early money, they help give the candidate the air of viability to the press and public.

"Viability" is especially crucial in a primary because in a race without the usual two-party labels, so much of voting is based on the bandwagon effect: people like to pick a winner. Furthermore, in a simple plurality system like America's, voting for someone other than the top two candidates is essentially throwing your vote away. So it's crucial to make sure everyone considers you one of the top two.

Once you've met the threshold to be viable, you need to actually start moving people toward your side: persuasion. In a typical campaign, there is a long-running argument held in the media—through debates, dueling quotes to the press, competing public events, and so on—which is then underscored through things like TV ads (in big campaigns) and mailers. The highly informed voters watch this argument like a prize fight, but they usually come into it rooting for a particular side and not waiting to be won over. The rest of the public glimpses it only through a dark glass. Key phrases and arguments glance their consciousness, perhaps enough to sway them one way or another, but rarely with any degree of significant thought.

As with the rest of campaign strategy, it's very unclear what affect any of this has. A massive experiment by Gerber et al. (2007) tested the effect of television and radio ad purchases during Rick Perry's (R-TX) 2006 campaign for governor. It was a four-way race pitting then Lieutenant Governor Perry against a Democratic House member, humorist Kinky Friedman, and the Republican comptroller, who was running as an independent. By randomizing when ads were purchased in different areas, and measuring their effects with follow-up polls, the study concluded that the television ads boosted Perry's vote share by about five points, irrespective of whether his opponents ran ads. However, the effects were short-lived, fading after a couple weeks.

All other measured effects have been on this scale. But such results are very hard to interpret because they come in the context of an already hard-fought race. We know the Republican is going to get a large percentage of the vote, and the Democrat will as well. But if Kinky Friedman bought a passel of television ads, would it boost his name recognition scores from zero percent to five percent (because TV ads are worth five points)? From zero percent to 25% (because they'd indicate he was a serious contender)? From zero percent to zero percent (because nobody will ever take him seriously)? It's hard enough to measure the effect of a simple action on the wider social world. It's practically impossible in a hard-fought zero-sum game like a political race.

But while time taken out to record ads is crucial, most of the candidate's days are spent on what's now called "earned media" (the old term, "free media," was deemed misleading because it required too much work to really be "free"). These are the endless series of bogus campaign "events" held in the hopes of persuading some reporter to write about it or, even better, some television station to cover it.

The candidate goes to a steel mill and shakes hands, the candidate declares his opponent a tax cheat, the candidate attends a debate. Ideally, it gets another mention for the candidate in the papers and maybe a quick chance to include a sound bite or two.

Finally, there is the issue of turnout. Campaign progress is always measured in percentages, as if there is a static population of voters and the goal is simply to win more and more of them over to your side. But in most elections, most eligible voters don't vote—and this is especially true in the crucial primaries.

Most voters are pretty firmly tied to a party identity—political scientists have found that even folks who identify as "independent" voters usually vote straight party tickets. (For example, Tea Party activists may consider themselves independent of the Republican Party, but they're never going to vote for the Democrat.) As a result, there's very little room for persuasion in a general election (though that hasn't ever stopped a major campaign from trying) and turnout becomes the crucial factor.

Despite that, turnout is treated with far less importance than persuasion in the average campaign. Part of this seems to be because of a widespread misconception among politicos about how persuadable people are. After all, the entire campaign seems to be a debate between competing ideologies—it'd be hard to understand why you'd go through all that effort if nobody ever changed their mind. Part of it seems to be a result of always seeing things in percentages. Part of it may be the result of the Median Voter Theorem.

The Median Voter Theorem, a key result in rational choice politics, says that candidates both move to adopt the policy views of the median voter so as to get the maximum number of votes. If both candidates are right in the middle, with one just slightly to the left and one just slightly to the right, then they pick up the most votes—any move to an extreme would cede moderate voters to the remaining centrist.

Even a cursory look at any recent campaign will make clear the Median Voter Theorem doesn't hold in real life. It's hard to even think of a federal election where the candidates were barely distinguishable. This could be because of persistent "irrationality" on the basis of voters and candidates, but it could also be because of turnout effects. If moving to the center causes people at the extremes not to show up, then it's not as costless as the MVT would suggest.

But there's also a rational reason for not focusing on turnout: convincing people to turn out is hard. Under some analyses turning out an average voter is actually more expensive than persuading one, when it'd have to be half the price to be cost-effective. That's because turning out a new voter increases your lead by just one vote, while persuading an existing voter increases it by two (one new vote for you and one vote less for your opponent). It takes a lot to get disaffected voters to the polls. By contrast, people who really like voting tend to do it every time no matter what's going on.

Those tend to be the people who vote in primaries, when turnout is especially low. As a result, even though there's more room to increase your vote through turnout, turnout is even less of a factor. Even if the entire primary electorate considers themselves to be hard-left Democrats, you can fight a vicious campaign about who's the real hard-left Democrat in the race and who's the corporate shill. Because turnout is so low these battles are usually fought among very high-information voters, who follow the twists and turns of a complicated campaign.

All the tactics of persuasion have been tested on turnout as well—and much more rigorously, since public voting records allow you to costlessly measure their effect. (There's no need to poll the potential voters; you just look up their voting history.) Tactics like knocking on voters' doors have been found to be surprisingly effective, and calling people up and even mailing them letters can be cost-effective under the right circumstances.* Measuring these effects is a burgeoning field of study, especially since IRBs will let you work to turn voters out but not to persuade them who to vote for.

Much of this work (calling, knocking on doors) can be done by well-harnessed volunteers. But even there, many campaigns turn to trained professionals (or in the case of phone calls, trained robots) to do the work for them—an expensive proposition. The ads and

---

*Gerber, Alan and Donald P. Green. September 14, 1999. "Does canvassing increase voter turnout? A field experiment." *Proceedings of the National Academy of Sciences* 96 (19): 10939–10942. <http:// www.pnas.org/content/96/19/10939.full>.

mailers are quite expensive as well, which is the main place where all those millions of dollars in campaign spending go.

Still, our understanding of what effect any of this has is still in its infancy. The first major study[*] was just over a decade ago; even basic methodological issues haven't been worked out. So while we know that everyone spends a ton of money campaigning, we don't really know what difference it makes.

After all this campaigning, Election Day arrives. The candidate goes out in the morning to vote—one more earned media event—and then spends the rest of the day running around town, shaking hands, trying to get people to go out and vote. The field team executes on their get-out-the-vote strategy, getting periodic check-ins from each of their branch offices.

Volunteers drop by the polls to make sure everything is in order. The more ambitious ones ask to see the list of people who have voted so far. This information is then reported back to headquarters and supposedly used to redeploy resources where they're most needed, although doing this intelligently during the rush of Election Day is rather difficult.

Some campaigns have so many volunteers that they can station people at key polling places to listen for each voter's name as they request a ballot. The volunteer can then check this voter's name off on their list and send the results back to HQ so the campaign has a live list of who's voted and who hasn't. People who haven't voted yet then get barraged with phone calls until the man at the polling place sees them get their ballot.[†]

But for campaign leadership, Election Day is often an anticlimax. Everything has already been planned—unless there's some late-breaking emergency, there's nothing more you can do except watch the staffers execute and check your email for exit poll data. As the

---

[*]Ibid.

[†]Herbert, David. November 10, 2008. "Obama's 'Project Houdini' Revealed: After Early Stumble, Ambitious Voter-Targeting Program Helped Streamline Get-Out-The-Vote Effort." *National Journal*; Thomas, Evan and the staff of Newsweek. November 7, 2008. "The Final Days: Obama was leading in the polls, even in red states like Virginia. But McCain almost seemed to glory in being the underdog." *Newsweek*. <http://www.newsweek.com/2008/11/06/the-final-days.html>.

polls begin to close, the staffers file out to the campaign party, usually held at a nearby hotel, while leadership stays back, continually reloading the early election returns and trying to decipher what it all means. ("We're doing surprisingly well in the south!")

Eventually even they head over to the party and, as the results come in, emotion starts to build in the crowd. The candidate is with his team of advisors in a decadent suite high above, praying he doesn't have to make The Call. But then reality sets in, his jaw sets, and he excuses himself to the other room to dial the number.

Or else—the phone rings! He goes to the other room, comes back with a big grin, bounds down the stairs, through the cavernous hallways, through the kitchen, and bounds out onstage! All smiles and waves! The crowd is cheering! They conceded! We won!

There's drinking and dancing and hugs and high-fives and all the stress of the campaign, of the months of ceaseless toil, the blood, sweat and tears—all drains away . . . at least for one night.

Part Two: Legislation

The next morning is like the hangover after any good party. The hotel room is trashed, the office is a mess, everyone's stumbling around in a daze, half dressed. But the job isn't over yet—it's just beginning.

As the campaign ends, the job begins. And like any new job, it has its orientation session. Every new member of Congress receives a passel of training: there are events held at Harvard's Kennedy School, orientations held on Capitol Hill, and education programs given by the Congressional Management Foundation.

The Congressional Management Foundation is an odd creature: a nonpartisan, independent foundation whose only goal is to teach members of Congress to be better managers. A newly elected member of the House of Representatives doesn't just get a key card valid for two years of voting—they also get a multimillion-dollar budget to spend on their official duties.

It's tempting to just hire the people from your campaign, but being a member of Congress is a serious job and requires serious skills—experience above all, according to those with experience. When searching for a new campaign staff, you can't just choose anyone off the street. You need someone who knows the Capitol—because you sure don't! This means typically hiring people from other offices, where they've been groomed in "the way things are done around here."

But these staffers also have divided loyalties. Most newly elected members come from either the handful of competitive districts, which are likely to swing back to the other party just as they've swung toward you, or are the result of a fluke or a wave year, in which case the other party will be heavily gunning to reclaim the seat in the next election. Either way, more often than not your new boss isn't going to still be here in two years.

So if you want long-term employment as a congressional staffer, it's not your boss you need to keep happy—it's your previous employer. Many long-serving members of Congress build a power base by grooming new staffers and sending them out into the world to serve other members. When they need that member's vote or some other favor, help is just a phone call away.

But even these staffers are chosen from a narrow pool. How does someone get experience in Congress in the first place? By applying to be an intern. Imagine the sort of college student whose idea of a great first job is to run errands and fetch coffee for whichever random person happens to represent their hometown. They're not likely to be someone who cares passionately about making the world a better place—if they were, they'd be working for some activism group. They're not someone who's interested in judiciously weighing the facts and trying to come up with good solutions—if they were, they'd be working for a think tank. Instead, they're someone who gets excited by proximity to power—who's turned on just by striding the Capitol's marble halls, by sitting in a closet next to a Man with a Vote, by running into the leaders of the Free World in the elevator. There are people who thirst for a chance at power, and for them, fetching coffee is a trifling price.

By and large, these people will not be powerful themselves. Some of them have the spark of ambition and will go far, will become one of the people they once longed to be near. But most aren't interested in power for themselves, but merely being in its good graces. They have a sensitive antenna for who's in charge and what it is they want. And the result is that a congressman who actually wants to accomplish things, who doesn't want to be just another pawn for the people who actually run the game, starts off with a team full of saboteurs.

At every turn, they will insist "that isn't the way things are done around here." Even when given direct orders, they will often find ways to shirk them, to avoid the stain of their boss's uncouth requests harming their own reputation. But most bosses never get that far. They don't want to stand out either—like any good politician, they yearn to fit in. So they follow their staff's instructions and fall in line.

There are many talented and competent people in the world —people who have risen to high positions in business or academia— who would gladly leave their post for a couple years to help run a congressional office. Think of the resources at their disposal! There's the millions of dollars, of course, but that's nothing. There are the votes, but even those are tiny. But there's the prestige—just say you're calling on behalf of a member of Congress and everyone returns your calls. And there's the attention—make a statement or a pronouncement and it's instantly newsworthy. "Area Man Calls for Higher Taxes"? It's a joke. But "Area *Congressman* Calls for Higher Taxes"— now that's news.

But more than all of that—much more—is the access. Every day, whizzing through the halls of Congress, are the words that will bind the world's only superpower. Even changing something as simple as a single letter can affect the lives of not just thousands, not just millions, but hundreds of millions of people—for good or ill. And as a member of Congress you can get those letters changed—just by asking! Where else can you regularly help millions of people just by asking someone to fix a typo?

Paul Thacker was a low-level journalist for the incredibly obscure journal *Environmental Science & Technology* (an official publication of the American Chemical Society). And he hadn't even had that position for very long. He had a taste for writing hard-hitting chemical exposés, including one about how a D.C. consulting firm, the Weinberg Group, helped corporate giant DuPont cover up how the toxic acid they produced was poisoning West Virginians. DuPont, as you might imagine, was not amused. Not long after that story came out, he was fired. Of course, even when he had his job, publishing hard-hitting pieces in *Environmental Science & Technology* wasn't exactly world-changing.

But—what a stroke of luck!—he found a new job working for Sen. Grassley (R-IA), who was then the top Republican on the Senate Finance Committee, with oversight responsibility for anything involving federal funds. Time after time, Thacker would send out letters on behalf of Grassley, looking into whether federally funded researchers were double-dipping and taking money from the drug companies at the same time. Thacker's repeated exposure of this web of corruption led to a number of prominent resignations and earned him a top spot on Big Pharma's Most Wanted list.[*]

It's a powerful example of what just one person in a congressional office can do. And the fact that it almost never happens shows how few congressional staffers dare to rock the boat.

So who does get hired? The vast majority of the budget goes to dealing with constituents. A team of district staffers run one or more offices back home that act almost as branch offices of the federal government. Do "you need assistance with a government agency?" asks Rep. Michael Capuano's (D-MA) website. "Congressman Capuano's office can help. Staff can answer basic questions, point constituents in the right direction, or work with the agency in question to resolve the constituent's case."[†]

In a television ad for his Senate campaign, Capuano dramatized the process. "Sally Bah was a refugee from the civil war in Sierra Leone. She was told that her husband and two little boys were killed," Capuano tells the camera. "Then they told me, 'No! Your sons are alive!' but they will not let them come to me," Sally explains. "Insane bureaucratic red tape left her little boys alone in Africa." "No

---

[*]Wadman, Meredith. September 16, 2009. "Money in biomedicine: The senator's sleuth." *Nature* 461:330–334. <http://www.nature.com/news/2009/090916/full/461330a.html><http://www.webcitation.org/5wCgNz5FX><doi:10.1038/461330a>

[†]Capuano, Michael E. no date [visited February 2, 2011]. "Casework and Constituent Assistance." <http://www.house.gov/capuano/services/casework.shtml> <http://www.webcitation.org/5wCgXIYxZ>

one could do anything, no one could help, until Mike Capuano made them give me back my boys. Mike cut the red tape. Mike cares about people."[*]

Most cases are much less exciting. A typical case is an elderly woman wondering why her Social Security check hasn't arrived yet. (The Centers for Medicare and Medicaid Services have a whole team dedicated to responding to requests from congressional offices.)[†] But, as the Congressional Research Service explains, despite "the widely held public perception that Members of Congress can initiate a broad array of actions resulting in a speedy, favorable outcome," members are prohibited by law from "forc[ing] an agency to expedite a case or act in favor of a constituent." Instead, they're limited to guiding constituents through the official process.[‡]

In a government as powerful and complicated as that of the United States, it's easy to understand the appeal of hiring someone to help you navigate the bureaucracy. And it's also easy to understand how members of Congress ended up with this job. After all, what other representative of the government is out there on the streets, shaking people's hands, trying to get folks to like them?

But in many ways congressional casework feels like a relic of a bygone age of transactional politics when government favors were doled out as personal patronage rather than provided by neutral agencies. For one thing, they have the same distributional concerns as patronage did. The people most in need of government support are not the sort of people who would ever think to pick up the phone and call their congressman. And I've never heard of a congressional office going out into impoverished neighborhoods and informing people about their services. Why would they? Poor people don't vote.

---

[*]Capuano, Michael E. October 16, 2009. "Sally" (television ad). <http://www .youtube.com/watch?v=Urg6s40GOiw>.

[†]CMMS (Center for Medicare & Medicaid Services). no date [visited February 2, 2011]. "Office of Legislation: Overview." <https://www.cms.gov/OfficeofLegisla tion/><http://www.webcitation.org/5wCglDHpm>.

[‡]Petersen, R. Eric. January 5, 2009. "Casework in a Congressional Office: Background, Rules, Laws, and Resources." *Congressional Research Service* RL33209. <http:// assets.opencrs.com/rpts/ RL3320920090105.pdf><http://www.webcitation.org /5wCgrxVjC>.

But getting rid of casework isn't really an option either, because the entitled upper middle class that takes advantage of it is comprised of just the sort of people who are likely to get upset and raise a fuss if it goes away. Perhaps the best solution is to transition the job to the executive branch, like all the others—an office of "Government Ombudsman" could be established at each major post office. On the other hand, whoever directs that office will have much less incentive to keep it from becoming another heartless bureaucracy than a congressman who must regularly face the wrath of the voters.

Just as the majority of in-district time is eaten up by staffers handling casework, the majority of staff time in Washington is spent responding to constituents. Especially in the age of the Internet petition, every congressional office is barraged with phone calls, faxes, and letters. None of this, naturally, ever makes it to the congressman. Instead it is dealt with by a team of fresh-faced staffers who tediously record the topic of each communication and mail them a bland but appropriate letter in response. Write your congressman complaining that the cost of health care is too damn high and you will get back a long and bland letter saying, "Thank you for contacting me to express your opposition to H.R. 4872, The Health Care and Education Affordability Reconciliation Act." Write saying that you'd like them to vote for the Polis-Pingree amendment to the bill and you'll get back the same thing.

With most of the budget blown on this electoral time wasting, there's only money left over for a small core staff of people to do the actual work of making laws. First and foremost, a chief of staff to manage the day-to-day. The chief of staff typically also has a second job as the congressman's campaign manager during the off-years and typically sees their job as figuring out how the congressman can use the powers of the office to maximize their chance of reelection.

As you might imagine, with every congressman trying to game the system, there is an arcane and lengthy set of "ethics rules" specifying the precise boundary between legislating and campaigning. You're not supposed to discuss raising money on Capitol property, so the chief of staff will often take a break from that job, walk outside, switch from their congressionally supplied BlackBerry to their personal cell phone, and make a call in their duty as campaign manager. But it's difficult to imagine that the things discussed there don't continue to have an impact when they walk back inside. (It's also difficult to imagine that every chief of staff always makes sure to walk outside.) Other key staffers do the same.

The most extreme version of these arcane rules comes up when exercising the privilege of "franking," or sending mail for free. If it's a matter of official business, a congressman can use the U.S. Postal Service without providing a stamp—instead they merely need to sign their name in the corner of the envelope where the stamp would normally go. To save them even this expense, every congressional office gets stacks of official stationary including boxes of pre-signed envelopes.

Naturally, the temptation to use this to send what amount to free campaign mailers is irresistible. As a result, all proposed mailings must be approved by a special Franking Commission, which decides whether they have enough substantive content to constitute official business.

The other top staffers include the scheduler, who deals with the endless requests for the congressman's time; the press secretary, who works hard to make sure the congressman gets plenty of earned media in the papers back home; and the legislative director, the one top-level staffer who focuses on the actual work of making laws. They usually direct one or two legislative assistants who tend to specialize on particular areas.

But even the work of the legislative director and her staff mostly consists of writing those bland responses to constituents. Actual legislative language is not written by members of the congressman's staff at all. It is typically written by lobbyists, although if the congressman has an actual idea for a bill or amendment, he can have it written up by the Office of Legislative Counsel. The Counsel's office employs forty or so lawyers who take ideas expressed in plain English by members of Congress and convert them into the formal language necessary for a bill. This includes researching previous and related legislation, figuring out how to operationalize what are often vague policy objectives, and publishing the result in the inimitable official congressional style—the official House style guide runs to almost eighty pages.[*]

In an act of (intentional?) self-parody, the style guide is written in the precise style it describes. An example:

SEC. 102. MAIN MESSAGE.
    (a) ORGANIZATION.—
        (1) EVERY DRAFT SHOULD BE ORGANIZED.—
        Every draft should be organized.

But the job does have one other big perk. The connections and experience built up from years of service in the halls of Congress are a valuable asset for lobbying firms—even a medium-level staffer can find themselves freed from the restrictions and low pay of public service into a lobbying job where they can help subvert or evade the regulations they once wrote. And their comrades congratulate them for such a promotion!

So how does a bill become a law? A member of Congress comes up with an idea—or is given it by a lobbyist—and sends it to Legislative Counsel for drafting. They produce a real bill, which gets dropped in "the hopper," a box at the front of the House for new bills. The bill is picked up by the clerk and the Speaker of the House refers it to the appropriate committee for more detailed consideration.

That's about as far as most bills get.

If the member wants to put some extra effort into it, they'll send out a "Dear Colleague" letter explaining the bill and imploring their fellow members of Congress to "co-sponsor" it. Dear Colleague letters were once actual letters sent around to each office, but now they're sent through an e–Dear Colleague mailing list system. Staffers sign up to receive e–Dear Colleague letters on the topic areas they work on, then when a new bill is introduced, a letter is sent to the list for that topic.

More ambitious staffers will contact their fellow staffers one-on-

---

[*]Forstater, Ira B. November 1995. "House Legislative Counsel's Manual on Drafting Style." *The Office of the Legislative Counsel, U.S. House of Representatives* HLC 104–1. <http://www.house.gov/legcoun/pdf/draftstyle.pdf><http://www.webcita tion.org/5wChLv2J8>.

one, while more ambitious members will take the co-sponsorship papers to the floor of the House and buttonhole other members to talk up the bill and pressure them to sign. The average bill has around five co-sponsors—usually the original sponsor's friends.

Co-sponsorship is a purely symbolic act, an official way of expressing strong support for a bill. Members can (and sometimes do) vote against bills they co-sponsor, but there are few other formal ways to express support for a bill before it comes to a vote. House Leadership often says that if a bill receives enough co-sponsors, they'll bring it up for a vote, but this isn't really true. Ron Paul's Federal Reserve Transparency Act received 320 co-sponsors in the House (you only need 218 for a majority and 290 for 2/3) but even so it never came to a vote on the floor.

Instead, legislation typically gets passed by getting attached to larger bills pushed by congressional leadership. If your bill has enough co-sponsors on the floor, perhaps you can bring it up as an amendment to some bigger bill, or maybe the committee chair will even add it himself. (Finance Committee chairman Barney Frank [D-MA] said he'd attach the Federal Reserve Transparency Act to the massive financial reregulation bill, but he backed out at the last minute and denounced it as too extreme. Rep. Paul and Rep. Alan Grayson [D-FL] proposed it as an amendment in committee and got it attached that way; it was later watered down by the Senate.)

This is because passing a disputed bill through the Senate is so onerous that only two sorts of bills pass: totally undisputed bills, which can be passed through the Senate by unanimous consent, and the huge priority bills, which can absorb weeks of debate. If a bill isn't uncontroversial enough to be passed unanimously but isn't important enough to deserve weeks of debate, the Senate leadership is unlikely to spend the floor time required to move it. Most of Congress's floor time is spent on the first sort of bill—hardly a day goes by without some member of Congress voting on a bill to rename a post office somewhere. Student loan reform, by contrast, was passed by being attached to the massive health care bill.

These massive bills are written largely by the relevant committees. The chair introduces a first draft, after holding hearings and talking to the "stakeholders." Then the bill goes to a "markup" where they walk through the bill section by section and any member of the committee can propose changes.

In practice, of course, the members mostly skip these boring markups. Those who are proposing changes are given a time to drop by, where they passionately argue their cause to an empty committee room. (The committee meetings are filmed but the footage typically isn't made available to the public.) The chairman can then decide which amendments pass or fail by scheduling the vote on the amendment for when the right mix of people are in the committee room. If the chairman wants the amendment to pass, he calls for a vote when the room is empty, and it passes unanimously. If he wants it to fail, he invites an opponent in to vote it down.

The big-deal votes are saved for marathon sessions when the whole committee drops by, although the chairman kindly provides them with a voting guide in advance telling them which amendments to support or oppose.

Once the markup concludes, there is a final vote on whether to send the revised bill to the full House for consideration. (If a bill touches on the topics of more than one committee, things get even more complicated and time-consuming. Let's ignore that for now.) Once the bill is voted out of committee, it then goes not to the full House, but to the Rules Committee, which sets the rules under which "debate" on a bill can be held in the House.

In the same way that the chairman can ensure whether amendments succeed or fail through clever scheduling, the Speaker can do the same through controlling the Rules Committee. The Rules Committee decides how long debate will be, whether amendments will be considered on the floor, and if so, in which order they'll be voted on and what those votes will mean.

For example, under a king-of-the-hill rule, a number of different amendments (providing for different versions of a bill) can be voted on and whichever one is the last to receive a majority is the one that ultimately gets passed. Or under the deem-and-pass rule, the rule will state that the House automatically passes a bill by agreeing to debate it. The debate is then just on various amendments; whatever bill results from the amendment process is "deemed" to have passed the House, even without an explicit vote.

These rules are themselves voted on by the full floor, but voting against your party's rule is seen as an incredibly reckless move, since without strong rules for debate the opposing party can take control of the floor and propose whatever amendments they like. (Given the chance, the opposing party will propose all sorts of "poison pill" amendments—things that it's seen as politically suicidal to vote against, but which will torpedo support for the bill or neutralize its effect.)

As a result, most debates are tightly controlled by the Speaker, who gets to pick the members of the Rules Committee. If the Speaker doesn't want a bill to come to the floor, she simply ensures the Rules Committee never votes on a rule for debating it.

If a bill survives both its initial committee and Rules, then it finally gets to go to the floor. There it gets voted on by the full House and, if it passes, sent on to the Senate.

The Senate is a whole other can of worms. Again, the bill has to pass through the appropriate committee. But instead of a rule, a bill typically comes to the floor under a "unanimous consent agreement" about the rules for debate. As the name suggests, such an agreement requires unanimous consent. It's typically negotiated between the majority leader and the minority leader, but if a member of either party feels strongly about opposing the bill, they can object to their leader and ask him not to let it come to the floor. (This is known as "placing a hold" on the bill.)

If no unanimous consent agreement is adopted, the Senate must break a filibuster to pass the bill. Unlike how it's depicted on TV, a real Senate filibuster doesn't actually require anyone to talk on the floor. (The reasons why are so ridiculous that to include them here would strain my credibility.) The mere objection to unanimous consent requires the majority leader to go through onerous Senate processes that require days of waiting and a 3/5 vote before a bill can be considered.

After all of that, there is a final vote on passage and the bill can pass the Senate. But wait—there's more! The bill was undoubtedly changed somewhat by the committee or by amendment on the floor. As a result, the Senate and the House have passed two different bills. To reconcile them, a team of negotiators from both the House and

Senate are assigned to meet in a special "conference committee" to hammer out their differences. It's in these typically closed-door meetings that the real bill is written, through a bizarre process of ping-pong between House and Senate negotiators. The House side goes through the bill and modifies it to come up with a proposal, then votes to send the proposal to the Senate side. The Senate side (seated on the other side of the table) goes through this new offer from the House and does the same. Eventually, theoretically, the two sides come to some agreement.

Once that's done, the newly revised bill goes back to the House and Senate for one more vote. If both pass it, it (finally) goes off to the president for his signature.

Political scientists measure a legislative system by its number of veto points. The fewer veto points, the easier it is to get stuff done. By any measure, the U.S. Congress has a record number of veto points. Even in this simplified description, we can see a bill requires the approval of:

- a member willing to sponsor it
- the chairman of the relevant House committee
- a majority of that committee
- a majority of the House Rules Committee
- the Speaker of the House
- a majority of the House
- the chairman of the relevant Senate committee
- a majority of that committee
- either unanimity in the Senate or 3/5 and days of patience
- a majority of the House conference committee
- a majority of the Senate conference committee
- the president of the United States

And even then, the bill sometimes gets struck down by the Supreme Court.

Ask any lobbyist or member of Congress about the relationship between the two and they'll always start off by saying the same thing: "It's not a quid pro quo." That's because quid pro quo deals with members of Congress are illegal and they want to begin by making it clear that they are not confessing to a crime—however much the rest of their story may make it sound like that.

Lobbyists deal with Congress in a relationship that's not quite quid pro quo, but about as close as you can get. No (well, not many) members of Congress say, "Make a hefty donation to my campaign and I'll give you my vote." That would be illegal. (Former Rep. Duke Cunningham [R-CA] is currently serving eight years in prison for sliding a "menu" of potential deals—e.g., a $50K contribution for a $1M government contract—across the table to defense contractor Mitchell Wade.) Instead they say, "I do him a favor, he does me a favor." Call it "quid *post* quo."

The difference is that there's no formal contract. I give you something, then you give me something, but we never explicitly say that one is for the other. Quid post quo is an example of the generalized reciprocity that underlies most personal relationships, particularly in business: you do a fellow businessman a favor, not because you're demanding anything in return at the moment (only the most crass would demand repayment for each favor) but because, in return, they will "owe you" and you can request a favor of your own at a later date. Think of *The Godfather*: "Someday, and that day may never come, I will call upon you to do a service for me." People in real life rarely state the situation so baldly; the principle is just commonly assumed.

And if the favor is not returned, you can cut the person off—or even take small steps (or, in the case of the Godfather, big steps) to hurt them. This was Lyndon Johnson's modus operandi: friends get anything they ask for, enemies get destroyed.

The economist Samuel Bowles calls this sort of system "contingent renewal" and he finds that it pops up wherever you have a trade that can't be perfectly contracted. (In this case, you can't write a contract for the trade because the trade is illegal.) Imagine you want to buy a nice bottle of wine. Well, you can't write a contract for "a nice bottle of wine"—aside from extreme cases, it's impractical to prove to a judge that the wine wasn't actually very nice. As a result, the normal economic logic—pay the marginal cost for the product in a perfectly competitive market—breaks down.

But there's another option: you can do the wine-making company a favor. You can pay them a premium for their bottle of wine and keep paying it as long as the wine is good. The stream of future surplus payments encourages the company not to cheat you on any individual bottle—if they did, they'd lose all that extra money.

Lobbyists work pretty much the same way. They contribute huge amounts to politicians and, as long as they keep doing so, politicians keep giving them favors. If either party breaks the informal relationship, the other party can stop as well: if he doesn't get his favor, a lobbyist can stop contributing and encourage his friends not to contribute; if he doesn't get his donation, a politician can stop helping a lobbyist's clients and even move to hurt them. It's a classic case of contingent renewal.

What are the favors that lobbyists get? The official story is that money merely buys "access." Lobbyists give their donation to the chief of staff/campaign manager and then, when they want a meeting, call her up to ask for one. She knows what they gave and instructs the scheduler to add it to the schedule. This is on top of all the direct access lobbyists get by buying invitations to expensive Capitol Hill fund-raisers.

But everyone knows major donors get more than merely access. The average constituent gets a couple seconds on the computer screen of a bored staffer who hits a button to send them a form letter. The average activist group gets a couple minutes with a low-level staff member. And when, on occasion, they do get some time with an actual member or a top staffer, they get a polite smile and some nods and a couple minutes to briefly air their concerns.

Contrast this with a lobbyist who is owed a favor. The meeting is not about simply listening to, and then ignoring, their requests. It's about strategizing together how to get things done, getting a commitment about a vote or a co-sponsorship or a phone call or one of the other myriad of favors a congressional office can give. It's about making a deal.

Members of Congress owe these lobbyists a favor because they gave money. The dreaded call time doesn't end with the end of the campaign. Instead it ramps up—now you're expected to raise money like an incumbent. The members with the most difficult seats are put on the most lucrative committees (Financial Services is a key example). Here they're all but required to demand large sums of money from the people they're supposed to oversee.

Every spare moment, the chief of staff/campaign manager is going to try to spirit them out of Congress to one of the phone bank operations across the street to do some more call time. Anything else would be irresponsible. Amassing a huge war chest as an incumbent is the most important piece of reelection campaign strategy—raise enough money and everyone will think twice before daring to challenge you.

And aside from the call time, every morning and night there are the fund-raisers in the nearby Capitol Hill hotels. A few examples just from February 2nd: $1,000 for a fund-raising breakfast with Rep. Elijah Cummings (D-MD) at 8 a.m., $5,000 for dinner with Sen. Ben Cardin (D-MD) at 6:30 p.m. These fund-raisers are a much more regular part of Capitol Hill life than debates, or even votes.

But sometimes even all the fund-raising in the world isn't enough and a campaign starts again in earnest. Back to the old days of turnout and persuasion, of TV ads and debates. And sometimes even all the money in the world can't win you reelection. The campaign party in the hotel ballroom isn't filled with whoops and cheers but a quiet and sad feeling of dejection.

But it's OK. The game isn't over. You can always show up back in town as a lobbyist. All the connections that you made during your career, all the access you had as a member, turn out to be worth something after all. And you can cash it in with one of those lobbyists who owe you a favor.

Part Three: Consequences

America often likes to think of itself as the greatest democracy in the world, but a clear-eyed evaluation of the consequences leaves great room for doubt. On every topic, ideas that meet with wide support from the public—as measured in a wide variety of ways—find themselves wrecked on the rocky shoals of Congress.

Take health care, for example. Polls consistently show that a majority of Americans support a Canadian-style single-payer system, which would save money and expand access. However, despite being popular among the public and a clear policy improvement, the idea is immediately derided as "politically impossible" in the American context. Why? Because it would destroy the business of wealthy insurance companies.

During the recent health care debate, even the moderate public option—supported by overwhelming majorities, including most Republican voters—was killed because it was too threatening to powerful corporate interests.

There are examples in every field. Most Americans support breaking up the big banks and putting the criminals who run them in jail, a position too extreme to even be proposed during the financial reregulation debate. Even commonsense measures, like accurate dietary guidelines or a reduction of economically harmful subsidies, face no chance in such a corporate Congress.

Even on that heated issue of the budget, the public's preferences are almost the reverse of the proposed policy: the public wants military spending to go down, but it goes up; the public wants spending on education, job training, and energy reform to be increased, but it gets cut.*

Clearly there is a democratic disconnect—the members of Congress are not executing the will of the voters. The analysis above suggests several possibilities why.

- *Candidate selection*: Perhaps only fans of insurance companies decide to run for Congress—or, more likely, only fans of business in general (who are predisposed to insurance companies' pleas).
- *Campaign finance*: Even if these aren't the only people who run, they are likely to be the people who best get along with the major fund-raisers, PACs, and other key sources of money.
- *Campaign tactics*: This money, in turn, is what's necessary to run a modern campaign—complete with TV ads and

---

*Chomsky, Noam. 2006. *Failed States: The Abuse of Power and the Assault on Democracy* (Macmillan). ISBN 0805079122, 234.

mailers and expert pollsters. As a result, it's the best fund-raisers who tend to win.

- *Staff selection:* When they get to Congress, even good candidates hire tired and acculturated staffers. Thus their ambitious reforms are sabotaged by internal defenders of the system with divided loyalties.
- *Staff ethics:* Attracted by their own "revolving door" (there's a lucrative market for former staffers), staffers are focused more on doing what their future employers might want than on what would best serve the public. And with their dual duties between congressional office and campaign, perhaps they get distracted by the pressing needs of the campaign and neglect what's best for the country.
- *Lobbyists:* Or maybe it's lobbyists who are screwing the whole thing up. The money they have to write bills and suggest strategies certainly gives them a big advantage over interests that can't afford to lawyer up. And the money they raise for candidates gives them a powerful hold on those candidates' attention. Finally, if you can't beat them—join them. Many former legislators get jobs as lobbyists where their past service for the industry is repaid with a lucrative position.

Part Four: Change

There have been many, many ideas about how to reform Congress. We can categorize them in two basic ways: by the part of the process they address (candidate selection, campaigns, staff, lobbyists) or by the tactics they adopt (restrictions, incentives, tools). Some of these ideas have even been adopted—but as members of Congress themselves must usually vote on them, it's not clear how much the proposed changes are intended to address the substance as opposed to the perception of corruption.

Candidate Selection

While it's commonplace for members of Congress to urge more people to "get involved in the process," I'm not aware of any examples of formal congressional attempts to recruit more candidates. (After all, who wants more competition?)

Instead, the biggest efforts have come from outside the official system. As mentioned above, Progressive Majority works hard to identify and recruit progressive activists. And each party has an arm focused on candidate recruitment—although the goal is usually finding someone who can raise enough money to win a seat for the party, rather than adjusting the makeup of Congress as a whole.

It's possible to imagine you could make a significant difference by increasing these efforts—finding more and better people to run. At the moment, even when someone wins by random fluke, it's rarely the sort of decent, honest person you'd want to win—and even when it is, the cult of experience forces them to behave the same way as everybody else. If more good people ran, even if nothing else changed, there's a chance they could win at least occasionally and thereby inject a modicum of decency into the process.

Campaign Finance

Since Watergate, the bulk of campaign reforms have consisted of caps and disclosures. At present, federal campaigns are not allowed to raise more than $2,400 from an individual and more than $5,000 from a bona fide political action committee (PAC) in any two-year cycle. (Corporations are prohibited from donating directly; instead their employees must voluntarily donate to a bona fide PAC.) At the same time, all major contributions and expenditures have to be publicly disclosed.

The main effect of disclosure has been to create a string of TV ads and campaign attacks along the lines of "You took X million dollars from Y bad guy." It's not clear how effective these attacks have been in any particular case, but they've undoubtedly contributed to a culture of assuming all legislators are bought and paid for. Unfortunately, the only people who can run campaigns without taking sizable amounts of money from bad guys are multimillionaires who self-finance, and on the whole they don't seem to be much of an improvement over the normal candidate.

The main effect of the caps has been to create a bustling market in figuring out how to evade them, culminating with the recent *Citi-*

zens United decision by the U.S. Supreme Court, which ruled that outside groups (including corporations) can spend unlimited campaign money on basically anything, as long as they don't coordinate their spending with the candidate. The result is a culture of coordination-without-coordination on top campaigns, where senior staffers will leak the details of their campaign strategy to the Capitol Hill press, where outside groups read it and figure out how to fill in the gaps. Obviously it's not the same as being able to direct how the money is spent, but it doesn't seem so different that it's made a noticeable impact on campaigning. As a result, campaign finance laws are largely seen as a dead letter.

The most serious proposal to address the problem is that of Fair Fight Funds. Under such a system, a candidate could opt-in to public financing of their campaign. In exchange for agreeing not to raise outside money, they would be given an initial chunk of money to fund a basic campaign (say $500,000), as well as an extra dollar for each dollar their opponent raises. (In some versions they receive $0.90 or $1.10 instead of $1.)

For example, imagine John Q. Public decides to run against Montague T. Moneybags. Public opts in to public financing and receives $500,000. Moneybags holds a big fund-raiser and raises $600,000. The government then gives Public an extra $100,000 to level the playing field. While the cost to the government is theoretically unlimited, there's not much incentive for Moneybags to keep raising big money if he knows Public is going to get another dollar for each new dollar Moneybags raises.

This plan really would neutralize the effect of money while being totally voluntary, but some legal experts believe the Supreme Court would find it unconstitutional, on the grounds that giving money to Public unconstitutionally discourages Moneybags's exercise of his First Amendment right to speech. (The present Supreme Court does seem to have an irrational distaste for campaign finance legislation. In response, some have argued that we need a constitutional amendment to push them to stop striking down strong laws.)

In the meantime, public financing supporters have scaled back their hopes. Instead, their current plan allows Public to receive the $500,000 but he then must raise the additional money through small-dollar contributions. Such a system has two major flaws: first, a well-connected Moneybags can still wildly outraise an honest Public; second, even raising small-dollar contributions will bias a member toward the affluent upper middle class that already has a strong taste for political engagement. (Recall that American inequality is so severe that anyone making over $87,000 a year is in the top 20% and anyone making over $154,000 is in the top 5%.* Having candidates responsive to them rather than major corporations would be an improvement, but perhaps not a major one.)

Some find even this implausible. Instead, in desperation, they've turned to the outside world—with ideas for new technology, like ActBlue, that makes it easier for average Americans to donate money to political candidates over the Internet.

There's an unresolved theoretical question that would determine whether such a path is actually practical. If the more money you raise, the more likely you are to win, then it's hard to imagine ever raising enough from individuals to be able to take on the hundreds of millions a major corporation can spend. But the stories of failed self-funding candidates suggest this isn't the case. Senate candidate Jeff Greene (D-FL) spent over $23 million trying to win the primary, while his opponent Kendrick Meek won by 26 points after spending closer to $7 million. Meg Whitman (I) spent $173 million trying to become governor of California, but still lost by 11 points to Jerry Brown (D), who spent $40 million.

A more hopeful answer is that there's some "threshold of viability" above which more money doesn't make a significant dent. In a $200 million race every voter has undoubtedly heard from every candidate, even if they hear from one candidate three times more than the other. If this were true, our new fund-raising technique would only need to get decent candidates up to that threshold. (This would also be good news for public financing techniques that only provide candidates with base funds.)

---

*DeNavas-Walt, Carmen, Bernadette D. Proctor, and Robert Mills. August 2004. "Income, Poverty, and Health Insurance Coverage in the United States: 2003." U.S. Census Bureau, *Current Population Reports* P60-226. <http://www.census.gov/prod/2004pubs/p60-226.pdf><http://www.webcitation.org/5wCm9AS48>.

The truth is probably somewhere in between—increasing amounts of money has diminishing returns, but they're still nonzero. And even raising Meek's $7 million would be difficult to do from independent donors. But perhaps it would not be impossible—small donors contributed hundreds of millions to the Obama campaign (although he picked up an equal amount from big donors). Figuring out how to harness that potential is a key goal for the campaign finance community going forward.

Campaign Tactics

Others, especially Sen. Ron Wyden (D-OR), have focused on changing the tenor of campaigns. Wyden's "Stand by Your Ad" provision attempted to discourage negative campaigning by forcing each candidate to say "I'm [STATE YOUR NAME] and I approved this message" once during each commercial. This doesn't seem to have done much to change the tenor of campaigns, although it does shorten ads by a few crucial seconds.

Wyden has also proposed limiting the amount of time during which members of Congress can fund-raise. This proposal has been much less successful and while it may help somewhat in lightening Capitol Hill's moneygrubbing culture, it's difficult to picture how it could have a significant impact on the overall problem.

There is room, however, for an outside revolution in campaign tactics. It's not enough to bring more people into the process if they're simply left as suckers to be ripped off by the existing pack of campaign strategists. Instead, someone needs to help them run innovative, cost-effective campaigns that give them a real shot even on a limited budget. The new science of effective campaigns can provide key guidance on what works and what doesn't, and innovative new technology can help lower the cost of campaign tactics.

Staff Selection

If, as I've argued, the cult of expertise is a key reason why the congressional offices of even courageous members are so timid, then the solution is simple: bringing more bold people from the outside world into the halls of Congress. This could be done with a large-scale cultural campaign to make working in Congress seem appealing, or with a smaller-scale campaign aimed at pressuring new members to hire from outside the inner circle.

Staff Ethics

Within the halls of Congress, staff behavior is regulated even more heavily than campaigns. But while requiring every political staffer to carry two phones may preserve some façade of decency, it seems difficult to say it's seriously lessened the amount of politics that occurs in Capitol office buildings. Nor is it at all clear that too much politics is a major cause of this democratic deficit.

As odd as it seems, I haven't seen anyone propose that Congress prohibit the dual-employment system of political/congressional staffers. Of course, the major problem with any such reform is that the man at the top—the member himself—inevitably has both jobs.

There are some constraints on "revolving-door" activity—including some outright prohibitions on becoming a lobbyist within a particular time and some "cooling-off" periods requiring delays before you go to lobbying your old colleagues. As with most such restrictions, these regulations help lessen the most egregious aspects but don't even come close to solving the problem. But revolving-door staffers seem like a minor enough phenomenon that even a total ban on the practice probably wouldn't make much of a dent in the democratic deficit.

Lobbyists

There's a further game of cat-and-mouse when it comes to taking gifts from lobbyists. With every scandal the rules get tighter and the lobbyists get cleverer. At the moment, for example, lobbyists are prohibited from buying members of Congress expensive meals, but there is a so-called appetizer exemption, with the ridiculous result that lobbyists are now forced to serve members of Congress expensive meals in small pieces while everyone stands up.

Lobbyists have similarly been forced into a system of restriction and disclosure. The restrictions are much more minor, amounting merely to a prohibition on outright bribes (strong restrictions on lobbying would presumably run afoul of the First Amendment) while the disclosure seems even more pointless (what is anyone going to do with the fact that Lobbyist X has been paid by Special Interest Y?).

An outside strategy again seems to have more promise. Just as the power of small contributions can be harnessed to make them more powerful in elections, they can be combined for lobbying purposes as well. A congressman doesn't owe a favor to a donor who gave him $15, but he does owe one to an online group that raised him $200,000 in $15 contributions. Existing online groups have been reluctant to take advantage of this influence, possibly because their natural transparency makes it harder for them to pretend they're not violating ethics rules, but it's a promising avenue for the future.

The alternative would be to figure out some way of severing campaign contributions from lobbying, but it's difficult to imagine how to do this practically. Even if lobbyists weren't permitted to touch campaign contributions themselves (and even that requirement is of dubious constitutionality), there's no reason their clients couldn't make contributions which the lobbyists could then call in as favors. Like campaign contribution caps, any regulation is likely to be full of loopholes.

Members have their own revolving door—and revolving-door restrictions. But as with staffers, the problem seems minor enough that even tough restrictions wouldn't make much difference. A cushy lobbying job is a nice dessert for a career well served, but the campaign contributions are the financial meat of the meal.

Conclusion

The good news, for those of us outside the Beltway, is that we don't need to wait for Congress to fix itself. The most effective solutions outlined here can be done by any outside group—and there are a number of people starting to do them. What's needed is not some final law that will solve our problems, but a group of outside activists creating their own reform. It may not be easy, but that just means we better get to work.

Keynes, Explained Briefly

http://www.aaronsw.com/weblog/keynes

September 24, 2009

Age 22

If you read the economic textbooks, you'll find that the job market is a market like any other. There's supply (workers) and demand (employers). And the incredible power of market competition pushes the price (wages) to where those two meet. Thus massive unemployment is about as likely as huge unsold piles of wheat: if people aren't buying, it's just because you're setting the price too high.

And yet, as I write, 17.5% of the country is unemployed. Are they all just insisting on being paid too much? Economists are forced into the most ridiculous explanations. Perhaps people just don't know where the jobs are, some say. (Maybe the government should run ads for Craigslist.) Or maybe it just takes time for all those former house-builders to learn new jobs. (This despite the fact that unemployment is up in all industries.) But they're typically forced back to the fundamental conclusion of the textbook: that people are just demanding to be paid too much. It might be for the most innocent of reasons, but facts are facts.

John Maynard Keynes' great insight was to see that all of this was nonsense. The job market is a very special market, because the people who get "bought" are also the people doing all the buying. After all, why is it that people are hired to farm wheat? It's because, at the end of the day, other people want to buy it. But if lots of people are out of a job, they're doing their best to save money, which means cutting back on purchases. And if they cut back on purchases, that means there are fewer people for business to sell to, which means businesses cut back on jobs.

Clearly something is badly wrong with the basic economic theory. So let's go through Keynes' masterpiece, *The General Theory of Employment, Interest, and Money*, and understand his theory of how the economy works.

When you get your paycheck at the end of the week, you spend it. But presumably you don't spend all of it—you put some money away to save, like you were told as a child. Saving is seen as a great national virtue—thus all those Public Service Announcements with talking piggy banks. Everyone knows why: put some money away today and it'll be worth more tomorrow.

But there's a kind of illusion involved in this. Money isn't worth anything on its own; it's only useful because it can buy things. And it buys things because it pays other people to make them for you. But you can't save people in your bank account—if fifteen million people are out of work, they can't put their time in a piggy bank for when things are looking up. The work they could have done is lost forever.

So yes, some people can save while others borrow from them—you can let your neighbor buy two iPods in exchange for letting you buy four next year—but the country, as a whole, cannot. At the end of the day, someone has to buy the things we can make. But if everyone's saving, that means people aren't buying. Which means the people making stuff are out of a job.

It's a vicious cycle: if people buy less, companies make less, which means people get paid less, which means people buy less. And so on, until we're all out of work. (Thankfully it doesn't get that bad—but only because some people are refusing to lower their wages. The thing that mainstream economists said was causing unemployment is actually preventing it!)

But this cycle can be run in reverse. Imagine Donald Trump hires unemployed people to build him a new skyscraper. They're suddenly getting paid again, which means they can start spending again. And each dollar they spend goes to a different business, which can start hiring people itself. And then those newly hired people start spending the new money they make, and so on. This is the multiplier: each dollar that gets spent provides even more than one dollar's worth of boost to the economy.

Now let's look at things from the employer's side—say you run a truck factory. How do you decide how many trucks to make? Obviously, you make as many as you think you can profitably sell. But there's no way to calculate something like that—it's a question about what customers will do in the future. There's literally no way to know. And yet, obviously, trucks get made.

It used to be, Keynes says, that wealthy men just thought investing was the manly thing to do. They weren't going to sit around and calculate what kind of bonds yielded the greatest expected return. Bonds are for wusses. They were real men. They were going to take their money and build a railroad.

But they don't make rich people like that anymore. Nowadays, they put their money in the stock market. Instead of boldly picking one great enterprise to invest in, they shift their money around from week to week (or hire someone else to do it for them). So these days, it's the stock market that stimulates most new investment.

But how does the stock market figure out what profits are supposed to be? In truth, it has no more clue than you do. It's really just based around a convention. We all pretend that whatever the stock price is now is a pretty decent guess and then we only have to worry about the various factors that will cause the stock price to change. We forget about the most basic fact: that nobody has any clue what the stock price should be to begin with.

So instead of people trying their best to figure out which businesses will make money in the future, and investing in those, we have people trying to figure out which stock prices will change in the future, and trying to get there first. It's like a giant game of musical chairs—everybody's rushing not to be the one left standing when the music stops.

Or, you could say, it's like those newspaper competitions where you have to pick the six prettiest faces from a hundred photographs. The prize goes to the person who picks the faces that are most picked, so you don't pick the faces you find prettiest, but instead the faces you think everyone else will find prettiest. But it's not even that, since everyone else is doing the same thing—you're actually picking the faces you think everyone else will think everyone else will find prettiest! And no doubt there are some people who take this even further.

You might think this means that someone who actually did the work and tried to calculate expected profits would clean up, taking money from all the people playing musical chairs. But it's not so simple. Calculating expected profits is really quite hard. To make money, you'd have to be unusually good at it, and it seems much easier to just guess what everyone else will do.

And even if you were somehow good at guessing long-term profits, where would you get the money to invest? It's in the fundamental nature of your strategy that your investments seem crazy to everyone else. If you're successful, they'll write it off as a lucky fluke. And when your stocks aren't doing well (which is most of the time—they're long-term picks, remember), people will take this as evidence of your failures and pull their money out.

The scary thing is that the more open our markets get, the faster people can move their money around and the more trading is based on this kind of speculation instead of serious analysis. And that's scary because—recall—the whole point of the stock market is to decide the crucial question of what we, as a society, should build for the future. As Keynes says, "When the capital development of a country becomes a by-product of the activities of a casino, the job is likely to be ill-done."

The best solution is probably a small tax on each trade. Not only would this raise a ton of money (modern estimates suggest even a tiny tax could raise $100 billion a year), it would help redirect all the brains on Wall Street from these wasteful games of musical chairs to something actually useful.

But even if we solve the problem of the stock market, there's still some irreducible uncertainty. Because whether new investment makes sense always depends on whether the economy will be doing well in the future. And whether the economy is doing well depends on whether there's new investment. So, at the end of the day, investment doesn't depend simply on a careful calculation of future expected yield, but on our "animal spirits," our optimism about the future. It's this factor that exaggerates booms and deepens slumps and makes it hard to get out of a bad situation.

Even more perversely, it means economic performance depends in no small part on keeping businessmen happy. If electing Obama gets businessmen depressed, they might pull back their investments and send the economy into a slump. It doesn't even have to be intentional—they may very well believe that a President Obama is bad for the economy. But when you have a system that only works when businesspeople feel good, their fears become a self-fulfilling prophecy.

The result, Keynes suggests, is that the government will have to step in to prevent the economy from crashing every time rich people get a bit of indigestion.

So that's how we calculate the income side of things, now what about costs? Most costs are pretty clear—you need to buy equipment and hire people. But since you need to make stuff now that you can only sell in the future, one of your big costs is going to be money to use in the meantime. And the cost of money is just the interest rate. (If you get a loan for a million dollars at 5% interest, you're essentially paying $50,000 for the right to use the money now.)

Thus lowering interest rates increases investment—it reduces the cost of getting money, which reduces the cost of making stuff, which means more things can make a profit. And if more things can make a profit, more things get made, which means more people get hired. So what determines the interest rate?

Well, if the interest rate is the cost of money, the obvious answer is the amount of money in circulation. If there's a lot of money lying around, you can get some pretty cheap. Which means that, fundamentally, unemployment is caused by a lack of money: more money (assuming people don't hoard it all) means lower interest rates, lower interest rates (assuming expected profits don't crash) means higher investment, higher investment (assuming people don't stop buying) means more employment, and more employment means higher prices, which means we're going to need more money.

Money is created by the central bank (the Federal Reserve in the U.S.), which decides what they want the interest rate to be and then prints new money (which they use to buy up government debt) until the interest rate is where they want. To get the economy back on track, all they have to do is keep lowering interest rates until investment picks up again and everyone has a job.

But there's one catch: the interest rate can't go below zero. (Keynes didn't think this problem was very likely, but in the U.S. we're facing it right now.) What do you do if the interest rate is zero and people are still out of work?

Well, you can pray that billionaires will start hiring us all to build them giant mansions, but that's no way to run a country. The government has to step in. Instead of waiting for billionaires to build pleasure domes, the government can hire people to build things we all need—roads, schools, houses, high-speed Internet connections. Although, honestly, it doesn't have to be things we all need. They could hire people to do anything. This is why inspecting the stimulus money for waste is so ridiculous—waste is perfectly fine, the important thing is to get the money into circulation so that the economy can get back on track.

Another good solution is redistributing income. Poor people are a lot more likely to spend money than billionaires. If we take some money from the billionaires and give it to the poor, the poor will use it to buy things they need and people will get jobs making those things.

Remember that money is just a kind of illusion. In reality, there are just people who want things and people who make things. But we're stuck in a completely ridiculous situation: there are lots of people who desperately want jobs making things—they're literally not doing anything else—while at the same time there are lots of people who desperately want things made. It seems ridiculous not to do something about this just because some people have all the little green sheets of paper!

Capitalism seems to go through frustrating cycles of booms and busts. Some people say the solution is just to prevent the booms—raise interest rates so the party doesn't get out of hand and we won't all be sorry the next morning. Keynes disagrees: the remedy "is not to be found in abolishing booms and thus keeping us permanently in a semi-slump; but in abolishing slumps and thus keeping us permanently in a quasi-boom."

Think back to the dot-com era, when venture capitalists were spending all their money laying fiber-optic cable under the street. The right solution wasn't for the Fed to raise interest rates until even punch-drunk venture capitalists could realize all this investment in fiber wouldn't be profitable. The right solution was to take their money away. Give it to the poor, who will spend it on something useful, like food and clothing.

So those are Keynes' prescriptions for a successful economy: low interest rates, government investment, and redistribution to the poor. And, for a time—from around the 1940s to the 1970s—that's kind of what we did. The results were magical: the economy grew strongly, inequality fell away, everyone had jobs.

But, starting in the 1970s, the rich staged a counterattack. They didn't like watching inequality—and their wealth—melt away. There was a resurgence in classical economics, Keynes was declared to have been debunked, and interest rates were raised drastically, throwing millions out of work. The economy tanked, inequality soared, and things have never been the same since. For a while people talked about levels of inequality that hadn't been seen since the 1920s. Then they talked about a recession the size of which hadn't been seen since the 1930s.

Once again, Keynes provides us with the instructions on how to get out of this mess. The question is whether we'll follow them.

Toward a Larger Left

http://crookedtimber.org/2009/08/04/toward-a-larger-left/

August 4, 2009

Age 22

Stanford, like many universities, maintains full employment for humanities professors by requiring new students to take their seminars. My heart burning with the pain of societal injustice, I chose the one on "Freedom, Equality, Difference."

Most of the other students had no particular interest in the topic—they were just meeting the requirement. But a significant minority did: like me, they cared passionately about it. They were the conservatives, armed with endless citations on how affirmative action was undermining American meritocracy. The only other political attitude I noticed was a moderate centrism, the view espoused by the teacher, whose day job was studying just war theory.

It quickly became clear that I was the only person even remotely on the left. And it wasn't simply that the others disagreed with me; they couldn't even *understand* me. I remember us discussing a scene in *Invisible Man* where a factory worker brags he's so indispensable that when he was out sick the boss drove to his house and begged him to come back, agreeing to put him in charge. When I suggested Ellison might be implying that labor, not management, ought to run workplaces, the other students (and the teacher) didn't just disagree—they found the idea incomprehensible. How could you run a factory without managers?

This is the reproduction of American intellectual culture: a large number of vocal and articulate conservatives, a handful of mushy moderately liberal centrists, and an audience that doesn't much care. (Completing the picture, the teacher later shouted me down for bringing up inconvenient facts during a discussion of Vietnam.)

It's a future that worries George Scialabba. He cares passionately about the humane left-wing tradition, but he's forced to watch it shrivel. As he observes, the conservatives receive prominent places in industry (including industry-funded think tanks), the centrists are quarantined in hyperspecialized programs at universities, and the real leftists can barely get a toehold. (*The Soviet Union fell*, seems to be the dominant position. *Why are you still here?*)

The question is what to do about it. George hails the few exceptions (Noam Chomsky, Alexander Cockburn—names presumably picked to provoke) who have managed to eke out a niche exposing the falsehoods and bucking the consensus, getting pushed to the cultural margins for their trouble. Henry proposes a more technical version, where left-wing critics don't argue to the public (which in practice seems to mean the 20,000 readers of *Z Magazine*) but instead to elites, especially disciplinary experts, using a field's flaws against itself (à la Doug Henwood). And Michael seems to make the usual retort that such extremism never gets an audience, let alone an accomplishment—only incrementalism and realist accommodation to power will make a difference in people's lives (perhaps Ezra Klein could be the poster boy here).

This debate is not dispassionate. It's a muddy mix of trying to work out what to do with our lives and how to justify what we've already done. Personally, I adore Chomsky, Henwood, and Klein—I find both their writing and their personalities incredibly inspirational. And while I could quibble with their strategies, it's difficult for me to imagine, let alone desire, a world in which they did anything particularly different. But my own plans—forged in that Stanford classroom and (to my surprise) unshakable ever since—take a different tack.

A new media world is emerging. The mainstream media outlets that won't even bother to print Chomsky's response when they libel him are fading, while alternative media explodes. Alexander Cockburn publishes not one, but a dozen articles each day at Counter-Punch.org. Amy Goodman has a daily television news show carried on over 700 stations. There's a whole Chomsky industry, which gets at least a shelf even at suburban chain bookstores. Socialist-feminists like Barbara Ehrenreich write *New York Times* bestsellers. Hell, we even have a socialist U.S. senator now!

Then there's the whole new generation of political bloggers. Daily Kos, Atrios, and so on have a combined readership in the millions and are all consistently venomous toward the bulk of the Democratic Party and the media. Their work is broadcast nightly on major networks by Jon Stewart and Rachel Maddow. (*The West Wing* even made Atrios a character.) Even Scialabba admits (although not in his book) that if he wants to spend time with like-minded friends, he heads to Crooked Timber.

But while this clearly has a salutary effect on mainstream political culture (witness Stephen Kinzer's transformation from Noam Chomsky's bête noire to Amy Goodman's guest), it hasn't exactly created an alternative culture of its own. Conservatives, centrists, liberals—they all repeat *their* fundamental premise: *We've got a pretty good system going here. Sure, there may be some trouble around the edges* (liberals think more, conservatives think less), *but, as McCain said, the fundamentals are still strong.* The lines are so well publicized that even college freshmen can repeat them down to the sound bite.

The left has succeeded in making it sound hollow and unconvincing. Your average liberal blogger is happy to admit all the papers are full of lies, all the politicians are bland sellouts, and the government is run by lobbyists and corporate hacks. And (nothing new here) your average citizen is happy to agree (it takes a lot of education to be dumb enough to think otherwise). But where do you go from there? Elect Howard Dean?

The Popular Front is long dead, the labor unions have all but fizzled out, the New Left never had much of a plan ("We must name that system," SDS cried. "We must name it, describe it, analyze it, understand it and change it"; apparently they never got past naming) and barely even exists anymore. The term *socialism* has become so watered down that it polls roughly equal with capitalism among the under-30 set—apparently it now means anything to the left of austere neoliberalism (except file sharing, of course).

If there was ever a time for a new program, this would seem to be it. The economic crisis has shattered the Washington Consensus more than a thousand Chomsky op-eds could, while the Internet has made it possible to organize people by the million. But the left can't seem to move beyond its reactive stance. If you want books that criticize the policies of the Bush administration, you can fill up a whole library. But if you want books on what to do instead, where do you go? The only left-of-center group seriously putting out policy proposals is Third Way. (Sample recommendation: "Moderniz[e] our intelligence force . . . [hold a p]ress conference highlighting the 20th anniversary of the creation of al Qaeda.")

There *is* a coherent, alternative ideology on the left. Scialabba, summarizing Chomsky, even takes a stab at laying it out: "The fundamental purpose of American foreign policy has all along been to maintain a favorable investment climate . . . the American intelligentsia, though less harshly and clumsily regulated than its Soviet counterpart, has been no less effectively subordinated to the goals of the state." (I would add only that the domestic economy is structured to make the majority of the population expendable servants of the rich.) Scialabba lays it out, but Chomsky (as far as I can find) never does.

I'll even go further and take a stab at describing Chomsky's solution: democracy. Media democracy, to prevent the population from being misled by deluded elites with big megaphones. Economic democracy, to promote a better mix and fairer distribution of societal goods and necessary evils. And political democracy, so that our military isn't led by murderous thugs into endless immoral engagements.

This philosophy is so different from the dominant consensus that it takes far more than two paragraphs to explain, let alone argue for. But who's even trying? Instead, the audience is forced to read a shelf of Chomsky and reverse-engineer the principles behind it.

This is better than nothing—it worked for me—but it obviously puts a hard limit on who can be persuaded. People without the time or the ability end up as the folks you see in liberal blog comments: people who know something is badly wrong, but aren't quite sure what it is or what to do about it.

In short, leftist intellectuals need to move from simply poking holes in the dominant consensus to clearly articulating their alternative and proposing a concrete method for promoting it (Chomsky, for all his brilliance, seems to espouse a theory of change that doesn't go much beyond getting people at his book readings to join the local ISM chapter). I hope that more people will, because I sometimes fear that if they don't, there may not be many leftist intellectuals anymore.

Professional Politicians Beware!

http://rebooting.personaldemocracy.com/node/5490

2008

Age 21

This essay first appeared in Rebooting America: Ideas for Redesigning American Democracy for the Internet Age, *edited by Allison Fine, Micah L. Sifry, Andrew Rasiej, and Joshua Levy (Personal Democracy Press, 2008).*

> "By the power of exponents, just five levels of councils, each consisting of only fifty people, is enough to cover over three hundred million people."

The government of a republic, James Madison wrote in Federalist No. 39 ("Conformity of the Plan to Republican Principles," 1788), must "be derived from the great body of the society, not from an inconsiderable proportion, or a favored class of it; otherwise a handful of tyrannical nobles, exercising their oppressions by a delegation of their powers, might aspire to the rank of republicans, and claim for their government the honorable title of republic."

Looking at our government today—a House of professional politicians, a Senate filled with multimillionaires, a string of presidential family dynasties—it seems hard to maintain that our officials are in fact "derived from the great body of the society" and not "a favored class" merely posing as representatives of the people.

Unless politics is a tradition in your family, your odds of getting elected to federal office are slim. And unless you're a white male lawyer, you rarely get to vote for someone like yourself in a national race. Nor, in reality, do we have an opportunity to choose policy positions: no major candidates support important proposals that most voters agree with, like single-payer health care.

Instead, national elections have been boiled down to simple binary choices, which advertising men and public relations teams reduce to pure emotions: Fear. (A bear prowls through the woods.) Hope. (The sun rises over a hill.) Vote Smith. Or maybe Jones. Nor does the major media elevate the level of debate. Instead of substantive discussions about policy proposals and their effects, they spend their time on horse-race coverage (who's raised the most money? Who's polling well in Ohio?) and petty scandals (how much did that haircut cost? Was someone somewhere offended by that remark?)

The result after all this dumbing down? In 2004, voters who said they chose a presidential candidate based on the candidate's agendas, ideas, platforms, or goals comprised a whopping 10% of the electorate. So it's not too surprising when political scientists find that voters' decisions can be explained by such random factors as whether they like red or blue, whether the economy is good or bad, or whether the current party has been in office for long or not.

Aside from the occasional telephone poll, the opinions of "the great body of the society" have been edited out of the picture. Way back in Federalist No. 10 ("The Utility of the Union as a Safeguard Against Domestic Faction and Insurrection [Continued]," 1787), Madison put his finger on the reason. "However small the republic may be," he noted, "the representatives must be raised to a certain number, in order to guard against the cabals of a few." But similarly, "however large it may be, they must be limited to a certain number, in order to guard against the confusion of a multitude."

The result is that the population grows while the number of representatives stays fixed, leaving each politician to represent more and more people. The first Congress had a House of 65 members representing 40,000 voters and three million citizens (they had a whopping 1.3% voter turnout back then). That's a representative for around every 600 voters or 46,000 citizens (the size of the average baseball stadium). A baseball stadium may be a bit of an unruly mob, but it's not unimaginably large.

Today, by contrast, we have 435 representatives and 300 million citizens—one for roughly every 700,000 citizens. There isn't a stadium in the world big enough to hold that many people. It's a number more akin to a television audience (it's about how many people tune in to watch Keith Olbermann each night).

Which is exactly what the modern constituency has become: the TV audience following along at home. Even if you wanted to, you can't have a real conversation with a TV audience. It is too big to convey a sense of what each individual is thinking. Instead of a group to represent, it's a mob to be managed.

I agree with Madison that there is roughly a right size for a group of representatives "on both sides of which inconveniences will be found to lie. By enlarging too much the number of electors, you render the representatives too little acquainted with all their local circumstances and lesser interests; as by reducing it too much, you render him unduly attached to these, and too little fit to comprehend and pursue great and national objects."

But what Madison missed is that there is no similar limit on the number of such groups. To take a technological analogy, the Internet is, at bottom, an enormous collection of wires. Yet nobody would ever think of it this way. Instead, we group the wires into chips and the chips into computers and the computers into networks and the networks into the Internet. And people only deal with things at each level: when the computer breaks, we can't identify which wire failed; we take the whole thing into the shop.

One of the most compelling visions for rebooting democracy adopts this system of abstraction for politics. Parpolity, developed by the political scientist Stephen Shalom, would build a legislature out of a hierarchical series of nested councils. Agreeing with Madison, he says each council should be small enough that everyone can engage in face-to-face discussion but large enough that there is a diversity of opinion and the number of councils is minimized. He estimates the right size is 25 to 50 people.

So, to begin with, let us imagine a council of you and your 40 closest neighbors—perhaps the other people in your apartment building or on your block. You get together every so often to discuss the issues that concern you and your neighborhood. And you may vote to set policy for the area which the council covers.

But your council has another function: it selects one of its own to send as a representative to the next council up. There the process repeats itself: the representative from your block and its 40 closest neighbors meet every so often to discuss the political issues that concern the area. And, of course, your representative reports back to the group, gets your recommendations on difficult questions, and takes suggestions for issues to raise at the next area council meeting.

By the power of exponents, just five levels of councils, each consisting of only fifty people, is enough to cover over three hundred million people. But—and this is the truly clever bit—at the area council the whole process repeats itself. Just as each block council nominates a representative to the area council, each area council nominates a representative to the city council, and each city council to the state council, each state council to the national council, and so on.

Shalom discusses a number of further details—provisions for voting, recalls, and delegation—but it's the idea of nesting that's key. Under such a system, there are only four representatives who stand between you and the people setting national policy, each of whom is forced to account to their constituents in regular, small face-to-face meetings. Politicians in such a system could not be elected through empty appeals to mass emotions. Instead, they would have to sit down, face-to-face, with a council of their peers and persuade them that they are best suited to represent their interests and positions.

There is something rather old-fashioned about this notion of sitting down with one's fellow citizens and rationally discussing the issues of the day. But there is also something exciting and new about it. In the same way that blogs have given everyone a chance to be a publisher, Wikipedia lets everyone be an encyclopedia author, and YouTube lets anyone be a television producer, Parpolity would let everyone be a politician.

The Internet has shown us that the pool of people with talent far outnumbers the few with the background, connections, and wealth to get to a place in society where they can practice their talents professionally. (It also shows us that many people with those connections aren't particularly talented.)

The democratic power of the net means you don't need connections to succeed. In a world where kids can be television stars just by finding a video camera and an Internet connection, citizens may begin to wonder why getting into politics is so much harder.

For many years, politicians had a ready excuse: politics was a difficult job, which required carefully weighing and evaluating evidence and making difficult decisions. Only a select few could be trusted to perform it; the vast majority of the population was woefully underqualified.

And perhaps in the era of a cozy relationship between politicians and the press, this illusion could be sustained. But as netroots activists and blogs push our national conversation ever closer to the real world, this excuse is becoming laughable. After all, these men and women of supposedly sober judgment voted overwhelmingly for disasters like the Iraq War. "No one could have ever predicted this," TV's talking heads all insist. No one, that is, except the great body of society, whose insistence that Iraq did not pose a threat and that an occupation would be long and brutal went ignored.

New online tools for interaction and collaboration have let people come together across space and time to build amazing things. As the Internet breaks down the last justifications for a professional class of politicians, it also builds up the tools for replacing them. For the most part, their efforts have so far been focused on education and entertainment, but it's only a matter of time before they turn to politics. And when they do, professional politicians beware!

The Attraction of the Center

http://www.aaronsw.com/weblog/whycentrism

July 12, 2006

Age 19

"Centrism" is the tendency to see two different beliefs and attempt to split the difference between them. The reason why it's a bad idea should be obvious: truth is independent of our beliefs, no less than any other partisans, centrists ignore evidence in favor of their predetermined ideology.

So what's the attraction? First, it requires little thought: arguing for a specific position requires collecting evidence and arguing for it. Centrism simply requires repeating some of what A is saying and some of what B is saying and mixing them together. Centrists often don't even seem to care if the bits they take contradict each other.

Second, it's somewhat inoffensive. Taking a strong stand on A or B will unavoidably alienate some. But being a centrist, one can still maintain friends on both sides, since they will find at least some things that you espouse to be agreeable with their own philosophies.

Third, it makes it easier to suck up to those in charge, because the concept of the "center" can easily move along with shifts in power. A staunch conservative will have to undergo a major change of political philosophy to get a place in liberal administrations. A centrist can simply espouse a few more positions from the conservatives and a few less from the liberals and fit in just fine. This criteria explains why centrists are so prevalent in the pundit class (neither administration is tempted to really force them out) and why so many "centrist" pundits espouse mostly conservative ideas these days (the conservatives are in power).

Fourth, despite actually being a servant of those in power, centrism gives one the illusion of actually being a serious, independent thinker. "People on the right and on the left already know what they're going to say on every issue," they might claim, "but we centrists make decisions based on the situation." (This excuse was recently used in a fund-raising letter by the *New Republic*.) Of course, the "situation" that's used to make these decisions is simply who's currently in power, as discussed above, but that part is carefully omitted.

Fifth, it appeals to the public. There's tremendous dissatisfaction among the public with the government and our system of politics. Despite being precisely in the middle of this corrupt system, centrists can claim that they're actually "independents" and "disagree with both the left and the right." They can denounce "extremism" (which isn't very popular) and play the "moderate," even when their positions are extremely far from what the public believes or what the facts say.

Together, these reasons combine to make centrism an especially attractive place to be in American politics. But the disease is far from limited to politics. Journalists frequently suggest the truth lies between the two opposing sources they've quoted. Academics try to distance themselves from policy positions proposed by either party. And, perhaps worst of all, scientists try to split the difference between two competing theories.

Unfortunately for them, neither the truth nor the public necessarily lies somewhere in the middle. Fortunately for them, more valuable rewards do.

Exercise for the reader: What's the attraction of "contrarianism," the ideology subscribed to by online magazines like *Slate*?

The Conservative Nanny State

http://www.aaronsw.com/weblog/cns

May 22, 2006

Age 19

For years, progressives have watched as both Democratic and Republican administrations have taken away what little remained of economic liberalism in this country. Bill Clinton, for example, took away what meager assistance the government paid to poor single mothers, signed NAFTA, and began attempting to chip away at Social Security.

But even worse than these policy defeats are the conceptual defeats that underlie them. As cognitive scientist George Lakoff has argued, people think about politics through conceptual moral frames, and the conservatives have been masterful at creating frames for their policies. If the left wants to fight back, they're going to have to create frames of their own.

Enter Dean Baker, co-director of the Center for Economic and Policy Research and one of the people instrumental in fighting back against the most recent attempt to privatize Social Security (as author of *Social Security: The Phony Crisis*, he had plenty of facts to demonstrate that the crisis was, in fact, phony). He has a new book out, *The Conservative Nanny State: How the Wealthy Use the Government to Stay Rich and Get Richer*, which takes decades of conservative frames and stands them on their head. (Disclosure: I liked the book so much I converted it to HTML for them and was sent a free paperback copy in return.)

His most fundamental point is that conservatives are *not* generally in favor of market outcomes. For far too long, he argues, the left has been content with the notion that conservatives want the market to do what it pleases while liberals want some government intervention to protect people from its excesses.

No way! says Baker. Conservatives *love* big government—only they use it to give money to the rich instead of the poor. Thus the conservative nanny state of the title, always looking out for crybaby moneybags to help.

Take, for example, trade policy. The conservative nanny state is more than happy to sign free trade agreements that let manufacturing jobs in the United States flee offshore. And they're happy to let immigrant workers come into the country to replace dishwashers and day laborers. But when it comes to the professional class, like doctors, lawyers, economists, journalists, and other professionals, *oh no!*, the conservative nanny state does everything it can (through licensing and immigration policy) to keep foreign workers out.

This doesn't just help the doctors, it hurts all of us because it means we have to pay more for health care. NAFTA boosters estimate that the entire agreement saved us $8 billion a year. Using competition to bring only doctors' salaries down [to] the levels seen in Europe would save us *eighty* billion dollars—nearly $700 per family per year, just from improved prices for doctors. You'd see similar amounts from other major professions.

Baker's book is also one of the few to reveal the shocking secret behind the Federal Reserve Board you always hear messing with interest rates on the news. This unaccountable technocracy, most of whose members are appointed by banks, uses its power over interest rates to drive the economy into a recession so that wages won't get too high. That's right, the government tries to slow down the economy so that you get paid less. (Full details are in the book.)

Baker's book is also chock-full of fascinating new policy ideas. He points out, for example, that corporations aren't part of the free market, but instead a gift offered by the government. (A very popular one too, since companies voluntarily pay $278 billion each year for it.) And because of this, there's absolutely no reason the government can't tweak its terms to make us all better off. For example, Baker points out that currently, corporate rules count shareholders who don't vote at all as voting in favor of whatever the directors of the corporation prefer. Baker suggests requiring that all CEO pay packages get approved by a majority of those actually voting, instead of letting major CEOs pick how much to pay themselves, as they do now.

Or what about copyright and patents? Again, this isn't a law of nature, but a big government gift. People who really care about shrinking government would want to try to get rid of or shrink the laws that say the government gets to make rules about what songs and movies we can have on our personal computers.

Americans spend $220 billion on prescription drugs, largely because of government-granted patents. Instead of handing that money to big drug companies, the government could spend far less (only a couple hundred million) funding researchers itself and making the resulting drug discoveries free to the public. College students spend $12 billion on textbooks alone. Again, the government could make free textbooks for one-thousandth that. And we spend $37 billion on music and movies. Why not create an "artistic freedom voucher" (vouchers—a conservative favorite!) that can only be spent on artists who place their work in the public domain?

None of these would require outlawing the existing system—they could work side by side, simply forcing the existing drug, textbook, and movie companies to compete with this alternate idea. If their version works better, then fine, they'll get the money. But if not, there'll be no conservative nanny state to protect them.

Similarly, the government could expand the Social Security program, allowing everyone to buy additional personal accounts from a system with amazingly low overhead (.5% versus the 20% of private funds) and a 70-year track record of success. Or it could try to improve our pitifully bad health care system by letting people buy into the government's Medicare program, which again has amazingly low administrative costs (did you know that, on a per person basis, we spend 80% of what Britain spends on health care altogether simply on administration?) and serious bargaining power to push down prices. Again, why not let the private companies try their best to compete?

The book itself also discusses bankruptcy laws, torts and takings, small businesses, and taxes. And it goes into far more detail on each of these subjects. And it's all available for free on the Internet, so there's no excuse for not reading it. It's a fun read, the kind of book that turns the way you think about the economy upside-down.

Political Entrepreneurs and Lunatics with Money

http://crookedtimber.org/2009/05/01/politicalentrepreneurs-and
-lunatics-with-money/

May 1, 2009

Age 22

One of the interesting things about capitalism is that, if you have money, people seem to just magically appear to meet your needs. When it rains in New York City, vendors materialize to sell me an umbrella. When I was walking to the inauguration, the streets were lined with people selling hats and handwarmers. I certainly didn't ask anyone to bring me a hat; I didn't even realize I would want one, or I would have brought it myself—but people predicted that I would and brought it for me.

The more money you have, the more crazy these desires can get. If you're rich, people offer to launch you into space, build large buildings with your name on them, or set up lavish cemetery plots. Or, as Steven Teles demonstrates, push the law to be more to your liking.

What's striking about the rise of modern conservatism is that it was *not*, in large part, the creation of big business. Big business, all things considered, was pretty happy with the liberal consensus. They weren't exactly itching to drown the government in the bathtub, especially when it did so much for them.

Teles makes this clear with his brilliant first chapter* on the *liberal* legal network. "From the perspective of the early twenty-first century," Teles notes, "it is perplexing why these wealthy, well-positioned, white men—presidents of the American Bar Associa-

---

*Actually the second—as with most academic books, the first chapter is theoretical background and the story doesn't begin until after.

tion, leaders of the nation's largest foundations—put their support behind a project to liberalize the legal profession." You had groups as respectable as the Ford Foundation, the ABA, and the OEO supporting a project as activist as the Legal Services Program, which, Teles writes, "helped transform the administration, and ultimately the politics, of public aid" (32). Law schools started pro bono clinics, and the Ford Foundation funded a dozen legal activist groups. (Admittedly, the other major foundations refused to join in.)

Corporations did attempt to strike back—as Teles documents in a chapter called "Mistakes Made." He quotes an influential report on these early attempts, complaining that they simply took money from a company and spent it fighting that same company's legal battles, a law firm structured as a tax dodge. Afraid of alienating the shareholders of their corporate donors, they shied away from principled ideological stands and didn't influence the larger political debate.

But the real conservative movement was funded instead by wealthy extremists on the fringes of the business world. It was the creation of people like Richard Mellon Scaife, who inherited part of the vast Mellon fortune from his alcoholic mother. Joseph Coors inherited a brewing company, John M. Olin ran a relatively obscure chemical company, R. Randolph Richardson inherited the money his father made by selling Vicks to Procter and Gamble.* None of them can exactly be called Titans of Industry, or even titans of industry. Yet these are the men who bankrolled not just the conservative legal movement, but the conservative movement in general.

This fact is sometimes obscured by a document called the Powell Memo. Written by Lewis Powell, shortly before Nixon made him a Supreme Court Justice, it calls on the U.S. Chamber of Commerce to defend "the free enterprise system" from "the college campus, the pulpit, the media, the intellectual and literary journals, the arts and sciences, and from politicians" that would dare to criticize it.

The Powell Memo kicks off most histories of the right-wing think tank, not because it was so clearly influential, but because it was

---

*Note how many of them directly inherited their fortunes. I'll leave it to someone more inclined to psychological speculation to comment on the relationship between a conservative philosophy and strong support for the system that let your father make his millions.

so clear: "The national television networks should be monitored," Powell wrote, "in the same way that textbooks should be kept under constant surveillance." What passionate critic of the free enterprise system could resist such a quote?[*]

But the quotes have disguised the fact that Powell's suggestions didn't exactly come to pass. It wasn't the Chamber of Commerce or major businesses that took on these tasks, but a network of independent, ideologically based think tanks. And these think tanks weren't founded by eminent Men of Business, but by a new class of people—a group we might call political entrepreneurs.

Dan Burt was a little-known Massachusetts lawyer when he took over the Capital Legal Foundation and turned it into one of the first effective conservative-movement law firms. Henry Manne was merely a legal scholar when he began pitching Pierre Goodrich (millionaire stockpicker) on building a new right-wing law school. Lee Liberman Otis was just a law student when she started pitching Scaife and others on the need for the Federalist Society.[†]

The field even has its serial entrepreneurs. Paul Weyrich was the press secretary for a Republican senator when he met Joseph Coors. Over the next few decades, Weyrich used Coors' money to start the Heritage Foundation, the Free Congress Foundation, Moral Majority, the American Legislative Exchange Council, and various other groups that haunt any history of modern conservatism's rise.

Just like the vendors at the inauguration, political entrepreneurs sought out people with money and tried to sell them something they didn't even know they wanted. (Manne to Goodrich: "The Augean stables were cleaned by diverting a stream of water through them. . . . One law school dedicated to propositions like those you

---

[*]Kim Phillips-Fein's excellent new history, *Invisible Hands*, is notable for how hard it works to put the Powell Memo in its proper context, noting how much was done before the memo was even written and casting a skeptical eye on claims of the memo's influence.

[†]For an example in another field, see my previous piece on Roger Bate, whose Africans Fighting Malaria spends its time trying to claim environmentalists kill African babies. Bate tried to start the organization by hitting up his friends at Philip Morris, but in the end could only get the money from a California mining magnate. (Interestingly, many find this hard to believe and argue that Philip Morris must have been the real funder.)

propound . . . would do more to discipline all the other[s] than any-thing I can think of." Note how Manne claims to promote the ideas "*you* propound.") Nonprofits are small enough and rich people are wealthy enough that it only takes a handful of lunatics with money to fund a whole forest of think tanks.

And yet, there must be crazy lefty billionaires too. So why do most lefty think tanks rarely go any farther than the Clintonite con-sensus? (To take a story in the news recently, conservatives have had some fun pointing out the Center for American Progress, like Obama, is in favor of sending *more* troops to Afghanistan.) It's easy to understand why big corporations wouldn't want to push left-wing ideas, but it's harder to understand why there aren't any brazen rich people who do.

Which leads me to suspect the limiting factor isn't the funders, but the entrepreneurs. The average lefty wants to *do stuff,* not hob-nob with rich people and manage a staff. They're not particularly cut out for organizational work nor do they hang around with the kind of people who are. If they do hang out with entrepreneurs, they're more likely to be the kind who start small, hip technology compa-nies, which just makes them wonder why they're not making mil-lions doing that instead of wasting time on this political bullshit. (One friend recently left lefty activism to make Firefox plug-ins.)

As a good institutionalist, I'm a bit uncomfortable proposing what basically amounts to a cultural explanation for this phenomenon, but while it's less intellectually satisfying it's at least more politically optimistic. If one of the things holding the left back is a lack of po-litical entrepreneurs, then all we need to do is make more.

Now I just need to find some lunatics with money.

Full disclosure: Aaron Swartz recently co-founded the Progressive Change Campaign Committee, making him something of a politi-cal entrepreneur himself. Before that he was one of those lame tech start-up entrepreneurs, founding reddit.com. This piece is written entirely in his personal capacity, of course.

People who didn't know Aaron remember him for his tireless work on behalf of a variety of public causes. They usually don't realize that this work went together with a myriad of private kindnesses. I got to know Aaron as an extraordinarily intelligent commentator on Crooked Timber, an academic blog that I contribute to. At first I didn't know about the other great things that he had done; he didn't talk about them unless he was pressed. He just wanted to get involved in conversations with other people who were interested in political inquiry and social justice the way he was.

He also wanted to help. When we had major technical difficulties because our audience was outpacing the capacities of the server space we had leased, he suggested, without any fuss, that he would be very happy to take over our technical responsibilities and provide us all the facilities we needed. He privately helped many other people in equally unfussy ways. Rick Perlstein, the political historian of the rise of the right, is now famous. Before he was well known, Aaron came across his work, realized that he didn't have a website, and offered to make one for him. Rick was a bit nonplussed to receive so generous an offer from a complete stranger, but he quickly realized that Aaron was for real. They became good friends.

We asked Aaron to guest-blog for us for seminars, but we also just published his work when he had something to say and asked us if we were interested (we said yes, and for good reason). He brought many worlds together. His activism went hand in hand with a deep commitment to the intellect and to figuring out the world through argument. This could discomfit other activists, since it meant that he often changed his mind. He had the profound intellectual curiosity of a first-rate scholar, without the self-importance that usually accompanies it. If he could be accused of arrogance (and some people did so accuse him), it was a curiously egoless form. He simply expected other people to live up to the same exacting standards that he imposed upon himself. But he could also take a joke. When the *New York Times* ran a story on him with an accompanying photo that portrayed him brooding and backlit behind the screen of his MacBook, I teased him about it, and he was clearly delighted to be teased.

It's hard to face up to what we've lost. He wasn't just an activist, or a programmer, or an intellectual. He was a builder of bridges between many different people from many different worlds. Only after he died did I begin to realize how many people he corresponded with. When I write now, it is often in an imaginary dialogue with him, where I imagine his impatience with this or that plodding sentence, too far removed from the real concerns of real people. That imaginary dialogue is no substitute for the real thing. He was smarter than I am, and always capable of surprising me. I miss him very much.

—Henry Farrell

MEDIA

L ike Aaron, I go around a lot and talk to people about stuff that I think is of burning importance: questions about whether the Internet will be a tool for unimaginable surveillance, control, and censorship, or whether it will be a tool for unprecedented democratic deliberation, collective action, creativity, and self-expression.

When it's over, inevitably someone will ask me how I think it'll all turn out. After all, I'm a science fiction writer. Isn't that a bit like being a futurist?

But being a science fiction writer is nothing like a futurist. Or shouldn't be, anyway. A science fiction writer who believes he can predict the future is like a drug peddler who starts sampling the product—it never ends well. The point of science fiction is to talk about the present—to build a counterfactual world that illustrates some important fact about the present that is so vast and diffuse that it's hard to put your finger on.

When you go to the doctor with a sore throat, she'll swab it and touch the swab to a petri dish that goes into a cupboard for a day or two. When she gets it out again, the stuff that was on the swab will have multiplied into something that is visible with a conventional microscope, ready for diagnosis. Science fiction writers do that to whole societies. We pluck a single technological fact out of the world around us, and we build a world in a bottle where that fact is the totalizing truth. Through a process of fiction, we take the reader on a tour of this thought experiment that gives him the power to intuit the way technology is flexing our reality, making the invisible visible.

The important fact about the petri dish with your throat gunk on it is that it is not an accurate model of your body. It's an incredibly simplified model of it, inaccurate in a specific and useful way. So it is with science fiction—its value is not in prediction but in description, in making the invisible visible.

Who wants to be a predictor, anyway? If the world was predictable, it would be foreordained, and what we do wouldn't matter. A world on rails is one in which everything we do is futile. Why, if you saw what Dante did to the fortune-*tellers* in Inferno, you'd—

So then they say, "Fine, fine, you're not a predictor. But what about optimism? Are you optimistic about the future or pessimistic?"

And that's when I really start to channel my inner Aaron. Because that's exactly the wrong sort of question to ask. Of course I'm pessimistic about what would happen if the forces of reaction triumph and the Net is irreversibly used to wire up a system of totalitarian control that combines Orwell (surveillance) with Huxley (ubiquitous corporate messaging) and Kafka (guilt by Big Data algorithm).

But so what? The fact that I'm still doing something tells you the answer to the optimism/pessimism question. If I didn't think there was any hope of salvaging things, I wouldn't be out there kicking at the walls and shouting from the hilltops. Is that optimism?

I don't know. Call it hope instead.

And on second thought, even if I was convinced that nothing I did mattered, I'd still be out there. Because this world is people I love—my wife, my daughter, other family members, friends, some of you reading these words. And just as I wouldn't stop treading water if I was trying to keep my daughter afloat in an open sea, not until my last breath was gone and my legs wouldn't kick another stroke, even if I knew it wouldn't make a difference, I'd still keep kicking. If I weren't capable of another stroke, I'd still keep advocating for Net freedom even if I knew my efforts wouldn't make a difference.

Don't ask yourself whether the future will be good or bad. Don't ask yourself whether you are an optimist or a pessimist. Ask what you can do to make the world better. Live as though these are the first days of a better nation. Never give up.

—Cory Doctorow

The Book That Changed My Life

http://www.aaronsw.com/weblog/epiphany

May 15, 2006

Age 19

Two years ago this summer I read a book that changed the entire way I see the world. I had been researching various topics—law, politics, the media—and become more and more convinced that something was seriously wrong. Politicians, I was shocked to discover, weren't actually doing what the people wanted. And the media, my research found, didn't really care much about that, preferring to focus on such things as posters and polls.

As I thought about this more, its implications struck me as larger and larger. But I still had no bigger picture to fit them in. The media was simply doing a bad job, leading people to be confused. We just had to pressure them to do better and democracy would be restored.

Then, one night, I watched the film *Manufacturing Consent: Noam Chomsky and the Media* (I think it had come up in my Netflix queue). First off, it's simply an amazingly good film. I've watched it several times now and each time I'm utterly entranced. It's undoubtedly the best documentary I've seen, weaving together all sorts of clever tricks to enlighten and entertain.

Second, it makes shocking points. I didn't understand all of what it was saying at the time, but I understood enough to realize that something was severely amiss. The core of the film is a case study of Indonesia's brutal invasion of the country of East Timor. The U.S. personally gave the green light to the invasion and provided the weapons, which allowed Indonesia to massacre the population in an occupation that, per capita, ranks with the Holocaust. And the U.S. media ignores it and, when they do cover it, inevitably distorts it.

Shocked and puzzled by the film, I was eager to learn more. Noam Chomsky has dozens of books but I was fortunate to choose to read *Understanding Power*, a thick paperback I picked up at the library. Edited by Peter Mitchell and John Schoeffel, two public defenders in New York, the book is a collection of transcripts of group discussions with Chomsky.

Chomsky lays out the facts in a conversational style, telling stories and explaining things in response to questions from the groups, covering an incredibly wide range of topics. And on every single one, what he tells you is completely shocking, at odds with everything you know, turning the way you see things upside-down. Mitchell and Schoeffel know you're unlikely to believe these things, so they've carefully footnoted and documented every claim, providing block-quote excerpts from the original sources to establish them.

Each story, individually, can be dismissed as some weird oddity, like what I'd learned about the media focusing more on posters than on policy. But seeing them all together, you can't help but begin to tease out the larger picture, to ask yourself what's behind all these disparate things, and what that means for the way we see the world.

Reading the book, I felt as if my mind was rocked by explosions. At times the ideas were too much, and I literally had to lie down. (I'm not the only one to feel this way—Norman Finkelstein noted that when he went through a similar experience, "it was a totally crushing experience for me. . . . My world literally caved in. And there were quite a number of weeks where . . . I just was in bed, totally devastated.") I remember vividly clutching at the door to my room, trying to hold on to something while the world spun around.

For weeks afterwards, everything I saw was in a different light. Every time I saw a newspaper or magazine or person on TV, I questioned what I thought I knew about them, wondered how they fit into this new picture. Questions that had puzzled me for years suddenly began making sense in this new world. I reconsidered everyone I knew, everything I thought I'd learned. And I found I didn't have much company.

It's taken me two years to write about this experience, not without reason. One terrifying side effect of learning the world isn't the way you think is that it leaves you all alone. And when you try to describe your new worldview to people, it either comes out sounding unsurprising ("Yeah, sure, everyone knows the media's got problems") or like pure lunacy and people slowly back away.

Ever since then, I've realized that I need to spend my life working to fix the shocking brokenness I'd discovered. And the best way to do that, I concluded, was to try to share what I'd discovered with others. I couldn't just tell them it straight out, I knew, so I had to provide the hard evidence. So I started working on a book to do just that. (I'm looking for people to help, if you're interested.)

It's been two years now and my mind has settled down some. I've learned a bunch more but, despite my best efforts, haven't found any problems with this frightening new worldview. After all this time, I'm finally ready to talk about what happened with some distance and I hope I'm now able to begin work on my book in earnest.

It was a major change, but I wouldn't give it up for anything.

The Invention of Objectivity

http://www.aaronsw.com/weblog/newobjectivity

October 19, 2006

Age 19

Big media pundits are always wringing their hands about how up-start partisan bloggers are destroying the neutral objectivity our country was founded on. (If there's one thing pundits love to do, it's hand-wringing.) Without major papers giving everyone an objective view of the facts, they insist, the very foundation of the republic is in peril.

You can criticize this view for just being silly or wrong, and many have, but there's another problem with it: it's completely ahistorical. As Robert McChesney describes in *The Problem of the Media*, objectiv-ity is a fairly recent invention—the republic was actually founded on partisan squabblers.

When our country was founded, newspapers were not neutral, nonpartisan outlets, but the products of particular political parties. The Whigs had their paper, the Tories theirs, both of which attacked their political opponents with slurs that would make even the most foul-mouthed bloggers blush. This behavior wasn't just permitted—it was encouraged.

You often hear the media quote Jefferson's comment that "were it left to me to decide whether we should have a government without newspapers, or newspapers without government, I should not hesi-tate a moment to prefer the latter." However, they hesitate to print the following sentence: "But I should mean that every man should receive those papers, and be capable of reading them." In particu-lar, Jefferson was referring to the post office subsidy the government provided to the partisan press.

In 1794, newspapers made up 70% of post office traffic and the big debate in Congress was not over whether the government should pay for their delivery, but how much of it to pay for. James Madison attacked the idea that newspaper publishers should have to pay even a token fee to get the government to deliver their publications, calling it "an insidious forerunner of something worse." By 1832, newspaper traffic had risen to make up 90% of all mail.

Indeed, objectivity wasn't even invented until the 1900s. Before that, McChesney comments, "such notions for the press would have been nonsensical, even unthinkable." Everyone assumed that the best system of news was one where everyone could say their piece at very little cost. (The analogy to blogging isn't much of a stretch, now is it? See, James Madison loved blogs!)

But as wealth began to concentrate in the Gilded Age and the commercial presses began to lobby government for more favorable policies, the size and power of the smaller presses began to dwindle. The commercial presses were eager to be the only game in town, but they realized that if they were, their blatant partisanship would have to go. (Nobody would stand for a one-newspaper town if the one paper was blatantly biased.) So they decided to insist that journalism was a profession like any other, that reporting was an apolitical job, based solely on objective standards.

They set up schools of journalism to train reporters in the new notion. In 1900, there were no J-schools; by 1920, the major ones were going strong. The "church and state" separation of advertising and reporting became official doctrine and the American Society of Newspaper Editors (ASNE) was set up to enforce it.

The entire foundation of press criticism was rebuilt. Now, instead of criticizing papers for the bias of their owners, press critics had to focus on the professional obligations of their writers. Bias wasn't about the slant of a paper's focus, but about any slanting put in by a reporter.

So that was the line of attack the house press critics took when the world of weblogs brought back the vibrant political debates of our country's founding. "These guys are biased! Irresponsible! They get their facts wrong! They're unprofessional!" they squeal. Look, guys. Tell that to James Madison.

Shifting the Terms of Debate: How Big Business Covered Up Global Warming

http://www.aaronsw.com/weblog/shiftingl

June 6, 2006

Age 19

In this series of blog posts, Aaron provided citations as links, many of which have broken since. Where the citations are broken, they have simply been elided, rather than replaced.—Ed.

> *[Here's the first part of an article I wrote last year about how right-wing think tanks shift the debate.]*

In 2004, Michelle Malkin, a conservative editorialist, published the book *In Defense of Internment*. It argued that declassified security intercepts showed that Japanese internment during World War II—the government policy that relocated thousands of Japanese to concentration camps—was actually justified in the name of national security. We needed to learn the truth, Malkin insisted, so that we could see how racial profiling was similarly justified to fight the "war on terror."

Bainbridge Island was the center of the evacuations; to this day, residents still feel ashamed and teach students a special unit about the incident, entitled "Leaving Our Island." But one parent in the district, Mary Dombrowski, was persuaded by Malkin's book that the evacuation was actually justified and insisted the school was teaching a one-sided version of the internment story, "propaganda" that forced impressionable children into thinking that the concentration camps were a mistake.

The school's principal defended the practice. As the *Seattle Times* reported:

"We do teach it as a mistake," she said, noting that the U.S. government has admitted it was wrong. "As an educator, there are some things that we can say aren't debatable anymore." Slavery, for example. Or the internment—as opposed to a subject such as global warming, she said.[†]

True, Japanese internment isn't a controversial issue like global warming, but ten years ago, global warming wasn't a controversial issue either. In 1995, the UN's panel on international climate change released its consensus report, finding that global warming was a real and serious issue that had to be quickly confronted. The media covered the scientists' research and the population agreed, leading President Clinton to say he would sign an international treaty to stop global warming.

Then came the backlash. The Global Climate Coalition (funded by over 40 major corporate groups like Amoco, the U.S. Chamber of Commerce, and General Motors) began spending millions of dollars each year to derail the Kyoto Protocol, the international treaty to help reduce global warming. They held conferences entitled "The Costs of Kyoto," issued press releases and faxes dismissing the scientific evidence for global warming, and spent more than $3 million on newspaper and television ads claiming Kyoto would mean a "50-cent-per-gallon gasoline tax."[‡]

The media, in response to flurries of "blast faxes" (a technique in which a press release is simultaneously faxed to thousands of journalists) and accusations of left-wing bias, began backing off from the scientific evidence.[‡] A recent study found only 35% of newspaper stories on global warming accurately described the scientific consensus, with the majority implying that scientists who believed in global warming were just as common as global warming deniers (of

---

[*]Florangela Davila, "Debate Lingers over internment of Japanese-Americans, *The Seattle Times*, September 6, 2004.

[†]PR Watch newsletter, Volume 4 Number 4, Fourth Quarter 1997 [PDF].

[‡]Ibid.

which there were only a tiny handful, almost all of whom had received funding from energy companies or associated groups).[*]

It all had an incredible effect on the public. In 1993, 88% of Americans thought global warming was a serious problem. By 1997, that number had fallen to 42%, with only 28% saying immediate action was necessary.[†] And so Clinton changed course and insisted that cutting emissions should be put off for 20 years.

U.S. businesses seriously weakened the Kyoto Protocol, leading it to require only a 7% reduction in emissions (compared to the 20% requested by European nations) and then President Bush refused to sign on to even that. In four short years, big business had managed to turn nearly half the country around and halt the efforts to protect the planet.

And now, the principal on Bainbridge Island, like most people, thinks global warming is a hotly contested issue—the paradigmatic example of a hotly contested issue—even when the science is clear. ("There's no better scientific consensus on this on any issue I know," said the head of the National Oceanic and Atmospheric Administration, "except maybe Newton's second law of dynamics.")[‡] But all this debate about problems has kept us away from talk about solutions. As journalist Ross Gelbspan puts it, "By keeping the discussion focused on whether there is a problem in the first place, they have effectively silenced the debate over what to do about it."[§] So is it any wonder that conservatives want to do the same thing again? And again? And again?

---

[*]Jules Boykoff and Maxwell Boykoff "Journalistic Balance as Global Warming Bias," *FAIR*, November 1, 2004.

[†]Cambridge Reports, Research International poll. "Do you feel that global warming is a very serious problem . . . ?" *Cambridge Reports National Omnibus Survey*, September 1993, in *Roper Center for Public Opinion Research* (0290350, 039). USCAMREP.93SEP, R40.

[‡]Warrick, Joby. "Consensus Emerges Earth Is Warming—Now What?" *Washington Post*, 12 Nov. 1997: A01.

[§]Ross Gelbspan, "The Heat Is On," *Harper's Magazine*, December, 1995.

Making Noise: How Right-wing Think Tanks Get the Word Out

http://www.aaronsw.com/weblog/shifting2

June 7, 2006

Age 19

Malkin's book on internment was no more accurate than the corporate misinformation about global warming. Historians quickly showed the book badly distorted the government records and secret cables it purported to describe. As just one example, Malkin writes that a Japanese message stated they "had [Japanese] spies in the U.S. Army" when it actually said they hoped to recruit spies in the army.* But it should be no big surprise that Malkin, who is, after all, an editorialist and not a historian, didn't manage to fully understand the complex documentary record in the year she spent writing the book part-time.

Malkin's motives, as a right-wing activist and proponent of racial profiling, are fairly obvious. But how did Mary Dombrowski, the Bainbridge Island parent, get caught up in this latest attempt to rewrite history? Opinions on global warming were changed because big business could afford to spend millions to change people's minds. But racial profiling seems like less of a moneymaker. Who invested in spreading that message?

The first step is getting the information out there. Dombrowski probably heard about Malkin's book from the Fox News Channel, where it was ceaselessly promoted for days, and where Malkin is a contributor. Or maybe she heard about it on MSNBC's *Scarborough*

---

*Greg Robinson, "Why the Media Should Stop Paying Attention to the New Book that Defends Japanese Internment," History News Network, 9-9-2004.

Country, a show hosted by a former Republican congressman, which had Malkin as a guest. Or maybe she heard it while driving and listening to Fox host Sean Hannity's radio show, or maybe Rush Limbaugh's. Or maybe she read a review in the *New York Post* (which, like Fox News, is owned by Rupert Murdoch). Or maybe she read about it on a right-wing website or weblog, like Townhall.com, which publishes 10 new conservative op-ed columns every day.

All of these organizations are partisan conservative outlets. Townhall.com, for example, is published by the Heritage Foundation, a right-wing Washington, D.C., think tank. Most people imagine a think tank as a place where smart people think big thoughts, coming up with new ideas for the government to use. But that's not how Heritage works. Nearly half of Heritage's $30 million budget is spent on publicity, not research. Every day, they take work like Malkin's that agrees with their ideological prejudices and push it out through the right-wing media described above (Fox News, Rush Limbaugh, *New York Post*) and into the mainstream media (ABC, NPR, *New York Times*, *Seattle Times*).

They use a variety of tactics. Heritage, for example, publishes an annual telephone directory featuring thousands of conservative experts and associated policy organizations (*The Right Nation*, 161). And if looking up somebody is too much work, Heritage maintains a 24-hour hotline for the media, providing quotes promoting conservative ideology on any subject. Heritage's "information marketing" department makes packages of colored index cards with preprinted talking points for any conservative who plans to do an interview (*The Right Nation*, 167). And Heritage computers are stocked with the names of over 3,500 journalists, organized by specialty, who Heritage staffers personally call to make sure they have all the latest conservative misinformation. Every Heritage study is turned into a two-page summary which is then turned into an op-ed piece which is then distributed to newspapers through the Heritage Features Syndicate (*What Liberal Media?*, 83).

It all adds up: a 2003 study by Fairness and Accuracy in Reporting, the media watch group, found conservative think tanks were cited nearly 14,000 times in major newspapers, television, and radio shows. (By comparison, liberal think tanks were cited only 4,000 times that year.) That means 10,000 additional quotes of right-wing ideology, misleading statistics, distorted facts, and so on. There's no way that doesn't unfairly skew the public debate.

Endorsing Racism: The Story of *The Bell Curve*

http://www.aaronsw.com/weblog/shifting3

June 8, 2006

Age 19

If you have any doubt about the power of the think tanks, look no further than the story of *The Bell Curve*. Written by Charles Murray, who received over $1.2 million from right-wing foundations for his work, the book claimed that IQ tests revealed black people to be genetically less intelligent than whites, thus explaining their low place in society. Murray published the 845-page book without showing it to any other scientists, leading the *Wall Street Journal* to say he pursued "a strategy that provided book galleys to likely supporters while withholding them from likely critics" in an attempt "to fix the fight . . . contrary to usual publishing protocol." Murray's think tank, the American Enterprise Institute, flew key members of the media to Washington for a weekend of briefings on the book's content (*What Liberal Media?*, 94).

And the media lapped it up. In what Eric Alterman has termed "a kind of Rorschach test for pundits" (*WLM?*, 96), every major media outlet reviewed the book without questioning the accuracy of its contents. Instead, they merely quibbled about its proposed recommendations that the dumb blacks, with their dangerously high reproductive rates, might have to be kept in "a high-tech and more lavish version of an Indian reservation" without such luxuries as "individualism, equal rights before the law," and so on. Reviewers proposed more moderate solutions, like just taking away their welfare checks (*WLM?*, 94).

But such quibbles aside, the amount of coverage alone was incredible. The book received cover stories in *Newsweek* ("the science behind [it] is overwhelmingly mainstream"), the *New Republic* (which dedicated an entire issue to discussion of the book), and the *New York Times Book Review* (which suggested critics disliked its "appeal to sweet reason" and are "inclined to hang the defendants without a trial"). Detailed articles appeared in *Time*, the *New York Times* ("makes a strong case"), the *New York Times Magazine*, *Forbes* (praising the book's "Jeffersonian vision"), the *Wall Street Journal*, and the *National Review*. It received a respectful airing on such shows as ABC's *Nightline*, PBS's *MacNeil/Lehrer NewsHour*, the *McLaughlin Group*, *Think Tank* (which dedicated a special two-part series to the book), ABC's *Prime Time Live*, and NPR's *All Things Considered*. With fifteen weeks on the bestseller list, it ended up selling over 300,000 copies in hardcover.[*]

This wasn't just a media debate about the existence of global warming or the merits of internment, this was a full-on media endorsement of racism, which the *American Heritage Dictionary* defines as "the belief that race accounts for differences in human character or ability and that a particular race is superior to others." Nor did the media mention the work's political intentions. On the contrary, they presented it as the sober work of social scientists: *Nightline*'s Ted Koppel lamented to Murray about how his "great deal of work and research" had become "a political football."[†]

Of course, this was almost certainly Murray's intention all along. In the book proposal for his previous book (*Losing Ground*, an attack on government welfare programs) he had explained: "Why can a publisher sell this book? Because a huge number of well-meaning whites fear that they are closet racists, and this book tells them they are not. It's going to make them feel better about things they already think but do not know how to say."[‡] That's certainly what *The Bell Curve* did, replacing a debate over how to improve black achievement with one about whether such improvement was even possible.

There was just one problem: none of this stuff was accurate. As

---

[*]Jim Naureckas, "Racism Resurgent," FAIR.org: Fairness and Accuracy in Reporting, January 1, 1995.

[†]Ibid.

[‡]Ibid.

Professor Michael Nunley wrote in a special issue of the *American Behavioral Scientist* on *The Bell Curve,* after a series of scientific articles debunked all the book's major claims: "I believe this book is a fraud, that its authors must have known it was a fraud when they were writing it, and that Charles Murray must still know it's a fraud as he goes around defending it. . . . After careful reading, I cannot believe its authors were not acutely aware of . . . how they were distorting the material they did include" (*WLM?*, 100).

Spreading Lies: How Think Tanks Ignore the Facts

http://www.aaronsw.com/weblog/shifting4

June 9, 2006

Age 19

But do the right-wing think tanks even care about the facts? In his autobiography, *Blinded by the Right*, David Brock describes his experience being recruited for one right out of college: "Though I had no advanced degrees, I assumed the grandiose title of John M. Olin Fellow in Congressional Studies, which, if nothing else, certainly impressed my parents. . . . My assignment was to write a monograph, which I hoped to publish as a book, challenging the conservative orthodoxy on the proper relationship between the executive and legislative branches of government." This topic was chosen, Brock explains, because with "a squish like Bush in the White House . . . the political reality [was] that the conservative agenda could be best advanced by renegade conservatives on Capitol Hill" (79f).

Needless to say, paying fresh-faced former college students lots of money to write articles that serve political needs is not the best way to get accurate information. But is accurate information the goal? Look at John Lott, a "resident scholar" at the American Enterprise Institute—the same right-wing think tank that promoted *The Bell Curve*. Lott's book *More Guns, Less Crime* claimed that his scientific studies had found that passing laws to allow people to carry concealed weapons actually lowered crime rates. As usual, the evidence melted away upon investigation, but Lott's errors were more serious than most.

Not content to simply distort the data, Lott fabricated an entire study which he claimed showed that in 97% of cases, simply brandishing a gun would cause an attacker to flee. When Internet critics began to point out his inconsistencies on this claim, Lott posted responses under the name "Mary Rosh" to defend himself. "I have to say that he was the best professor I ever had," Lott gushed about himself in one Internet posting. "There were a group of us students who would try to take any class that he taught. Lott finally had to tell us that it was best for us to try and take classes from other professors."

Confronted about his alternate identity, Lott told the *Washington Post* "I probably shouldn't have done it—I know I shouldn't have done it." And yet, the very next day he again attacked his critics, this time under the new pseudonym "Washingtonian." (It later got so bad that one of Lott's pseudonyms would start talking about posts from another Lott pseudonym.)[*]

Lott, of course, is not the only scholar to make things up to bolster his case. For comparison, look at Michael Bellesiles, author of the anti-gun book *Arming America*, which argued guns were uncommon in early America. Other scholars investigated and found that Bellesiles had probably fabricated evidence. Emory University, where Bellesiles was a professor of history, began an investigation into the accuracy of his work, eventually forcing him to resign. His publisher, Knopf, pulled the book out of print. Libraries pulled the book off their shelves. Columbia University revoked the Bancroft Prize the book had been awarded. The scandal was widely covered in academic circles. Bellesiles was firmly disgraced and has not shown his face in public since.

And what happened to Lott? Nothing. Lott remains a "resident scholar" at the American Enterprise Institute, his book continues to sell well, his op-ed pieces are still published in major papers, and he gives talks around the country. For the right-wing scholar, even outright fraud is no serious obstacle.

---

[*]Link goes to blog of Tim Lambert on ScienceBlogs.com http://scienceblogs.com/deltoid/category/lott/

Saving Business: The Origins of Right-wing Think Tanks

http://www.aaronsw.com/weblog/shifting5

June 10, 2006

Age 19

Since the goal of these think tanks clearly isn't to advance knowledge, what are they for? To understand their real goals, we have to look at why they were created. After the tumultuous 1960s led a generation of students to start questioning authority, business decided something had to be done. "The American economic system," explained Lewis Powell in a 1971 memo for the U.S. Chamber of Commerce, "is under broad attack" from "perfectly respectable elements of society: from the college campus, the pulpit, the media, the intellectual and literary journals, the arts and sciences, and from politicians."

And business has no one to blame but itself for not getting these things under control: the colleges are funded by "contributions from capital funds controlled or generated by American business. The boards of trustees . . . overwhelmingly are composed of men and women who are leaders in the system." And the media "are owned and theoretically controlled by corporations which depend upon profits, and the enterprise system to survive." So business must "conduct guerilla warfare" by "establishing a staff of highly qualified scholars" who can be paid to publish a "steady flow of scholarly articles" in magazines and journals as well as books and pamphlets to be published "at airports, drugstores, and elsewhere."

William Simon, president of the right-wing Olin Foundation (the same one that later funded Brock), was more blunt: "The only thing that can save the Republican Party . . . is a counter-intelligentsia. . . . [Conservative scholars] must be given grants, grants, and more grants in exchange for books, books, and more books" (*Blinded by the Right*, 78).

The Powell memo was incredibly influential. Soon after it was written, business began following its advice, building up its network of think tanks, news outlets, and media pressure groups. These organizations began to dot the landscape, hiding behind respectable names like the Manhattan Institute or the Heartland Foundation. While these institutions were all funded by partisan conservatives, news accounts rarely noted this fact. (Another FAIR study finds the Heritage Foundation's political orientation—let alone its funding—was only identified in 24% of news citations.)

As the conservative message machine grew stronger, political debate and electoral results began to shift further and further to the right, eventually allowing extreme conservatives to be elected, first with Ronald Reagan and now with George W. Bush. More recently, conservatives have managed to finally win not only the White House but both houses of Congress. While their policy proposals, when understood, are just as unpopular as ever, conservatives are able to use their media power to twist the debate.

Hurting Seniors: The Attack on Social Security

http://www.aaronsw.com/weblog/shifting6

June 11, 2006

Age 19

Recent events provide a compelling case study of how this process works. Conservatives have wanted to get rid of Social Security for years. The most successful anti-poverty program in history, it clearly shows how the government can be used to help people—anathema to conservative ideology. Now, with a secure lock on government, is their time to strike. As a White House deputy wrote in a memo that was later leaked, "For the first time in six decades, the Social Security battle is one we can win—and in doing so, we can help transform the political and philosophical landscape of the country."

There's extremely strong public support for Social Security—conservatives could certainly never just come out and say they wanted to end it—so their plan is to deceive the public: First, persuade people that Social Security is facing some sort of crisis and won't be around for the next generation. Second, convince them to begin replacing Social Security with a privatized version. Privatization, the logic goes, will naturally keep increasing until all of Social Security is eliminated. The only problem is that Social Security isn't facing a crisis and any form of privatization, which would require both paying out to existing retirees and saving away money for the private accounts of the current generation, would worsen whatever financial problems Social Security does have.

But think tanks have been preparing for this moment for years, floating privatization plans and doing their best to persuade the media that Social Security was in imminent danger. So when the Bush administration started up their anti–Social Security campaign, the media knew exactly what to say.

CBS, for example, presented a segment featuring man-on-the-street Tad DeHaven. "I don't expect to get anything from Social Security, OK?" said young DeHaven. "It's not going to be there—that's my assumption." DeHaven had good reason to say these things: for years, he's been one of the leading Republican activists in the fight to get rid of Social Security. CBS never mentioned the connection.

A later CBS report boosted fears that Social Security was going bankrupt by displaying a graphic on the screen that read "2042: Insolvent = 0 benefits??" [sic] ("In 2042, Social Security will become insolvent, and today's young workers risk losing their benefits," a voiceover explained.) But this just isn't true: even the pessimistic Social Security Administration concedes that by 2042 Social Security will be able to pay nearly 80% of scheduled benefits, which is still far more than what it pays out today.

Other networks were no better. NBC's report features quotes from Bush saying the system would go "flat bust" and an interview with a Heritage Foundation scholar—identified only as a "Social Security expert"—but allowed no critics to contradict their claims. Meanwhile, an ABC report claimed, "One thing everyone agrees on, the Social Security system as it exists now won't be able to afford those payments for long after the Wilsons retire." In fact, it's quite the opposite: even the most pessimistic predictions say that Social Security will be fine until the Wilsons are statistically dead. Again, no critics got a voice.

Fighting Back: Responses to the Mainstream Media

http://www.aaronsw.com/weblog/shifting7

June 15, 2006

Age 19

Unlike the conservative media, it does not appear the national media is intentionally partisan. But it exists in a very specific structural context. A recent study found that two-thirds of journalists thought bottom-line pressure was "seriously hurting the quality of news coverage" while around half reported their newsrooms had been cut. 75% of print and 85% of broadcast journalists agreed that "too little attention is paid to complex issues." When you're short on staff and stories are shallow, reporters become even more dependent on outside sources—and the right-wing think tanks are more than willing to help out, while further pulling coverage to the right.

But one obvious solution—creating a matching set of left-wing think tanks—while perhaps helpful in balancing the debate, will not solve the problem. Media norms of balance mean that even qualified experts will always be presented as "just one side of the story," balanced directly against inaccurate conservatives—recall how the handful of corporate-funded global warming deniers are still balanced against the overwhelming scientific consensus.

Ideally, viewers would be able to hear both perspectives and decide which they thought was accurate. But since, as the journalists conceded, so little time is spent explaining complex issues, in practice very little information is presented that can help the viewer decide who's correct. So they're left to decide based on their existing ideological preferences, further splitting the country into two alternate realities.

Figuring out what is true—especially when it's so obvious, as in the examples above—is precisely what the mainstream media should be doing. Partisan pundits would be replaced with thoughtful scholars. Non-peer-reviewed books would be ignored, not endlessly promoted. Scientific facts would be given precedence over political arguments. Political commentary would be replaced by factual education.

Don't hold your breath. Six major companies own nearly 90% of all media outlets.* And they—and their advertisers—don't mind how things are going. Sumner Redstone, CEO of Viacom (Paramount, CBS, Blockbuster, MTV, Comedy Central, etc.), told a group of CEOs that "I look at the election from what's good for Viacom. I vote for what's good for Viacom." And, "from a Viacom standpoint, the election of a Republican administration is a better deal. Because the Republican administration has stood for many things we believe in, deregulation and so on." Better news reporting wouldn't just be more expensive, it would threaten these business interests.

To get the straight story, it's necessary to turn to independent and community sources which don't have such conflicts of interest. One possibility is the daily news show *Democracy Now!*, hosted by Amy Goodman, which is funded only by viewers and foundations. Broadcast on 150 radio stations, 150 television stations, and the Internet, the show presents stories from activists, journalists, authors, and public interest organizations from around the world.

When outlets from ABC to the *New York Times* began claiming Iraq had weapons of mass destruction, *Democracy Now!* was one of the few sources to take a contrary view. It presented the testimony of Iraq's top weapons official, who defected to the U.S. and explained that all the weapons had been destroyed. (Other stations, ironically, parroted the Bush administration in promoting the information he presented about the weapons Iraq *had*, without mentioning they had been destroyed.)†

And when U.S. soldiers kidnapped Jean-Bertrand Aristide, the

---

*Charlene LaVoie, "Media Juggernaut Grows," *The Winsted Voice*, April 11, 2003.

†"Top Iraqi Defector Says Iraq Destroyed Its WMDs, but Bush and Blair Continue to Cite Him to Drum Up Support for the War: An Interview with Former Unscom Chair Rolf Eke," *Democracy Now*, March 3, 2003.

democratically elected president of Haiti, and flew him to the Central African Republic, where they locked him in a hotel room, he managed to quietly phone out while armed guards stood outside his door. *Democracy Now!* was alone in airing his incredible story. When Aristide was finally freed, he insisted on returning to his country, and again Amy Goodman was the only U.S. television journalist who dared to accompany him back.*

Still, *Democracy Now!*'s audience is rather small compared to that of the mainstream media. But stories from overseas hint at what could happen if enough people began paying attention to such sources. In South Korea, the country with the highest rate of broadband adoption, politics has been turned upside down by OhmyNews, a five-year-old website. Founded by Oh Yeon Ho, OhmyNews has a feature unlike any other paper: more than 85% of its stories are contributed by readers.

Almost anyone can write for OhmyNews: the site posts 70% of all stories that are submitted, over 15,000 citizen-reporters have published stories. OhmyNews copyedits their work but tries to leave their differing styles intact. The citizen-reporters write about things they know about and that interest them; together they end up covering most of the traditional spectrum. Yet their new voices end up providing coverage on things which typically get ignored by the mainstream media.†

This is most evident in their political coverage. Before Ohmy News, conservatives controlled 80% of Korea's newspaper circulation. Then OhmyNews gave a voice to progressives, inspiring massive nationwide protests against the government. The protests, in turn, led to the election of reformist Roh Moo Hyun, now known as "the first Internet president." The furious conservative National Assembly responded by voting to impeach Roh on technical grounds. OhmyNews readers again organized and overthrew the Assembly in the next election, reinstating Roh. There's no reason why what happened in South Korea can't happen here. Overcoming the tide

---

*"President Aristide Says 'I Was Kidnapped'" *Democracy Now!*, March 1, 2004. [LINK]

†Todd Thaker, "OhmyNews a 'Marriage of Democracy and Technology," Oh mynews.com, 12-15-2004.

of misinformation is hard work, but working together committed citizens can make amazing progress, even when up against the most powerful interests. Our society has an extraordinary level of freedom and openness. Whether we use that freedom to seek out the truth or remain content with conventional platitudes is up to us.

What Journalists Don't: Lessons from the *Times*

http://www.aaronsw.com/weblog/001677

April 10, 2005

Age 18

Speech to the Bay Area Law School Technology Conference blogs panel, as prepared.

So I was asked to speak about bloggers and journalists—it seems like people are always finding an excuse to talk about this. In fact, the National Press Club had a panel on it just yesterday. Most of the discussion focuses on what bloggers do—is it trustworthy? Is it right?—but I'd like to take a different tack. I'd like to discuss what journalists *don't*.

Last summer, during the election campaign, I decided to take on a little project. Every day for a month I would read all the political articles in the *New York Times* and take notes on them on a blog. A number of things stood out and I thought I would discuss them. Keep in mind that this is the *New York Times*, widely recognized to be the most serious of newspapers. So everything that applies to them applies to an even greater extent to all the lesser newspapers, the evening news, the talking-head shows, and so on.

The first was the extreme conservative bias. One day, they ran a front-page story that claimed Kerry was, quote, like a caged hamster. Another, claiming, quote, life is like high school, decided to interview various Kerry classmates. So they got two quotes. On the right was the guy who thought Kerry "seem[ed] ruthless" and on the left was the one who insisted "hatred is too strong a word" for what his classmates felt. These are just fun examples—I found hundreds of these things in just a month. And many were on more serious issues as well.

The constant theme was that *Times* reporters would repeat Republican talking points and images and so on. Kerry was elitist, Kerry was a flip-flopper, the Kerry campaign was failing. One reporter even had his own cottage industry in stories of that last type. Adam Nagourney ran 22 consecutive stories claiming Democrats were worried about themselves.

But we shouldn't forget the more important things as well. The *Times* was, of course, one of the major outlets for false claims that Iraq had WMDs. My understanding is that it's a sort of cardinal rule in journalism that if you're going to make a claim, especially a big, important front-page claim, you get two sources. Well, the *Times* didn't do that on WMDs—they just printed whatever the administration said. And when the administration used their bogus reporting to go to war, the *Times* did its best to ignore the fact that the war was a blatant violation of international law.

In all these areas, the blogs bested the *Times*. Some tracked the spreading meme that Kerry was elitist, others pointed out that Bush wasn't much of a down-home cowboy himself, still others carefully debunked each new right-wing myth. Blogs pointed to people like weapons inspector Scott Ritter, who correctly pointed out there were no WMDs, or the Iraqi defector who explained they had all been destroyed. Blogs 1, *Times* 0.

The second thing I noticed during my study was that reporters rarely pointed out Bush was lying, corrected his lies, or even conceded that an objective reality containing a truth existed. You don't have to trust me on this one; I spoke to *Washington Post* campaign reporter Jim VandeHei about it when he visited Stanford. Some things are undoubtedly true, he said—he got very animated—but editors won't let reporters print the facts. He wanted to do a piece where he compared Bush and Kerry's stump speeches to see how many lies they contained, but editors just wouldn't let him.

So instead you get the results so perfectly parodied by Paul Krugman, who commented that if the administration announced the Earth was flat, the lead story in the *Times* the next day would be "Shape of Earth: Views Differ." In fact, we don't really need to leave that sort of thing to the imagination anymore. The other month ABC ran a show which balanced people who claimed they had been abducted by aliens against respected doctors who explained that their experiences resulted from a condition called sleep paralysis. Who was right? ABC refused to say.

Even when facts are reported, they don't seem to stick. Just last month, a Harris poll found that 47% of adults think Saddam helped plan 9/11 and 36% think Iraq had WMDs. But if the media sends the message that it's unnecessary to check your beliefs against the facts, should we really be so surprised that so many Americans don't?

Blogs suffer from no such compulsions. They're happy to tell you the facts and show you the evidence. They're happy to tell you that some things are just wrong and often furious against those who dare to lie. The incredible blog Media Matters, for example, diligently tracks right-wing lies spread through the media, citing all the sources that prove them false.

But the most important thing, and the thing that nobody really seems to talk about, was how completely empty the *Times*'s coverage was. It was entirely focused on who the candidates were giving stump speeches to or what ads they were buying this week.

The only time an actual policy proposal was mentioned was deep inside a discussion of how a candidate played with a certain group. You know, "Kerry has had problems with the Teamsters, even though they support his health care plan" or something. That was basically it. And this is supposed to be the high point of journalism! If the *Times* won't talk about policy then no one will.

And if nobody talks about policy then nobody votes on the basis of it. A September 2004 Gallup poll found that only 10% of registered voters said that they voted based on the candidates', quote, agenda/ideas/platforms/goals—6% for Bush, 13% for Kerry.

And it's at this point that you really have to ask yourself: "Is this really a democracy?" It's the most contested election of our time, coverage is lavished on the topic, the nation is closely divided, and yet the media completely ignores the issues. There's no policy debate. And if the media doesn't report the policy proposals and the media doesn't report the facts, then we're right back to my first point: vague emotional claims about Kerry being a rich elitist flip-flopper, or, from the other side, Kerry was a brave soldier who blew stuff up in the Vietnam War.

This wasn't your grand democratic election: The people didn't get together and look at the facts and have a debate about issues. They didn't look at facts and they didn't discuss issues at all! They sat in their houses, watched a bunch of fuzzy TV commercials, and took in news coverage that recited the same vague themes. And then they voted based on which fuzzy image they liked the best. There's a word for stuff like that. It's not pretty, but I think it's appropriate. It's called propaganda. This was an election on the basis of propaganda.

And so I believe blogs are important insofar as they help us move away from this sorry spectacle and towards a real democracy. Blogs, of course, can help spread propaganda—and no doubt, most do—but they can also help stem it. Political blogs can help pull people into politics, tell them things they wouldn't otherwise hear, and lead them to organize their own projects—like building support for Howard Dean or trying to save Social Security.

One of the most important things I think blogs do, though, is teach people. The media, as I've noted, is supremely unintelligent. But I don't think the people of this country are. And one of the most striking things about blogs to me is how they almost never talk down to their readership. Indeed most seem to think higher of their readership than they do themselves.

Atrios doesn't hesitate before explaining some piece of economics that the *Washington Post* finds too complex. Tim Lambert will teach you the statistical theory you need to understand why some right-wing claim is wrong. And Brad DeLong has taught me more about what it's like to be an economics guy in the government than I got from Paul O'Neill's book.

The media isn't going to come save us from this nightmare. But maybe blogs can. Or at least they can help. The more people learn, the smarter they become. The smarter they become, the more they understand the way the world really works. The more they understand, the more they can do to fix things. And that is the truly important goal. Thank you.

*　　*　　*

So, what I did was I took the above speech, bolded the key words and numbers, and printed it out. Then I gave it mostly from memory, occasionally looking down to get the next bolded word or a particularly well-worded phrase. It worked really well, I think.

The speech touched quite a nerve, as I hoped. My two conservative co-panelists (Zack Rosen failed to show) immediately demanded a chance to respond and then cut off my rebuttals. One of them (Mike) started insisting there was no such thing as objective truth, at which point I cut in and said, "Well, I can see why Republicans would want to deny that truth exists since it often cuts against them!" which was hailed as the best line of the night.

After the talk I got a lot of compliments and a guest blogger for Daily Kos said he'd talk to Markos about getting me an occasional spot on Daily Kos, which is something like the liberal blogger equivalent of a regular gig on the *Tonight Show*. So I think it went well. (:)

Rachel Carson: Mass Murderer?

http://fair.org/extra-online-articles/Rachel-Carson,-Mass-Murderer/

October 2007

Age 20

Originally appeared in Extra! *The magazine of FAIR, September/October 2007*

Sometimes you find mass murderers in the most unlikely places. Take Rachel Carson. She was, by all accounts, a mild-mannered writer for the U.S. Fish and Wildlife Service—hardly a sociopath's breeding ground. And yet, according to many in the media, Carson has more blood on her hands than Hitler.

The problems started in the 1940s, when Carson left the Service to begin writing full-time. In 1962, she published a series of articles in the *New Yorker*, resulting in the book *Silent Spring*—widely credited with launching the modern environmental movement. The book discussed how pesticides and pollutants moved up the food chain, threatening the ecosystems for many animals, especially birds. Without them, it warned, we might face the title's silent spring.

Farmers used vast quantities of DDT to protect their crops against insects—80 million pounds were sprayed in 1959 alone—but from there it quickly climbed up the food chain. Bald eagles, eating fish that had concentrated DDT in their tissues, headed toward extinction. Humans, likewise accumulating DDT in our systems, appeared to get cancer as a result. Mothers passed the chemical on to their children through breast milk. *Silent Spring* drew attention to these concerns and, in 1972, the resulting movement succeeded in getting DDT banned in the U.S.—a ban that later spread to other nations.

And that, according to Carson's critics, is where the trouble started. DDT had been sprayed heavily on houses in developing countries to protect against malaria-carrying mosquitoes. Without it, malaria rates in developing countries skyrocketed. Over 1 million people die from it each year.

To the critics, the solution seems simple: Forget Carson's emotional arguments about dead birds and start spraying DDT again so we can save human lives.

Worse than Hitler?

"What the World Needs Now Is DDT" asserted the headline of a lengthy feature in the *New York Times Magazine* (4/11/04). "No one concerned about the environmental damage of DDT set out to kill African children," reporter Tina Rosenberg generously allowed. Nonetheless, *"Silent Spring* is now killing African children because of its persistence in the public mind."

It's a common theme—echoed by two more articles in the *Times* by the same author (3/29/06, 10/5/06), and by *Times* columnists Nicholas Kristof (3/12/05) and John Tierney (6/05/07). The same refrain appears in a *Washington Post* op-ed by columnist Sebastian Mallaby, gleefully headlined "Look Who's Ignoring Science Now" (10/09/05). And again in the *Baltimore Sun* ("Ms. Carson's views [came] at a cost of many thousands of lives worldwide"—5/27/07), *New York Sun* ("millions of Africans died . . . thanks to Rachel Carson's junk science classic"—4/21/06), the *Hill* ("millions die on the altar of politically correct ideologies"—11/02/05), *San Francisco Examiner* ("Carson was wrong, and millions of people continue to pay the price"—5/28/07), and *Wall Street Journal* ("environmental controls were more important than the lives of human beings"—2/21/07).

Even novelists have gotten in on the game. "Banning DDT killed more people than Hitler, Ted," explains a character in Michael Crichton's 2004 bestseller, *State of Fear* (p. 487). "[DDT] was so safe you could eat it." That fictional comment not only inspired a column on the same theme in Australia's Sydney *Morning Herald* (6/18/05), it led Sen. James Inhofe (R-Ok.) to invite Crichton and Dr. Donald R. Roberts, a longtime pro-DDT activist, to testify before the Senate Committee on Environment and Public Works.

But other attacks only seem like fiction. A web page on Junk

Science.com features a live Malaria Death Clock next to a photo of Rachel Carson, holding her responsible for more deaths than malaria has caused in total. ("DDT allows [Africans to] climb out of the poverty/subsistence hole in which 'caring greens' apparently wish to keep them trapped," it helpfully explains.) And a new website from the Competitive Enterprise Institute, RachelWasWrong.org, features photos of deceased African children along the side of every page.

Developing Resistance

At one level, these articles send a comforting message to the developed world: Saving African children is easy. We don't need to build large aid programs or fund major health initiatives, let alone develop Third World infrastructure or think about larger issues of fairness. No, to save African lives from malaria, we just need to put our wallets away and work to stop the evil environmentalists.

Unfortunately, it's not so easy.

For one thing, there is no global DDT ban. DDT is indeed banned in the U.S., but malaria isn't exactly a pressing issue here. If it ever were, the ban contains an exception for matters of public health. Meanwhile, it's perfectly legal—and indeed, used—in many other countries: 10 out of the 17 African nations that currently conduct indoor spraying use DDT (*New York Times*, 9/16/06).

DDT use has decreased enormously, but not because of a ban. The real reason is simple, although not one conservatives are particularly fond of: evolution. Mosquito populations rapidly develop resistance to DDT, creating enzymes to detoxify it, modifying their nervous systems to avoid its effects, and avoiding areas where DDT is sprayed—and recent research finds that that resistance continues to spread even after DDT spraying has stopped, lowering the effectiveness not only of DDT but also other pesticides (*Current Biology*, 8/9/05).

"No responsible person contends that insect-borne disease should be ignored," Carson wrote in *Silent Spring*. "The question that has now urgently presented itself is whether it is either wise or responsible to attack the problem by methods that are rapidly making it worse. . . .

Resistance to insecticides by mosquitoes . . . has surged upwards at an astounding rate."

Unfortunately, her words were ignored. Africa didn't cut back on pesticides because, through a system called the Industry Cooperative Program, the pesticide companies themselves got to participate in the United Nations agency that provided advice on pest control. Not surprisingly, it continued to recommend significant pesticide usage.

When *Silent Spring* came out in 1962, it seemed as if this strategy was working. To take the most extreme case, Sri Lanka counted only 17 cases of malaria in 1963. But by 1969, things had once again gotten out of hand: 537,700 cases were counted. Naturally, the rise had many causes: political and financial pressure led to cutbacks on spraying, stockpiles of supplies had been used up, low rainfall and high temperatures encouraged mosquitoes, a backlog of diagnostic tests to detect malaria was processed, and testing standards became more stringent. But even with renewed effort, the problem did not go away.

Records uncovered by entomologist Andrew Spielman hint at why (*Mosquito*, p. 177). For years, Sri Lanka had run test programs to verify DDT's effectiveness at killing mosquitoes. But halfway through the program, their standards were dramatically lowered. "Though the reason was not recorded," Spielman writes, "it was obvious that some mosquitoes were developing resistance and the change was made to justify continued spraying."

But further spraying led only to further resistance, and the problem became much harder to control. DDT use was scaled back and other pesticides were introduced—more cautiously this time—but the epidemic was never again brought under control, with the deadly legacy that continues to this day.

Instead of apologizing, the chemical companies went on the attack. They funded front groups and think tanks to claim the epidemic started because countries "stopped" using their products. In their version of the story, environmentalists forced Africans to stop using DDT, causing the increase in malaria. "It's like a hit-and-run driver who, instead of admitting responsibility for the accident, frames the person who tried to prevent the accident," complains Tim

Lambert, whose weblog, Deltoid, tracks the DDT myth and other scientific misinformation in the media.

Front and Center

Perhaps the most vocal group spreading this story is Africa Fighting Malaria (AFM). Founded in 2000 by Roger Bate, an economist at various right-wing think tanks, AFM has run a major PR campaign to push the pro-DDT story, publishing scores of op-eds and appearing in dozens of articles each year. Bate and his partner Richard Tren even published a book laying out their alternate history of DDT: *When Politics Kills: Malaria and the DDT Story.*

A funding pitch uncovered by blogger Eli Rabbett shows Bate's thinking when he first started the project. "The environmental movement has been successful in most of its campaigns as it has been 'politically correct,'" he explained (*Tobacco Archives*, 9/98). What the anti-environmental movement needs is something with "the correct blend of political correctness (. . . oppressed blacks) and arguments (eco-imperialism [is] undermining their future)." That something, Bate proposed, was DDT.

In an interview, Bate said that his motivation had changed after years of working on the issue of malaria. "I think my position has mellowed, perhaps with age," he told *Extra!*. "[I have] gone from being probably historically anti-environmental to being very much pro–combating malaria now." He pointed to the work he'd done making sure money to fight malaria was spent properly, including a study he co-authored in the respected medical journal the *Lancet* (7/15/06) on dishonest accounting at the World Bank. He insisted that he wasn't simply pro-DDT, but instead was willing to support whatever the evidence showed worked. And he flatly denied that AFM had ever received money from tobacco, pharmaceutical, or chemical companies.

Still, AFM has very much followed the plan Bate laid out in his original funding pitch to corporations: first, create "the intellectual arguments to make our case," then "disseminate these arguments to people in [developing countries]" who can make convincing spokespeople, and then "promote these arguments . . . in the West." The penultimate page gives another hint that stopping malaria isn't the primary goal: "Is the DDT problem still relevant?" is listed as an "intellectual issue to be resolved"—once they got funding. (When asked for comment on this, Bate became upset and changed the subject.)

Bate continues to insist that resistance isn't much of an issue, because its primary effect is to keep mosquitoes away from DDT-covered areas altogether. Instead he claims "resistance was a useful device by which it was easy to pull the plug" on an anti-malaria campaign that was failing because of administrative incompetence. "You're not likely to see an aid agency [admit this]," he said when asked for evidence. "I'm not sure what you want me to say. If you read enough of the literature, you get that strong impression." But few experts aside from those affiliated with AFM seem to have gotten the same impression.

DDT's Dangers

These myths can have serious consequences. For one thing, despite what is claimed by the right, DDT itself is quite harmful. Studies have suggested that prenatal exposure to DDT leads to significant decreases in mental and physical functioning among young children, with the problems becoming more severe when the exposure is more serious (*American Journal of Epidemiology*, 9/12/06; *Pediatrics*, 7/1/06), while the EPA classifies it as a probable human carcinogen.

For another, resistance is deadly. Not only has DDT's overuse made it ineffective, but, as noted, it has led mosquitoes to evolve "cross-resistance": resistance not only to DDT but also to other insecticides, including those with less dangerous environmental effects.

And perhaps most importantly, the pro-DDT line is a vast distraction. There are numerous other techniques for dealing with malaria: alternative insecticides, bed nets, and a combination of drugs called artemisinin-based combination therapy, or ACT. ACT actually kills the malaria parasite fast, allowing the patient a quick recovery, and has a success rate of 95 percent (World Health Organization, 2001). Rollouts of ACT in other countries have slashed malaria rates by 80 to 97 percent (*Washington Monthly*, 7/06).

But such techniques require money and wealthy nations are

hesitant to give it, especially when they think they can just avoid the whole problem by unbanning DDT. "DDT has become a fetish," says Allan Schapira, a former senior member of the malaria team at the World Health Organization (*Washington Monthly*, 7/06). "You have people advocating DDT as if it's the only insecticide that works against malaria, as if DDT would solve all problems, which is obviously absolutely unrealistic."

As a result, senators and their staff insist that DDT is all that's necessary. And the new director of WHO's malaria program, Arata Kochi, kicked off his tenure by telling the malaria team that they were "stupid" and issuing an announcement that "forcefully endorsed wider use of the insecticide DDT" while a representative of the Bush administration stood by his side. Half his staff resigned in response (*New York Times*, 9/16/06).

There are genuine issues with current malaria control programs: incompetent administration, misuse of funds, outdated techniques, a lack of funding and concern. And, much to their credit, many on the right have drawn attention to these problems. Africa Fighting Malaria has frequently called for more effective monitoring, and conservative Sen. Tom Coburn (R-Ok.) has used his influence to fight corruption in anti-malaria programs.

But the same Tom Coburn recently held up a bill honoring the 100th anniversary of Rachel Carson's birth on the grounds that "millions of people . . . died because governments bought into Carson's junk science claims about DDT" (*Raw Story*, 5/22/07). Even AFM's Bate was quoted as finding this a bit too much, pointing out that Carson died in 1964, just two years after *Silent Spring* was published (*Washington Post*, 5/23/07). But apparently getting a few digs in at the environmental movement is just too hard for conservatives to resist.

Is Undercover Over? Disguise Seen as Deceit by Timid Journalists

http://fair.org/extra-online-articles/Is-Undercover-Over/

March 1, 2008

Age 21

Originally appeared in Extra!, *the magazine of FAIR, March/April 2008*

This past February, the famed lobbying firm APCO was approached by a man named Kenneth Case. Case said he represented the Maldon Group, an obscure firm that wished to improve the public image of Turkmenistan, where it had some investments. It was nothing out of the ordinary—private firms often lobby on behalf of foreign countries, either because they think it will increase the value of their investments or because they are acting as a front for the foreign government.

APCO happily met with them, despite the fact that the Stalinist regime of Turkmenistan is one of the most noxious on the planet, after North Korea. In a recent report, Human Rights Watch (11/02/07) called it "one of the most repressive and authoritarian [governments] in the world," noting it had "untold numbers of political prisoners . . . draconian restrictions on freedom of expression . . . [and] foreign travel restrictions."

All of which would normally be considered just another day of doing business in D.C., except for one thing: "Kenneth Case" was a fiction, and his "Maldon Group" a ruse cooked up by *Harper's* magazine editor Ken Silverstein to demonstrate what D.C. lobbying was really like.

"His Ethics, Not Ours"

The resulting piece, "Their Men in Washington" (*Harper's*, 7/07), won immediate acclaim. Silverstein was interviewed on everything from NPR (6/19/07) to Al-Jazeera (7/3/07), and the article quickly became widely linked and reposted in the blogosphere. It gave a rare look at the inner workings of public relations firms, from how they pitched themselves to prospective clients to the little-known behind-the-scenes work they offered to do.

APCO proposed laundering money through academic groups to fund congressional delegations or special conferences, as well as hiring "think-tank experts who would say, 'On the one hand this and the other hand that,'" writing pieces for them to sign and placing them as op-eds in major newspapers. Meanwhile, Cassidy & Associates, another lobbying firm hoping to receive the Turkmenistan account, bragged that they had "strong personal relationships" at every major level of government and had recently succeeded in keeping Equatorial Guinea's dictator Teodoro Obiang off the list of the world's Top 10 dictators.

Not everyone, however, was happy to have this information made public. APCO sent their PR people into damage control, issuing a press release insisting, "Silverstein's charade is a comment on his ethics, not ours. [His] claim that he was working in the 'public interest' [because going undercover was] the only way he could get information is as false as his story." APCO also insisted that Silverstein's "suggestion" that APCO offered to get others to work secretly on behalf of Turkmenistan could not be true because "current law REQUIRES disclosure" in such situations (emphasis in original).

In an NPR discussion between Ken Silverstein and APCO representative B. Jay Cooper (*Talk of the Nation*, 6/19/07), Cooper justified taking Turkmenistan as a client because, before doing so, they'd run the idea past their contacts in the government and they thought it would be a positive development. He also explained that writing op-eds and getting other people to sign on to them was standard practice—he'd done it dozens of times, for example. Cassidy & Associates, the more expensive firm, did little to respond to Silverstein's charges in the press. Seeing APCO's "defense," this seems like a wise choice.

"A Web of Deceit"

Of course, it's not surprising that the companies exposed would be opposed to the article. More surprising was the response from the supposed arbiters of journalistic ethics. CBS's Public Eye blog (6/28/27) insisted that the operation was inappropriate because everyone already knows that lobbyists deceive the public about their clients. "When you indulge in subterfuge to merely provide the conventional wisdom with a concrete example," they wrote, "that's when the cost . . . isn't worth the benefit."

Bill Buzenberg, the executive director of the Center for Public Integrity, an independent investigative reporting group, told reporters that "misrepresenting yourself is not a good idea. We're with Howard Kurtz on this one." Kurtz, media critic for the *Washington Post* and CNN, had sided with APCO in a *Post* column titled "Stung by *Harper's* in a Web of Deceit" (6/25/07). (Silverstein had long criticized Kurtz for, among other things, biased media criticism—*Washington Babylon*, 7/24/06.)

Kurtz reported that the editor of *Harper's* defended the practice by pointing to "a long history of sting operations" by journalists. But, Kurtz wrote, "that undercover tradition has faded in recent years. No newspaper today would do what the *Chicago Sun-Times* did in the 1970s. . . . Fewer television programs are doing what ABC did in the 1990s. . . . NBC's *Dateline* joins in stings against child predators, but by tagging along with law enforcement officials."

Why this decline in undercover reporting? Kurtz had an explanation: "The reason is that, no matter how good the story, lying to get it raises as many questions about journalists as their subjects." But maybe that isn't the whole story.

Undercover History

Undercover reporting has a storied history. Nellie Bly, famous for traveling around the world in 80 days, also did a famed investigation of the conditions in insane asylums for the *New York World*. Bly feigned insanity for a series of physicians before being committed to a lunatic asylum. There she documented rotten and spoiled food, freezing living conditions, frigid bathwater, abusive nurses, and relatively sane fellow residents. "What, excepting torture, would produce insanity quicker than this treatment?" she wondered. The series, later published as the book *Ten Days in a Mad-House*, created a sensation, and Bly was asked to join a government investigation of asylum conditions.

More recently, as Kurtz points out, Chicago in the 1970s and 1980s was something of a golden era of undercover reporting, in no small part because of the efforts of one woman: Pam Zekman. She and her investigative crew at WBBM-TV used undercover reporting to break dozens of stories. She got a job at a nursing home so she could verify allegations of filth and mistreatment made by relatives. She got a job as a dance instructor to prove a local dance studio was cheating money from seniors. She had a team work at an abortion clinic to prove they were performing abortions on women who weren't pregnant. And she had a staffer apply for a job at the airport to see what kind of background checks they did on bag screeners.

But Zekman's biggest story came while she worked at the *Chicago Sun-Times*. Everyone knew Chicago's government was corrupt, but Zekman proved it. She purchased a seedy tavern on Chicago's Near North Side with "more code violations than barstools," renamed it the Mirage Tavern, and recorded everything as a long string of officials—the fire inspector, the plumbing inspector, the ventilation inspector, the county clerk, accountants, landlords—took bribes while overlooking violations. Even the people who maintained the pinball machine dropped by to show the management how to skim profits.

The resulting 25-part series was full of juicy details like the "business broker" who advised them to bribe everyone except cops, because cops "keep coming around every month, like flies, looking for a payoff." It led to a stream of tourists visiting the bar, and hundreds calling the paper with new tips. There was coverage in outlets like *Time* (1/23/78) and *60 Minutes* (1/15/78), and in newspapers from Denmark to Australia. A federal investigation of the inspectors quickly led to indictments for 29 electrical inspectors, while the Illinois Revenue Department created a 12-man "Mirage Audit Unit" (*Chicago Sun-Times*, 1/10/88).

In more recent years, Barbara Ehrenreich went undercover for *Harper's* as a maid, a waiter, a Wal-Mart employee, and a nursing home assistant. She argued that such "unskilled" jobs were much harder than the white-collar work she was used to and found that even working by herself, eating little, and living in pitiful conditions, she still was unable to make ends meet. The result was the bestselling book *Nickel and Dimed*, which led to a resurgence of interest in the conditions of the "working poor."

Food Lion Fallout

But, outside of *Harper's*, undercover reporting has largely dried up in recent years, and many point to the Food Lion case as the reason. In 1992, ABC's *PrimeTime Live* sent reporters undercover at the Food Lion grocery store to investigate claims of unsanitary food handling practices. The reporters falsified their resumes ("I really miss working in a grocery store. . . . I would love to make a career with the company," one wrote on her application), donned hidden camera rigs, and got the story.

The pictures were vivid: "old meat being redated and put out again for sale, old ground beef being mixed with new, out-of-date chicken getting a coating of barbecue sauce before being relaunched in the gourmet section" (*CJR*, 3/97). Viewers came away convinced of Food Lion's wrongdoing.

But Food Lion fought back, filing a lawsuit against ABC—not challenging the accuracy of the story (although they did do that in public), but charging the reporters who got it with dishonesty. The chain sued ABC for fraud (for lying on their application), trespassing (for coming to Food Lion without permission), and breach of loyalty (for videotaping bad practices when they were supposed to be working for the company). After years of legal wrangling, in 1997 a jury awarded Food Lion a $5.5 million verdict. In 1999, the case was overturned on appeal on somewhat technical grounds.

But by then it was too late—the case had been grinding through the legal system for nearly seven years, and journalists and news outlets had gotten the message: undercover reporting has serious costs. Looking back in 1997, the editor of the *Columbia Journalism Review*

(3/97) declared the 1990s "a humbling time for journalism, particularly investigative television journalism." Among those humbled: *20/20* had to pay $10 million for claiming BankAtlantic Financial had hoodwinked investors, the Minnesota News Council upheld a complaint against a Minneapolis TV station for painting "a distorted, untruthful picture" of Northwest Airlines safety practices, a Houston TV station paid $5.5 million for charging a state representative with an insurance scam, Michael Moore's *TV Nation* paid $5 million for claiming a company had spread toxic sludge over a Texas ranch.

"You can expect journalists in the wake of this to give us more stories about Dennis Rodman and Madonna instead of more stories that are important to us," 1st Amendment lawyer Bruce Sanford said at the time of the Food Lion case. "The specter of a verdict of this magnitude . . . will have a chilling effect on investigative journalists all over the country," proclaimed Jane Kirtley, then executive director of the Reporters Committee on Freedom of the Press.

Out of Fashion

They appear to have been right (although, thankfully, the spate of Dennis Rodman stories has since abated). Undercover reporting has fallen out of fashion. Ken Silverstein argues that this is because reporters, especially Washington reporters, have grown complacent. In an *L.A. Times* op-ed on the controversy (6/30/07), he wrote:

> The decline of undercover reporting—and of investigative reporting in general—reflects, in part, the increasing conservatism and cautiousness of the media, especially the smug, high-end Washington press corps. As reporters have grown more socially prominent during the last several decades, they've become part of the very power structure that they're supposed to be tracking and scrutinizing.

The piece on lobbyists, he and his editor insist, was not just done to investigate the particular lobbying firms, but to reawaken journalists to the power of undercover reporting. "There was this meta level in the planning that asked, 'How will the journalism establishment react?'" *Harper's* editor Roger Hodge told a reporter (*AJR*, 10/07). "The fact that undercover journalism has fallen out of fashion seems to be a problem with the profession."

Investigative journalism has gotten so rare that foundations have stepped into the gap. A collection of funders has joined to form the new nonprofit ProPublica, which will have an annual budget of $10 million, already making it the largest investigative journalism team in the country.

It's unclear if anything will wake news organizations from their slumber. Perhaps someone should go undercover inside them to find out.

BOOKS AND
CULTURE

After I wrote a draft of this introduction, I asked the Aaron in my head about it, and he yelled at me. *All you can say is that he liked books? How unoriginal! You need more* This American Life–*type details, things that sound irrelevant but aren't.* So I threw out that draft and started again.

Aaron was unafraid to throw things out and start again—laws, ideas, essays. You will not be surprised to know that he was obsessed with the craft of writing. (He was obsessed with a lot of things. That was Aaron.) He held Malcolm Gladwell the "scientist" in contempt, but he pored over Gladwell's *Outliers* to understand how it worked. Writers he loved got even more attentive treatment. When Aaron found a passage he admired, he read it aloud "to get a feel for the sound of the voice." His own literary voice was like his personality: nerdy, focused, funny, and a little pushy. No, *very pushy: Why are you wasting your time on things you're good at? Lean into the pain.*

Aaron's book reviews—and he wrote a lot of them—are pushy, too: *This book shocked and confused me. Read it.* Even when he loved a book, he argued with it, or told the author about the book she should have written. The reviews are funny, too. His gut punches come wrapped in punch lines. (Aaron's entire review of *On Writing Well:* "This book is really dreadful, mostly because the author actually cannot write well.")

Hyperarticulate, hyperkinetic, attuned to the black comedy of America's contradictions, and with plenty of contradictions of his own, Aaron would have been the perfect subject for a David Foster Wallace profile. As it was, Aaron found a literary lodestar in the wordy moody warmhearted maddening saddening uplifting brilliant DFW. As a writer, Aaron played with imitating Wallace's digressive footnote-freckled voice, but he quickly fell back into his own. As a reader, though, Aaron latched on to this grandmaster of seeing people as they really are and loving them nonetheless. Aaron maintained comprehensive Wikipedia bibliographies of DFW's works and is responsible for the only truly convincing explanation I have seen of what happens at the end of Wallace's thousand-page novel *Infinite Jest:* a masterful close reading he penned while busy with his usual million other things.

Later, Aaron would write, "DFW's suicide hit me very hard. I ended up coping by reading every piece of nonfiction he'd ever published. He was a brilliant, tortured man and I see so much of myself in him. His nonfiction was fantastic and I will consider my life a success if I can do half of what he did."

I would say that Aaron was the David Foster Wallace of his generation, but you already know how that story ends.

—James Grimmelmann

Recommended Books

Aaron posted annual lists of the books he read, with notes on his favorites (and sometimes his not-so-favorites). Below is a representative sample of his recommendations, drawn from his lists from 2006 through 2011. —Ed.

G. H. Hardy, *A Mathematician's Apology* (PDF)

Godfrey Hardy was a great mathematician. But, looking back on his life, he wondered what it was he had actually contributed to society. In this, his classic defense of his pragmatically worthless profession, he examines what it means to have spent your life wisely. (Previous thoughts: my apology, Legacy.)

Raymond Smullyan, *5000 BC (And Other Philosophical Fantasies)*

In this bizarrely delightful little book, Smullyan, the famed recreational logician, addresses topics from the annoyances on long car rides to the most difficult problems in philosophy, often at once, using stories that are so delightfully amusing that it seems hard to believe they could have any educational value.

George Saunders, *In Persuasion Nation: Stories*

I have to be honest with you. I'm not really one for science fiction. Indeed, I'm not a big fan of fiction in general. But George Saunders is different: I'll read just about anything by him. Saunders' stories manage to combine a whimsically imagined future, biting critique of our present era, along with a use of language so delightfully varied that one wonders how one man can have such control over his authorial voice.

Thomas Geoghegan, *Which Side Are You On?: Trying to Be for Labor When It's Flat on Its Back*

One would think a book on labor history would be dreadfully dull and, more to the point, depressing. And yet, in the first chapter of this book, I found something that made me laugh or smile widely on practically every page. My friend Rick Perlstein got me to read this book by telling me it was "the best political book of the last 15 years[—]the best book of the last 15 years." (He's since taken me to meet Geoghegan several times.) It's hard to imagine a book more important and touching.

Robert Karen, *Becoming Attached: Unfolding the Mystery of the Infant-Mother Bond and Its Impact on Later Life*

At the beginning of the last century, doctors thought parental love was unimportant: parents weren't allowed to even visit their kids in the hospital, psychology experts encouraged moms not to hug or kiss their children, the U.S. government handed out pamphlets on how to be firm with your children. This *tour de force* book tells the amazing story of how all that was overturned by a group of dedicated scientists whose research into the subject of parental love brought some of the most stunningly strong results in the entire field of psychology. Thrillingly good story, textbook on the science, and self-help guide all in one—I can't recommend this book enough.

David Feige, *Indefensible: One Lawyer's Journey into the Inferno of American Justice*

Being a public defender is a fairly interesting job, but David Feige manages to make it downright fascinating in this in-depth description of his career. Feige describes his life in luscious detail, from the urine on his doorstep to the gritty details of the courtroom, and doesn't hesitate to name names or dig into unpleasant subjects. If only there was a book this good on every career.

Scott McCloud, *Making Comics: Storytelling Secrets of Comics, Manga and Graphic Novels*

Any Scott McCloud book is a treasure, but this one is especially probing. Essentially, McCloud asks what it is a writer does and what it takes to be a good one. His medium is comics, but a lot of the rules are applicable to other formats and it's hard to imagine a book this curious or this well written about them.

Matt Taibbi and Mark Ames, *The eXile: Sex, Drugs, and Libel in the New Russia*

Matt Taibbi is my favorite political journalist. He writes with a raw honesty that manages to be both politically biting and hilarious. This book tells the story of how, after playing professional basketball in Inner Mongolia, he met up with co-founder Mark Ames and started an independent newspaper that danced in the flames of Russia's dying society. The result is a strange and incredible book: stories of seedy dive bars full of drugged-up loose women, intermixed with incredible feats of investigative journalism into the oligarchs dragging Russia down—without any change in tone. It's wonderful.

Joan Didion, *Political Fictions*

Damn, this book is good. Nobody knows how to take a book and skewer it like Didion. The *New York Review of Books* pieces reprinted in here are simply some of the best eviscerations of any genre. It's hard to imagine how people can walk after a review like that.

Rick Perlstein, *Nixonland*

Perlstein's last book, *Before the Storm*, managed to turn the story of a largely dismissed political figure, Barry Goldwater, into a lesson on how the left can take over the country. Now, in *Nixonland*, he examines the turmoil of the 1960s with fresh eyes and the perfidy of the Nixon administration with new depth. I read the book as he was writing it and sent comments—apparently I was the first outside his home to finish it—and the final version hasn't been published. But do be sure to pick it up as soon as it is.

Lodge, *Changing Places*

Typical campus novel fun, but with some great People's Park stories.

Poundstone, *Fortune's Formula*

Fantastic fun. Math, mafiosi, movies.

Hoopes, *False Prophets*

A wonderful series of profiles of the most prominent management theorists going back to slavery and Taylor. The book's editorial line is a bit marred by the inability of the author (a B-School prof and manager) to reconcile his belief that management power is unjust and that it is necessary. But solid history and good takedowns of some important figures.

Wilson, *To The Finland Station*

Really, really good. Edmund Wilson was the incredible writer you'd expect and this is his masterpiece.

Maurer, *The Big Con: The Story of the Confidence Man*

Luc Sante's intro alone is worth the price of the book, but the rest of the book is fantastic as well. Everyone should know about con men. (The BBC's *Hustle* is obviously a television adaptation of the book.)

DFW, *Consider the Lobster*

DFW's suicide hit me very hard. I ended up coping by reading every piece of nonfiction he'd ever published. He was a brilliant, tortured man and I see so much of myself in him. His nonfiction was fantastic and I will consider my life a success if I can do half of what he did. . . .

Love at Goon Park by Deborah Blum

The first section is a (confessed!) retread of *Becoming Attached*, one of my very favorite books. But after that it gets much better and the interplay of animal and human stories is a lot of fun. I've been reading it to the five-year-old, who loves animal stories of all sorts, and she just laps it up. (I skip the incredibly dark parts, of course.)

The Power Broker by Robert Caro

I cannot possibly say enough good things about this book. Go read it. Right now. Yes, I know it's long, but trust me, you'll wish it was longer. I think it may be simply the best nonfiction book.

The Social Life of Small Urban Spaces by William H. Whyte

If Feynman was a sociologist, this is probably the book he'd write. A delightful little thing.

American Apartheid by Douglass Massey and Nancy Denton

This book is criminally under-publicized. Everyone has their own crazy theories about why it is that blacks are disadvantaged in our society. Massey and Denton show it's much more obvious than any of that: they're victims of extreme segregation, with all the negative effects that entails. An absolutely brilliant book.

The Liberal Defence of Murder by Richard Seymour

This book is like a little miracle. I'm not even sure how to describe it, except to say that it turns one's understanding of history completely upside down.

The Fox and the Hedgehog [*The Hedgehog and the Fox* by Isaiah Berlin – Ed.]

Absolutely delightful.

Bat Boy: The Musical

If you ever get a chance, go see it. It's the greatest musical ever.

Bad Samaritans by Ha joon Chang

The best introduction to the real issues of globalization and international development.

If You're an Egalitarian, How Come You're So Rich? by G. A. Cohen

I really enjoyed this book. It starts with a simple thought experiment: imagine you had a long-lost identical twin who grew up in a conservative home and became a conservative. You, by contrast, grew up in a liberal home and became a liberal. Wouldn't meeting him make you question your beliefs? And thus, shouldn't the possibility that you *could* meet him make you question your beliefs? (I'm not totally convinced by this; my beliefs are much more shaken by converts—people who were strong believers in X but converted to believing in Y.)

From this, Cohen heads to a reminiscence of his own upbringing, which I found especially touching, perhaps because he has the identity I wish I had: a Canadian communist in an antireligious Yiddish-speaking home. . . .

Secrets by Daniel Ellsberg

A fantastic book. Ellsberg turns out to be an incredible writer and he tells not only his own incredible story of the fight to release the Pentagon Papers (did you know the *New York Times* actually stole them from his house?), but, even more interestingly, recounts a great deal of fascinating personal experience about what it was like working with McNamara and Kissinger and trying to maintain your sanity in the highest levels of government. . . .

Prince of the Marshes by Rory Stewart

I occasionally have this fantasy, while reading the news, that whatever person I'm reading about has been fired and, through some miraculous fluke, I have been given their job. Would I make a hash of it? Or, would my naive mind and outsider's expertise allow me to do it in a fascinating new way?

In this book, Rory Stewart describes what happened when he was made a colonial governor of a province in Iraq. Brilliant fellow that he is, he does a remarkably good job all things considered, but also writes a questioning, soul-searching, fascinating book about the experience that highlights what an impossible task it really is.

False Profits: Recovering from the Bubble Economy by Dean Baker

A short, clear book on why the economy failed, who did it, and how to set it right by someone who was absolutely right about it all along. If you only want to read one book about the economic crisis, this would be an excellent choice.

The Accidental Theorist by Paul Krugman

A collection of Krugman's columns for *Slate*. It was before he really came off his neoliberal high, but after he learned to write, so while they're not always right, they're almost always delightful (and *Slate* gave him a lot more freedom to be playful than the *Times* does). A very fun book about a wide range of issues in economics. . . .

Eating the Dinosaur by Chuck Klosterman

Absolutely fantastic. Could hardly put it down. Chuck Klosterman is definitely in the running for greatest living essayist. The book is a collection of essays, but not, as far as I can tell, essays that were ever published anywhere else. They're each just magical gems that fit together just perfectly. I even liked the stuff about football (and I've never seen a game of football).

I liked this so much I went on to read all his other books in reverse chronological order.

Why Not Socialism? by G. A. Cohen

A great little book from the late philosopher Jerry Cohen. Not quite as great as his comments about the shmoos, but a wonderful (and, sadly, all too rare) attempt to get people thinking about what socialism really means and whether it would be practical.

The Persistence of Poverty by Charles Karelis

I feel like I've written so much about this book, but none of it appears to have made it to this blog. A great little book, just enough to explain one big idea and how it overturns what you think about classical economics and poverty and much else besides.

Acme Novelty Library, #19 by Chris Ware

Chris Ware is magic. This book consists mostly of a chapter from the work-in-progress Rusty Brown, which I was initially skeptical about, but turns out to be just amazingly great. And Building Stories is incredible too.

Ware's method is to publish a page each week or so in a weekly paper (the Sunday New York Times, the Chicago Reader), then redraw the entire chapter and send it out as an edition of the Novelty Library, then redraw it a third time when the entire book is published. So this is a way of getting intermediate results, but you could just wait for the final books themselves (if they are ever finished).

Bonfire of the Vanities by Tom Wolfe

Absolutely fantastic. A rare must-read novel—packed full of information about society, journalism, activism, race, etc. I can't convey just how good it really is. It's like The Power Broker of fiction.

How to Win Friends and Influence People (reread) by Dale Carnegie

There's a reason this is a classic. It articulates a way of dealing with people, founded on concern and empathy, and convincingly argues that this kind style is actually the more productive one for getting things done. Instead of yelling at people to do things, you make them *want* to help you. And the book itself is a genius exemplar of this practice. Instead of berating you for being a jerk, like most people would, it persuades you to *want* to change.

[REDACTED]

Managing to Change the World by Allison Green and Jerry Hauser

The best book on the practicalities of management I've ever read. Whereas most books focus on vague and meaningless advice, this book is clear about the nuts and bolts.

Workers in a Labyrinth by Robert Jackall

Not as great as my favorite book of all time, Jackall's *Moral Mazes*, but a fascinating look at how normal people make sense of their daily work lives.

The Possessed: Adventures with Russian Books and the People Who Read Them by Elif Batuman

Hilarious, brilliant, fantastic. There's no justification for this book being as good as it is. Even I wasn't interested in reading a book about Russian literary scholars, but it's just incredibly good and I'm glad I did.

This Is Your Country on Drugs by Ryan Grim

I would not have thought the world needed another book on drugs, but this one turns out to be basically perfect. Comprehensive, erudite, funny, and realistic—Grim definitely inhales.

Microeconomics by Samuel Bowles

A textbook that totally upends the field of classical economics. Sadly, it can be a bit hard to follow, but I wrote summaries of it here.

All Art is Propaganda: Critical Essays by George Orwell (with introduction by Keith Gessen)

Orwell is magic.

Dancing in the Streets: A History of Collective Joy by Barbara Ehrenreich

Ehrenreich makes a convincing case for the ecstatic tradition in American life. My only regret is that it lacks a chapter on raves.

The Lifecycle of Software Objects [online] by Ted Chiang

Read it! Even people who know much more about sci-fi than me agree this is one of the great science fiction books of all time. It's a novel about the ethical issues with AI.

Short: Walking Tall When You're Not Tall At All by John Schwartz

Surely you've heard about the studies showing short people don't make as much as tall people. John Schwartz set out to write a book to cheer kids up about this fact, but looking into them he found it wasn't a fact at all. The result is a model of self-help through science and media criticism. Schwartz playfully teaches you enough math and science to be able to debunk the studies and enough personal advice to make a life on your own terms.

The Halo Effect by Phil Rosenzweig

Last year, I recommended *Good to Great*, calling it "actual science." Dave Bridgeland quickly corrected me and recommended this book, which is vastly better. Not only does it systematically debunk the pretensions to science in *Good to Great* and the other management bestsellers in an absolutely delightful manner, it provides a short but very thought-provoking discussion of strategy in its own right.

You can mock the banality of its recommendations, but there's no question: this book is well worth it just for the way it encourages habits of genuine scientific thought. I knew I never should have fallen so low as to trust a business book!

The Trial by Franz Kafka (translated by Breon Mitchell)

A deep and magnificent work. I'd not really read much Kafka before and had grown up led to believe that it was a paranoid and hyperbolic work, dystopian fiction in the style of George Orwell. Yet I read it and found it was precisely accurate—every single detail perfectly mirrored my own experience. This isn't fiction, but documentary.

Spoilers follow. . . .

The bulk of the book is about K trying to find someone to fight his case for him, and failing miserably. As an individual in a world of bureaucracies, he concludes there's no substitute but to do the work himself.

This is set against the backdrop of his "day job" at the bank—about as characteristic a bureaucracy as you can imagine. The bank, by contrast, has no difficulty finding people to do its work for it. Even when K slacks off or gets distracted, the bank continues chugging along just fine—as seen in the vice president who leaps to take K's work from him. (Compare: The independent lawyer is under no such pressure to actually get K's work done.)

A vivid illustration that bureaucracies, once they get started, continue doing whatever mindless thing they've been set up to do, regardless of whether the people in them particularly want to do it or whether it's even a good idea. At the same time, individual people have an incredibly hard time executing long-term or large-scale tasks on their own, even when they're quite motivated.

But what of the priest? The priest tells K a story about how as an individual in a bureaucracy, it's a losing game to try to ask permission. You have to persuade your boss, your boss's boss, and your boss's boss's boss (so terribly powerful that your boss can't even bear to look at him). If you wait for your request to be approved by the chain of command, it won't happen at all.

K argues with the priest about how horribly unfair this is: isn't your boss (the individual) doing the wrong thing somehow? The priest maintains there are many different theories about this question of individual responsibility. But K is missing the larger point: this is just how bureaucracy works.

K takes the lesson to heart and decides to stop fighting the system and just live his life without asking for permission. It goes well . . . for a while. But it still seems a better option than the alternatives.

Poor Economics by Abhijit Banerjee and Esther Duflo

God, what a book! *Poor Economics* is a series of tales of foreigners trying to save the far-flung poor, while failing to realize not only that their developed-country ideas are terrible disasters in practice, but also that everything they've learned to think of as solid—even something as simple as measuring distance—is far more fraught, and complex, and political than they ever could have imagined. It's a stunning feeling to have the basic building blocks of your world questioned and crumbled before you—and a powerful lesson in the value of self-skepticism for everyone who's trying to do something.

The Inner Game of Tennis by Timothy Gallwey

This book touched me deeply and made me rethink the entire way I approached life; it's about vastly more than just tennis. I can't really describe it, but I can recommend this video with Alan Kay and the author that will blow your mind.

Rick Perry and his Eggheads by Sasha Issenberg

Sasha Issenberg is a miracle worker. This book (really an excerpt from his forthcoming book) is so very, very good that it just blows me away. Issenberg tells the tale of everything I've been trying to say to everyone in politics, but he does it in a real-life three-act morality play that's so good it could be a model on how to tell a story.

The Lean Startup by Eric Ries

Ries presents a translation of the Toyota Production System to start-ups—and it's so clearly the right way to run a start-up that it's hard to imagine how we got along before it. Unfortunately, the book has become so trendy that I find many people claiming to swear allegiance to it who clearly missed the point entirely. Read it with an open mind and let it challenge you, so you can start to understand how transformative it really is.

CODE: The Hidden Language of Computer Hardware and Software by Charles Petzold

A magnificent achievement. Charles Petzold starts with the story of two kids across the street who wish to communicate with each other and, from this simple beginning, builds up an entire computer without ever making it seem like something that should be over your head. I never really felt I understood the computer until I read this book.

What It Takes: The Way to the White House by Richard Ben Cramer

Were this just the story of how George H. W. Bush got elected, it'd be one of the few biographies that belonged in the same league as Robert Caro. But it's so much more than that: Richard Ben Cramer gives the same treatment to dozens of candidates in the 1988 presidential election: Gary Hart, Bob Dole, Joe Biden, Dick Gephardt, and on and on. Even if you didn't care about politics, this book would be worth reading simply because the writing is so good. But if you do, there's never been a better exposition of what drives these men who wish to be our leaders and what they have to go through to get there.

Guest Review by Aaron Swartz: Chris Hayes' *The Twilight of the Elites*

http://crookedtimber.org/2012/06/18/guest-review-by-aaron-swartz -chris-hayes-the-twilight-of-the-elites/

June 18, 2012

Age 25

In his new book, *The Twilight of the Elites: America After Meritocracy*, Chris Hayes manages the impossible trifecta: the book is compellingly readable, impossibly erudite, and—most stunningly of all—correct. At the end, I was left with just two quibbles: first, the book's chapter on "pop epistemology" thoroughly explicated how elites got stuff wrong without bothering to mention the non-elites who got things right, leaving the reader with the all-too-common impression that getting it right was impossible; and second, the book never assembled its (surprisingly sophisticated) argument into a single summary. To discuss it, I feel we have to start with remedying the latter flaw:

Our nation's institutions have crumbled, Hayes argues. From 2000–2010 (the "Fail Decade"), every major societal institution failed. Big businesses collapsed with Enron and WorldCom, their auditors failed to catch it, the Supreme Court got partisan in *Bush v. Gore*, our intelligence apparatus failed to catch 9/11, the media lied us into wars, the military failed to win them, professional sports was all on steroids, the church engaged in and covered up sex abuse, the government compounded disaster upon disaster in Katrina, and the banks crashed our economy. How did it all go so wrong?

Hayes pins the blame on an unlikely suspect: meritocracy. We thought we would just simply pick out the best and raise them to the top, but once they got there they inevitably used their privilege to entrench themselves and their kids (inequality is, Hayes says, "autocatalytic"). Opening up the elite to more efficient competition didn't make things more fair, it just legitimated a more intense scramble. The result was an arms race among the elite, pushing all of them to embrace the most unscrupulous forms of cheating and fraud to secure their coveted positions. As competition takes over at the high end, personal worth resolves into exchange value, and the elite power accumulated in one sector can be traded for elite power in another: a regulator can become a bank VP, a modern TV host can use their stardom to become a bestselling author (try to imagine Edward R. Murrow using the nightly news to flog his books the way Bill O'Reilly does). This creates a unitary elite, detached from the bulk of society, yet at the same time even more insecure. You can never reach the pinnacle of the elite in this new world; even if you have the most successful TV show, are you also making blockbuster movies? Bestselling books? Winning Nobel Prizes? When your peers are the elite at large, you can never clearly best them.

The result is that our elites are trapped in a bubble, where the usual pointers toward accuracy (unanimity, proximity, good faith) only lead them astray. And their distance from the way the rest of the country really lives makes it impossible for them to do their jobs justly—they just don't get the necessary feedback. The only cure is to reduce economic inequality, a view that has surprising support among the population (clear majorities want to close the deficit by raising taxes on the rich, which is more than can be said for any other plan). And while Hayes is not a fan of heightening the contradictions, it is possible that the next crisis will bring with it the opportunity to win this change.

This is just a skeletal summary—the book itself is filled with luscious texture to demonstrate each point and more in-depth discussion of the mechanics of each mechanism (I would call it Elster meets Gladwell if I thought that would be taken as praise). So buy the book already. Now, as I said, I think Hayes is broadly correct in his analysis. And I think his proposed solution is spot on as well—when we were fellows together at the Harvard Center for Ethics, I think we annoyed everyone else with our repeated insistence that reducing economic inequality was somehow always the appropriate solution to each of the many social ills the group identified.

But when talking to other elites about this proposal, I notice a confusion that's worth clarifying, about the *structural* results of inequality, rather than the merely quantitative ones. Class hangs over the book like a haunting specter (there's a brief comment on p. 148 that "Mills [had] a more nuanced theory of elite power than Marx's concept of a ruling class") but I think it's hard to see how the solution relates to the problem without it. After all, we started by claiming the problem is meritocracy, but somehow the solution is taxing the rich?

The clue comes in thinking clearly about the alternative to meritocracy. It's not picking surgeons by lottery, Hayes clarifies, but then what is it? It's about ameliorating power relationships altogether. Meritocracy says, "There must be one who rules, so let it be the best"; egalitarianism responds, "Why must there?" It's the power imbalance, rather than inequality itself, that's the problem.

Imagine a sci-fi world in which productivity has reached such impressive heights that everyone can have every good they desire just from the work young kids do for fun. By twiddling the knobs on their local MakerBot, the kids produce enough food, clothing, and iPhones to satisfy everyone. So instead of working, most people spend their days doing yoga or fishing. But scarcity hasn't completely faded away—there's still competition for the best spots at the fishing hole. So we continue to let those be allocated by the market: the fishing hole spot is charged for and the people who really want it earn the money to pay for it by helping people with various chores.

In this sort of world, inequality doesn't seem like much of a problem. Sure, some people get the best fishing hole spots, but that's because they did the most chores. If you want the spot more than they do, you can do more work. But the inequality doesn't come with power—the guy with the best fishing hole spot can't say, "Fuck me or you're fired."

This sci-fi world may sound ridiculous, but it's basically the one Keynes predicted we'd soon be living in:

> Now it is true that the needs of human beings may seem
> to be insatiable. But they fall into two classes—those

needs which are absolute in the sense that we feel them whatever the situation of our fellow human beings may be, and those which are relative in the sense that we feel them only if their satisfaction lifts us above, makes us feel superior to, our fellows. Needs of the second class, those which satisfy the desire for superiority, may indeed be insatiable; for the higher the general level, the higher still are they. But this is not so true of the absolute needs—a point may soon be reached, much sooner perhaps than we are all of us aware of, when these needs are satisfied in the sense that we prefer to devote our further energies to non-economic purposes.

[. . .] But, of course, it will all happen gradually, not as a catastrophe. Indeed, it has already begun. The course of affairs will simply be that there will be ever larger and larger classes and groups of people from whom problems of economic necessity have been practically removed.

And that's what a reduction in economic inequality could achieve. The trend in recent decades (since the fall of the Soviet Union and the ruling class's relief that "There Is No Alternative") has been for the people at the top to seize all the economic gains, leaving everyone else increasingly insecure and dependent on their largesse. (Calling themselves "job creators," on this view, is not so much a brag as a threat.) But with less inequality, it could be otherwise. Instead of a world in which there are a handful of big networks with the money to run television shows, everyone could afford to have their Sunday morning conversations filmed and live-streamed. Instead of only huge conglomerates having the capital and distribution to launch new product lines, everyone could make and market their own line of underwear or video games (instead of just elite Red Sox pitchers).

Even on strict efficiency grounds, this strikes me as a more alluring view than the usual meritocracy. Why put all your eggs in one basket, even if it's the best basket? Surely you'd get better results by giving more baskets a try.

You can argue that this is exactly where technology is bringing us—popular kids on YouTube get made into huge pop sensations, right?—and the genius of Hayes' book is to show us why this is not enough. The egalitarian demand shouldn't be that we need more black pop stars or female pop stars or YouTube sensation pop stars, but to question why we need elite superstars at all. I hope Hayes' next book shows us what the world without them is like.

Freakonomics

http://www.aaronsw.com/weblog/001688

April 23, 2005

Age 18

I happen to be taking a class on sociological methods. The other day we had a section where the TA showed us how to use SPSS, a GUI statistical analysis program. Usually such computer demos are pretty boring—pull down this menu here, click this button here, and so on—but this demo was magical: it used real data.

The TA downloaded a listing of venture capitalists from the state of California. Then he downloaded the records of political campaign contributions from the Federal Election Commission. He merged the two files and calculated an index of party loyalty—how likely each person was to donate to the Democrats or Republicans. Then he graphed it. He found an anomaly in the data and went back and investigated it.

The whole performance was oddly enthralling, and I went up to ask him questions afterwards. "So you're interested in statistics?" he asked me, and I said yes, and began to think about why. I've decided it's because I like truth. If you like finding out the truth—which is often surprising—the best technique to use is science. And if you want to do serious science, sooner or later you'll probably need statistics.

In the field of surprising statistics, one name comes up frequently: Steven D. Levitt. And—surprise, surprise—Levitt has a new book out, *Freakonomics*. (As an aside, Levitt must have a great publicist, because the book has been receiving tons of hype. It's a good book, but not as good as the hype would make it seem.* Nonetheless, I will put this

---

*The stuff that Levitt is interested in—the reason why his book is interesting—is

aside in reviewing it.) The book consists of a popularization of the papers of Levitt and other interesting economists.

As a result, the book doesn't have much of a theme but covers a bunch of bizarre topics: how school teachers and sumo wrestlers cheat, how bagel eaters don't, how real estate agents and surgeons don't have your best interests at heart, how to defeat the Ku Klux Klan, how *The Weakest Link* contestants demonstrate racism, how online daters lie, how drug dealing works like McDonald's, how abortion overthrows governments and fights crime, how to be a good parent, and what you can learn from children's names.

Despite his unusual interests and open mind, Levitt remains an economist and has the economist's typical right-wing assumptions: most notably, a strong commitment to incentives and an unquestioning faith in societal order. For the former, it makes fun of criminologists by insisting the evidence that punishment deters criminals is "very strong," but fails to provide a single citation (almost everything else in the book, even well-known facts, is scrupulously cited). For the latter, they simply assume that IQ is an accurate and inherited measure of intelligence, despite a rather glaring lack of evidence for this.

Furthermore, in a section that uses parental interviews to pick out which parenting techniques are most effective, the authors almost entirely ignore the possibility that parents are lying—an omission they don't make elsewhere. For example, they find no correlation between saying that you read to your children and your children

---

society, the field studied by sociology. In this sense, *Freakonomics* is really a sociology book. Yet its attitude toward sociologists could be parodied as "And thank goodness a sociologist risked his life by spending four years embedded with a drug gang because he managed to find a couple notebooks of business transactions that he could give to an economist!" One might expect that the picture of a drug gang resulting from four years of embedded research might be more interesting than a couple of notebooks, but apparently no.

Sociologists write many amazingly well-written and fascinating books, even without the help of a professional co-author, yet none of them have seen anything like the publicity this book has. I don't think it's a coincidence that it took an economist to write a sociology book before it could be given publicity. Sociology raises too many problematic questions about society, but an economist can do somewhat interesting things while continuing to endorse the status quo. (Even Levitt's most radical finding—that legalizing abortion cut crime rates in half—leads him to insist that the finding has no direct relevance for public policy.)

doing well in school. From this they conclude that reading doesn't matter; a far more likely explanation seems to be that nearly all parents *claim* they read to their children. (Thanks to Brad Delong for this criticism.)

But it's still a fun and interesting book. However, I believe its most important point is one that's not stated explicitly: that through the proper investigation of the numbers we can better understand our world.

The Immorality of Freakonomics

http://www.aaronsw.com/weblog/immoralfreaksDate June 17, 2005

Age 18

As the hype around the book *Freakonomics* reaches absurd proportions (now an "international bestseller," the authors have been signed for a monthly column in the *New York Times Magazine*), I think it's time to discuss some of the downsides that I mostly left out of my main review. The most important of which is that economist Stephen Levitt simply does not appear to care—or even notice—if his work involves doing evil things.

The 1960s, as is well-known, had a major civilizing effect on all areas of American life. Less well-known, however, was the immediate pushback from the powerful centers of society. The process involved a great number of things, notably the network of right-wing think tanks I've written about elsewhere, but in the field of education it led to a crackdown on "those institutions which have played the major role in the indoctrination of the young," as a contemporary report (*The Crisis of Democracy*) put it.

The indoctrination centers (notably schools) weren't doing their job properly and so a back-to-basics approach with more rote memorization of meaningless facts and less critical thinking and intellectual development was needed. This was mainly done under the guise of "accountability," for both students and teachers. Standardized tests, you see, would see how well students had memorized certain pointless facts and students would not be allowed to deviate from their assigned numbers. Teachers too would have their jobs depend on the test scores their students got. Teachers who decided to buck the system and actually have their students learn something worthwhile would get demoted or even fired.

Not surprisingly, as always happens when you make people's lives depend on an artificial test, teachers began cheating. And it is here that Professor Levitt enters the story. He excitedly signed up with the Chicago Public School system to try to build a system that would catch cheating teachers. Levitt and his co-author write excitedly about this system and the clever patterns it discovers in the data, but mostly ignore the question of whether helping to get these teachers fired is a good idea. Apparently even rogue economists jump when the government asks them to.

Levitt has a few arguments—teachers were setting students up to fail in the higher grade they would be advanced to—but these are tacked on as afterthoughts. Levitt never stops to ask whether contributing to the indoctrination of the young or getting teachers fired might not be an acceptable area of work, despite being an economist, he never weighs any benefits or even considers the costs.

Levitt, by all appearances, was not, like some of his colleagues, a self-conscious participant in this regressive game. He was just a rube who got taken in. But surely preventing others from the same fate would be a more valuable contribution.

In Offense of Classical Music

http://www.aaronsw.com/weblog/classicalmusic

June 20, 2006

Age 19

I recently had to sit through a performance of Bach's *Well-Tempered Clavier* at the Chicago Symphony Orchestra (it was the conductor's farewell concert). At first it was simply boring, but as I listened more carefully, it grew increasingly painful, until it became excruciatingly so. I literally began tearing my hair out and trying to cut my skin with my nails (there were large red marks when the performance was finally over). The pianist, I was certain, kept flubbing the notes and getting the timing off. But few around me seemed to agree. "Well, he certainly plays it differently from Gould," was the most they could say.

The audience, like that of private libraries and the Fox News Channel, was decidedly old. I don't recall seeing *anyone* who looked younger than thirty. And, aside from thoughts of this whole orchestras-playing-classical-music thing dying out, it made me wonder: what's so great about classical music?

Ask the old folks there and they'll tell you that nothing really compares. Listen to the stuff on the radio today and it's all simply repetitive melodies with stupid lyrics. And the thing is, they're right: the stuff on the radio does suck for the most part. But that's not really a fair comparison.

When I listen to good modern music, it takes my heart in its hands and plays with it as it pleases—makes me soar, makes me sad, excited, and mad. But when I listen to classical music, at most it simply occupies my brain for a while. Is this simply a flaw in my perception or has music really improved?

I think it's possible to argue that music is actually getting better. As humans, we clearly share a number of genetically encoded similarities, perhaps with some variation. For example, we almost all have two eyes, although in different shapes, sizes, and colors. Imagine that we are similarly endowed with some shared sense of musical appreciation (or, put another way, emotional susceptibility). We all fall for the same musical things, again with some variation.

If this is the case (and while I can't really prove it, it seems at least plausible to me that it is), then there would indeed be objective standards for measuring music: better music would be more appreciated by the "average person" or the majority of people or some such. And if there are objective standards for measuring music, then music can get better.

And, if we again imagine that what's appreciated in music isn't simply random, that it involves certain traits (which seems pretty clear, although again hard to prove), then not only can music get better, but it probably *will*. Musicians will listen to old music, the majority of them will enjoy the good songs of the past, and they'll try to build upon and improve that good material, following its patterns, creating even better music. And the next generation will do the same, from a further along starting point.

Does this prove that the latest Aimee Mann album (*The Forgotten Arm*) is the best work of music yet to be created by humans? Of course not. But it does mean it's at least *possible*, that I'm not completely crazy for thinking so.

A Unified Theory of Magazines

http://www.aaronsw.com/weblog/unifiedmagazines

September 28, 2006

Age 19

For as long as I've been building web apps, it's been apparent that most successful websites are *communities*—not just interactive pages, but places where groups of like-minded people can congregate and do things together. Our knowledge of how to make and cultivate communities is still at a very early stage, but most agree on their importance.

A magazine, we may imagine, is like a one-way website. It doesn't really allow the readers to talk back (with the small exception of the letters page), it doesn't even have any sort of interactivity. But I still think communities are the key for magazines; the difference is that magazines *export* communities.

In other words, instead of providing a place for a group of like-minded people to come together, magazines provide a sampling of what a group of like-minded people might say in such an instance so that you can pretend you're part of them. Go down the list and you'll see.

The magazines of Condé Nast, for example, export "lifestyles." Most readers probably aren't the "hip scene" the magazines supposedly cover, but by reading these things they learn what to wear and what to buy and what these people are talking about. Even their highbrow magazines, like the *New Yorker*, serve the same purpose, only this time it's books instead of clothes.

The late, great *Lingua Franca* exported the university. Academe-philes, sitting at home, probably taking care of the kids, read it so they could imagine themselves part of the life of the mind. Similarly, the new *SEED* magazine is trying to export the culture of science, so people who aren't themselves scientists can get a piece of the lab coat life.

Alumni magazines similarly export college life, so that graying former college students can relive some of their old glory days, reading pieces about library renovations as they recall having sex in the stacks. And house organs export a particular kind of politics, telling you what a party or organization's take is on the issues of the day, giving you a sense of the party line.

Run down the list and in pretty much every case you scratch a magazine, you find an exported community. Magazines that want to succeed will have to find one of their own.

On Intellectual Dishonesty

http://www.aaronsw.com/weblog/intellectualdishonesty

December 14, 2011

Age 24

Dishonesty has two parts: 1) saying something that is untrue, and 2) saying it with the intent to mislead the other person. You can have each without the other: you can be genuinely mistaken and thereby say something false without intending to mislead, and you can intentionally mislead someone without ever saying anything that's untrue. (The second is generally considered deceit, but not dishonesty.)

However, you can be intellectually dishonest without doing *either* of these things. Imagine that you're conducting an experiment and most of the time it comes out exactly the way you expect but one time it goes wrong (you probably just screwed up the measurements). Telling someone about your work, you say: "Oh, it works just the way I expected—seven times it came out exactly right."

This isn't untrue and it isn't intentionally misleading—you really do believe it works the way you expected. But it is intellectually dishonest: intellectual honesty requires bending over backwards to provide any evidence that you might be wrong, *even if you're convinced that you are right.*

This is an impractical standard to apply to everyday life. A prospective employer asks you in a job interview if you can get to work on time. You say "Yes," not "I think so, but one time in 2003 the power went out and so my alarm didn't go off and I overslept." I don't think anyone considers this dishonesty; indeed, if you were intellectually honest all the time, people would think you were pretty weird.

Science has a higher standard. It's not just between you and your employer; it's a claim to posterity. And you might be wrong, but what if you're not around for posterity to call you up and ask you to show your work? That's why intellectual honesty requires you show your work in advance, so that others can see if you're missing something.

The Smalltalk Question

http://www.aaronsw.com/weblog/smalltalkq

August 16, 2006

Age 19

One of the minor puzzles of American life is what question to ask people at parties and suchly to get to know them.

"How ya doin'?" is of course mere formality; only the most troubled would answer honestly for anything but the positive.

"What do you do?" is somewhat offensive. First, it really means "What occupation do you hold?" and thus implies you do little outside your occupation. Second, it implies that one's occupation is the most salient fact about them. Third, it rarely leads to further useful inquiry. For only a handful of occupations, you will be able to say something somewhat relevant, but even this will no doubt be slightly annoying or offensive. ("Oh yeah, I always thought about studying history.")

"Where are you from?" is even less fruitful.

"What's your major?" (in the case of college students) turns sour when, as is tragically all too often the case, students feel no real passion for their major.

"What book have you read recently?" will cause the majority of Americans who don't read to flail, while at best only getting an off-the-cuff garbled summary of a random book.

"What's something cool you've learned recently?" puts the person on the spot and inevitably leads to hemming and hawing and then something not all that cool.

I propose instead that one ask "What have you been thinking about lately?" First, the question is extremely open-ended. The answer could be a book, a movie, a relationship, a class, a job, a hobby, etc. Even better, it will be whichever of these is most interesting at the moment. Second, it sends the message that thinking, and thinking about thinking, is a fundamental human activity, and thus encourages it. Third, it's easiest to answer, since by its nature it's asking about what's already on the person's mind. Fourth, it's likely to lead to productive dialog, as you can discuss the topic together and hopefully make progress. Fifth, the answer is quite likely to be novel. Unlike books and occupations, people's thoughts seem to be endlessly varied. Sixth, it helps capture a person's essence. A job can be forced by circumstance and parentage, but our thoughts are all our own. I can think of little better way to quickly gauge what a person is really like.

"What have you been working on lately?" can be seen, in this context, to be clearly inferior, although similar.

So, what *have* you been thinking about lately?

UNSCHOOL

When I first met Aaron and he told me that Grace Llewellyn's *The Teenage Liberation Handbook: How to Quit School and Get a Real Life and Education* had been a big influence on him, I laughed in recognition. Chances are you haven't heard of the book, but trust me, it's a cult classic in certain circles. Over the years I've met countless curious, energetic, and always slightly rebellious young people who were emboldened to forge their own unique educational path after reading it.

Unlike Aaron, who discovered the book on his own, I got a copy from my parents. I was raised an "unschooler," which means I grew up without classes or coursework or grades. I was raised, in other words, according to the free-form child-centered pedagogy that so inspired Aaron. Part of what I find so captivating about Aaron's writing on education is his exuberance at discovering a philosophy of learning that aligns with his instincts and experiences. Aaron was nothing if not a compulsively curious and hardworking person, yet, as these pages make viscerally clear, he felt profoundly stifled in school. He laments the ways time is wasted, important topics are trivialized, and teachers are forced by the administration to fixate on testing instead of teaching for its own sake, which means that students become correspondingly blinkered, obsessed with passing or failing instead of getting truly absorbed in the subject at hand.

Online, Aaron found a community that pointed to the possibility of another way of doing things. Far-flung Internet users helped him master the art of computer programming, offering feedback and assistance and encouraging his love of coding—of knowledge—instead of enforcing rote memorization and instilling fear of failure, as a more orthodox student-teacher relationship might. Fear is a big theme of Aaron's writing on education, as is boredom, and for him the two go together. Like most prominent unschooling advocates, Aaron believes human beings are naturally curious; the problem is that conventional schooling stamps this inherent inquisitiveness out of us. Students are so afraid of getting answers wrong, so terrified of seeing a big F written in red pen, that they retreat into apathy, hedging their bets to finish the required assignments instead of taking the risks true engagement requires. Fear of humiliation, in other words, squelches experimentation. And as Aaron argues, this suits the powers that be just fine, because contemporary schooling is more about instilling discipline than imparting information, let alone wisdom. Fear tends to toe the line, while curiosity interrogates and crosses it.

It's this bigger story, about how our educational system evolved hand in hand with the rise of industrial capitalism, that Aaron begins to tell here. Though only a fragment of what he envisioned as a larger project, the essays that follow are a welcome and thought-provoking contribution to a long-standing and ongoing debate about learning, freedom, pedagogy, economics, and the public good. What's more, these pieces provide a valuable window on the learning process, an illustration of Aaron's fundamental argument about curiosity engaged. We witness Aaron maturing, transforming from a teenage student struggling in school to a young adult and independent scholar studying the academic system from the outside, asking why it evolved the way it did and whether it could be another way. What a gift to see such a keen and conscientious mind at work, striving to understand a world he cared so much about.

—Astra Taylor

School

Spring 2011

Age 24

Given as a lecture at the Safra Center at Harvard University.

From their very first moments on Earth, babies get bored.

Babies get so bored, in fact, that this is the basis of all modern baby research. Show a baby three dots (...) and they'll stare at it intently for a while, before getting bored and looking away. Vary the position of the dots (∴) and they'll look at it for a bit, then get bored again. But add another dot (....) and they'll go back to intent staring. The scientists are thrilled: babies can count! But they overlook something even more important: babies get bored.

In another study, babies were given a special pillow so that by adjusting their head they could control the movement of a mobile. Not only did these infants quickly learn how to move the mobile, this discovery was followed by what the researchers called "vigorous smiling and cooing."* As a later study observed, "Even casual observations of infants reveals their delight in making events occur."† In other words, infants aren't just playing around because they're bored—from birth, they know the pleasure of figuring things out.

And honestly, it makes sense that babies want to figure things out. The world is confusing! It's filled with strange sights and sounds and smells, a new world of taste and touch. The only way to make sense of any of it is to work at it as best you can, looking at all the new things you see and trying desperately to figure them all out.

Note: Some citations were added by the editor.

*John S. Watson, "Smiling, Cooing, and 'The Game.'"

†Neal W. Finkelstein and Craig T. Ramey, "Learning to Control the Environment in Infancy," *Child Development,* 1977, **48**, 806–819.

Give a six-month-old a new toy and they will "systematically ex-
amine [it] with every sense they have at their command (including
taste, of course)," write a leading team of baby researchers. "By a
year or so, they will systematically vary the actions they perform
on an object: they might tap a new toy car gently against the floor,
listening to the sound it makes, then try banging it loudly, and then
try banging it against the soft sofa. By eighteen months, if you show
them an object with some unexpected property, like a can with a
mooing noise, they will systematically test to see if it will do other
unexpected things."*

They apply such dedication to everything in their world. Soon
they begin to learn faces—to distinguish between their mom and
other people—and what those faces mean. They learn baby physics—
when a car rolls behind a screen they know exactly when to look for
it to come out the other side—and get surprised when it comes out
faster or slower than it should. They listen to what people say—the
baby talk we all naturally lapse into around little kids helps them
detect vowels—and learn to imitate those noises for themselves. In
short, little kids are curiosity machines.

In one experiment, the researchers put a toy slightly out of reach
and then gave the babies a rake they could use to get the toy. At first
the kids reach for it, then they look at their parents pleadingly to
get it for them, but then they quickly set about figuring it out for
themselves—and eventually realize they can use the rake to do so.
Their faces light up with that joy of discovery. They reach out, fum-
ble, but eventually get the toy and pull it to them.

But that's not enough—it's not just about getting the toy. "[They]
forget all about the toy after a trial or two. They often deliberately
put the toy back far out of reach and experiment with using the rake
to draw it toward them. The toy itself isn't nearly as interesting as the
fact that the rake moves it closer."

"It's not just that we human beings *can* do this; we *need* to do it,"
the researchers write. "We seem to have a kind of explanatory drive,
like our drive for food or sex. When we're presented with a puzzle,
a mystery, a hint of a pattern, something that doesn't quite make

---

*The Scientist in the Crib.

sense, we work until we find a solution. In fact, we intentionally set ourselves such problems, even the quite trivial ones that divert us from the horror of airplane travel, like crossword puzzles, video games, or detective stories. As scientists, we may stay up all night in the grip of a problem, even forgetting to eat, and it seems rather unlikely that our paltry salaries are the sole motivation."

Think back to the "secure home base" experiments [. . .]. When put in a strange situation, the toddlers are terrified—they cling to their mothers for support. But soon enough, their curiosity gets the better of them. They begin, at first tentatively but soon with abandon, to explore the rest of the room. The explanatory drive is so powerful it can even overcome fear.

And it doesn't go away as they get older. In one experiment with kids ages 4 to 10, the kids were given a variety of problems to work on—some easy, some hard. Obviously the kids didn't work on problems that were too hard for them, but they also didn't pick the problems that were too easy. They sought out the problems that were just right for them—providing a little bit of a challenge, but not so much that they were impossible. Unless they were rewarded, that is—when they were given rewards for solving puzzles, they headed straight back for the easy ones.[*]

Anyone who's been around preschoolers knows they don't need to be motivated to learn. "Rarely does one hear parents complain that their pre-schooler is 'unmotivated,'" notes one child psychologist.[†] Instead, the parenting books are filled with just the opposite complaint: all their preschoolers do is ask them why, why, why. "Why are we getting into the car?" "Why are we going to the grocery store?" "Why is all the food kept at the grocery store?" "Why do people use money to buy things?"[‡]

It's almost kind of annoying, really. So we ship them off to school.

It is difficult for most to recall what school was really like. If we did well, we focus on the positive memories and do our best to ignore

---

[*]http://www.jstor.org/pss/1129110.

[†](James Raffini 1993.)

[‡]http://family.go.com/parentpedia/preschool/milestones-development/pre school-asking-why/.

the rest. If we did poorly, we try to block out the memory of the in-
dignities we suffered. It's not a place we're usually eager to revisit.
But, for a moment, try to imagine it: torn away from your family,
shipped off daily to a strange and uncomfortable place, thrown into
a sea of unfamiliar faces, each scared in his or her own way and often
taking it out on you.

But what strikes me most when I revisit the classrooms I grew up
in is how small they seem now. In my memory, the teachers are giants and the rooms were designed for other giants like them. The
desks were big and dangerous contraptions, the blackboards seemed
endless, the desks and tables imposing figures.

But that was my world: day in and day out, those giants controlled
my life, those children were my only companions. And what happened in these classes? I did not get to explore or experiment as I did
at home. I did not learn things the way I had learned them the rest
of my life—through trial and error, through experience and experiment. No, school was the place for Real Learning and, I was told,
Real Learning was Work.

Most classes I was in, most classes I've seen since—even at the
most progressive schools—were much the same. The teacher sat at
the front of the class and talked while the kids sat in front of them
and listened. Occasionally there'd be a picture or a diagram or a
worksheet, but for the most part it was simply talk. Think of how
many hours you spent sitting at those desks—6 hours a day, 180 days
a year, for 12 years—listening to those teachers. That's nearly *thirteen thousand* hours, probably more time than you've spent watching
movies or playing sports. How much of it do you remember? I can
remember a few snapshots here and there, but as much as I try, I can't
even remember a single sentence I was told. All that talking, and I
can hardly recall a thing they said.

And I guess that's not a surprise. All those lectures were boring.
I'm sure I zoned out for most of them; I'm sure most everybody else
did as well. The teachers weren't oblivious to this, of course—that's
why they'd call on us, punctuating the long hours of boredom with
moments of panic and terror. You'd hear your name being called and,
suddenly awake, find the eyes of the teacher and the rest of the class
all on you—your whole world, watching to see if you'd screw up.

The radical educator John Holt once asked his class about this:

> We had been chatting about something or other, and everyone seemed in a relaxed frame of mind, so I said, "You know, there's something I'm curious about, and I wonder if you'd tell me." They said, "What?" I said, "What do you think, what goes through your mind, when the teacher asks you a question and you don't know the answer?"
>
> It was a bombshell. Instantly a paralyzed silence fell on the room. Everyone stared at me with what I have learned to recognize as a tense expression. For a long time there wasn't a sound. Finally Ben, who is bolder than most, broke the tension, and also answered my question, by saying in a loud voice, "Gulp!"
>
> He spoke for everyone. They all began to clamor, and all said the same thing, that when the teacher asked them a question and they didn't know the answer they were scared half to death. I was flabbergasted—to find this in a school which people think of as progressive, which does its best not to put pressure on little children, which does not give marks in the lower grades, which tries to keep children from feeling that they're in some kind of race.
>
> I asked them why they felt gulpish. They said they were afraid of failing, afraid of being kept back, afraid of being called stupid, afraid of feeling themselves stupid. [. . .] Even in the kindest and gentlest of schools, children are afraid, many of them a great deal of the time, some of them almost all the time. This is a hard fact of life to deal with. [70f]

And it doesn't let up—even law school students live in fear of the infamous "cold call," the moment when their professor will expect them to answer an obscure question in front of the whole class. If it has the power to shake these accomplished college grads, imagine how terrifying it must be for powerless, friendless first-graders!

Fear makes you dumb. Your field of vision literally narrows, you start thinking desperately about the problem at hand—not what you know or what it means, but just whatever you need to say to escape the moment safely. When the teacher asks you a question, there's no time to try to understand what they're really saying or how it fits into some bigger picture. It's not the time to get clarification on some point that's confused you. And it's not the time to make an honest mistake and learn from it. It's about getting the right answer, fast, through whatever means necessary.

Kids develop amazing strategies for dealing with these situations. They mumble, in the hope that the teacher will hear what they want to hear. They hedge, covering all their bases so it's harder to accuse them of being wrong. They study the teacher's face and body language for a clue—quickly correcting themselves if the teacher gives any hint that their answer is wrong. This isn't about learning, this is about survival.

Yet schools seem almost perfectly designed to keep kids scared. Even if kids can survive the embarrassment of being wrong in front of their peers, there are other punishments and rewards to keep them focused on answers instead of understanding. Do poorly on a test or an assignment and you get criticized for your failure. It goes down in the record books and gets reported to your parents, who usually chew you out and punish you further. The tests are presented as a race against the clock—no time to think about the bigger picture!— and when those are done, there's more busywork and drudgery to complete.

And it doesn't even stop when the school day ends, as desperate as you are for that blissful moment. No, you get home only to find that you must do homework, the same old busywork all over again. You never get a moment to pause, to think for yourself. Your entire life is monitored—either by your parents at home or a teacher at school.

There's never time to stop and ask why. Asking why isn't your job. If you think the teacher has it wrong, tough luck. There's no court of appeal. You are wrong, even if you're right. How is anyone supposed to develop self-respect, let alone self-esteem, in that sort of situation?

How is one supposed to develop anything? We understand the world by making models, generalizing from the patterns we experience and testing those generalizations against the real world. We learn because something puzzles us—we want to understand what it is or how it works, and we set off on the trail of adventure to figure it out. But there's no time for this in school. We're supposed to sit in class, not explore the world. Indeed, we don't get to explore at all—the real world is kept carefully at bay.

Instead we're spoon-fed an endless stream of predigested facts: definitions, names, dates, places, equations—all disconnected from reality and from each other. Instead of learning about the world, we learn random facts and rules. But even those you're not allowed to care about. When the fifty minutes are up and the bell rings, you have to stop being interested in this and switch over to being interested in that. But curiosity cannot be ordered around via remote control, the channel changed at fifty-minute intervals. The only way to survive is by giving up on curiosity altogether, not caring about the subjects you're supposed to be learning, just letting it all become a blur.

And that's fine, because it *is* all a blur. A class in physics isn't much different from one in biology or grammar. All education becomes memorization. The only difference between the subjects is the kind of stuff you need to memorize—is it animal names or parts of speech? Instead of trying to understand something, you just try desperately to remember it—at least long enough to repeat it back on the test.

It's a wonder anyone learns anything.

Perhaps they don't. That was the thought that haunted Eric Mazur.

Now, all the signs said that Eric Mazur was a good teacher—a great one, in fact. He taught at Harvard—the most prestigious school in the country, if not the world. I've talked to plenty of Harvard professors and believe me, just that is enough to make most of them feel pretty good about themselves. But even at Harvard, he stood out.

Take the teacher evaluations the students had to fill out at the end of the course, "the dreaded end-of-semester questionnaire." Mazur taught introductory physics, and physics was not exactly a popular course with most students. "Most of my colleagues, when they taught this introductory pre-med class, would come close to suicide when they saw the results . . . because these pre-meds were not too kind to their physics instructors. But not so for me—I got 4.5, 4.7 on a 5-point scale."

Was Mazur getting good ratings by just making things too easy? For that he looked at the exams. "I could give these students questions that I considered quite complicated—questions that I wasn't even sure *I* could do flawlessly under the pressure of an exam. I mean, a stick is lying on a frictionless surface, a puck hits it, the two stick together and start to rotate, now calculate the angle and rotational position as function of time. No problem for most of these pre-meds."

There were some warning signs. "For example, some students would write, at the bottom of their end-of-semester evaluation, 'Physics is boring.' Even though they gave me [a] high rating, they would write that down. Or, 'Physics sucks.' I could never make any sense of it and, therefore, preferred to concentrate on the positive signs and ignore the negative ones.

"You know, my dentist once told me—and I couldn't even speak back because I had the thing in my mouth—'Oh, you're a physicist. I got an A for physics in college but I really didn't understand anything.' It always bothers me when I hear these things and I never know how to react. I never understood what the cause was."

Then, in 1990, after six years of teaching, he saw an odd little article in an old copy of the *American Journal of Physics*. Ibrahim Halloun and David Hestenes, two physicists at Arizona State, had given their students a physics exam, but a very strange one. Most physics exams ask fairly complicated questions requiring a bunch of math to solve, like the one with the stick and the puck. But instead of making their physics exam harder, Halloun and Hestenes decided to make it easier. It involved no jargon or advanced math; indeed, it didn't require any calculation at all. The questions were so simple and understandable you could even give the test to someone who had never taken physics.

For physics students, they should be trivial. They didn't require much more than understanding Newton's laws. "The first week we describe motion—velocity, acceleration, and so on. The second week you talk about Newtonian mechanics—Newton's three laws. And then . . . things start to build on top of that."

Now, we've probably all heard Newton's laws. Take number three: "For every action, there is an equal and opposite reaction." Even English majors are fond of quoting that. Now, maybe we don't know exactly what it means, but surely physics students should—especially those doing pretty advanced physics at Harvard.

Well, in their test, Halloun and Hestenes asked students a fairly simple question about Newton's third law. It's question number two—and it ended up being the hardest question on the test:

2. Imagine a head-on collision between a large truck and a small compact car. During the collision,

   (a) the truck exerts a greater amount of force on the car than the car exerts on the truck.

   (b) the car exerts a greater amount of force on the truck than the truck exerts on the car.

   (c) neither exerts a force on the other, the car gets smashed simply because it gets in the way of the truck.

   (d) the truck exerts a force on the car but the car doesn't exert a force on the truck.

   (e) the truck exerts the same amount of force on the car as the car exerts on the truck.

Now, by Newton's third law, the answer has to be (e). The reason the car gets smashed and the truck doesn't is because an equal force translates into much greater acceleration in the smaller, stationary car. But, of course, most people don't understand that. (You may not even understand it after my one-sentence explanation.) Like most people, 70–80% of physics students say (a).

This wouldn't be such a big problem, except that, for a physics student, this question is incredibly basic. "The whole rest of the semester—another nine weeks or so—builds on top of Newton's laws. In other words, if you don't understand Newton's laws, you can't really make much sense of anything else in the entire semester." And yet, in question after question like this, it became clear: the students didn't understand Newton's laws.

"When I read that, it didn't really register," Mazur said. "After all, this is high school stuff"—how could university students flunk it? Especially Harvard University students, most of whom had aced AP Physics.

Knowing that most people wouldn't believe them, Halloun and Hestenes had repeated the study in all sorts of schools with all sorts of teachers. They tested a physicist who emphasized basic concepts, one who used lots of exciting lecture demonstrations (and won multiple awards), one who teaches problem solving by example, and a new teacher who was unsure of himself and just read straight from the textbook. They couldn't detect any difference—not even between the award-winning teacher and one who read from the textbook. Measured by a simple test like this, all were equally bad. It didn't make a difference what the teachers did; the students still didn't learn anything.

"Well, I felt challenged," Mazur recalls. "My reaction, you can probably already predict this: 'Not *my* students!' After all, I was at Harvard—maybe this was some problem that was in the Southwest of the United States, right? . . . I wanted to show that my students could ace this test. . . . At that time we were dealing with rotational dynamics, and the students had to calculate triple integrals of complicated bodies with different moments of inertia. You know, we were so *way* beyond Newtonian mechanics there was no comparison between [this test] and what we were actually doing in class.

"But I was so desperate to get this data, I walked into class and told my students I was going to give them this quiz. I called it a quiz because I didn't want to scare them—you know how pre-meds are. . . . But I had to give them some incentive to take this test seriously, so I told them, 'Look, if you take this test seriously, you can use your score to help you study for the upcoming midterm examination.' Now, I told you, the midterm examination dealt with far more complicated materials, and I realized as soon as I said that, it was actually a huge lie. And I was worried that as soon as I said that my students would be offended by the simplicity of this test as soon as they started on it.

"Oh, boy, were my worries quickly dispelled. Hardly had the first group of students taken their seats in the classroom when one student raised her hand and she said, 'Professor Mazur, how should I answer these questions? According to what you taught me, or according to the way I usually think about these things?'" How was he supposed to answer that?

Sure enough, the results came back and Mazur's class wasn't very different from any of the others. "When I saw how poorly my students had done, my first reaction was 'Well, maybe you're not such a great teacher after all.' But that could obviously not be true, right? So I didn't think about that too long. Well, what's another reason the score could be low? Dumb students. But that's pretty hard to say at [Harvard]; we have a very selective group of students. So I thought about it a little bit more and then, my mind, my twisted mind came up with the perfect excuse: . . . the test! There had to be something wrong with the test!

"Take this question about the heavy truck and the light car, right? You don't need to have taken physics to know you're much better off in the heavy truck than the light car. So maybe students were confusing damage or acceleration with force—maybe it's just a matter of semantics!

"So I decided to do some testing of my own. I decided to pair, on an exam, two questions of different types on the same subject. One was a typical question out of the textbook, on which I knew students would do well, and another was a word-based question a little bit like the one with the heavy truck and the light car. And I decided to stay away from Newtonian mechanics, because we all have some intuitive notions of Newtonian mechanics before taking physics. I decided to do some testing in DC circuits, direct current circuits. I think very few people have any intuitive notions about circuits."

All right, so here's the standard question (don't worry if you don't understand it):

> 5. For the circuit shown, calculate (a) the current in the 2-resistor and (b) the potential difference between points P and Q.

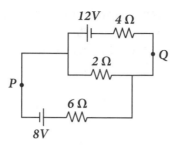

To you, this question may seem impenetrable. But for the physics students, this was the standard sort of problem they were used to answering. "This is straight out of the textbook. It's not a particularly hard problem, it's about 2/3 of a page of cranking numbers—but it's not a completely trivial question either."

Now, for comparison, here's the conceptual question:

1. A series circuit consists of three identical lightbulbs connected to a battery as shown here. When the switch

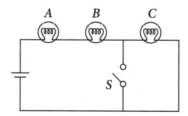

S is closed, do the following increase, decrease, or stay the same?

(a) The intensities of bulbs A and B

(b) The intensity of bulb C

(c) The current drawn from the battery

(d) The voltage drop across each bulb

(e) The power dissipated in the circuit

This question does not involve any numbers at all. "If you understand DC circuits, it takes 30 seconds to answer this question. And 25 of those 30 are spent on part I.

"Now at Harvard, large courses are taught by two faculty members. So in order to put this on the exam, I had to convince my colleague that this was a good exam problem. So I showed him the problem and after reading it he looked at me and said, 'Eric, you're out of your mind.' . . . He said, 'Eric, we only have 5 problems on this exam. We cannot give away 20% of the exam!' . . . We argued and argued . . . finally, he reluctantly agreed, mostly because we didn't have any other problem. And we made it problem number one—the warm-up problem.

"Well, it turns out the students overheated. 'Professor Mazur, this problem number one is the hardest problem on the exam!' Another student said, 'I didn't know how to get started on this problem.' What do you mean, getting started? I mean, if you're started you're done! . . . Students had freaked out. Some had taken up more than six pages in their blue books, writing down absolutely everything they knew about DC circuits in hopes of somehow covering the right answer somewhere. And I had to read through all of it, hunting for the right answer!"

A few words about this physics problem. The basic question is pretty simple: when you close the switch, the current now has two ways to form a circuit instead of just one. It can take its old path, all the way around (including through lightbulb C), or it can just go through the switch.

Now, one of the most basic things about circuits is that the current takes the shortest path it can. (Current is lazy, you might say.) If you close the switch, the current travels through that path (the short) and lightbulb C turns off. This is why things go off when they short-circuit. But that's not what the Harvard students thought. Most students figured that when the current had two ways it could go, it split half and half and took both. Thus, in their view, lightbulbs A and B stayed the same, while C decreased to half brightness.

You can't say this is simply a semantic argument—anyone with a little basic circuit equipment lying around can wire this up and see what happens. (But don't; short-circuiting things is a little dangerous.) Either lightbulb C goes out or it doesn't—and one would think that a student who aced circuits at Harvard would know which. But they didn't. When he looked at the results, Mazur was shocked to see that there were students who aced the traditional question but flunked the conceptual one. Even more shocking, there were no students who did the reverse—there was nobody who answered these basic questions perfectly and then went on to fail the harder parts of the test. No one.

But this is just the tip of the iceberg, even in physics. In one experiment, Andrea DiSessa had kids play a computer game that simulated basic Newtonian physics. The goal was to kick a simulated ball into a goal. Psychologist Howard Gardner describes one typical subject:

> Consider what happened to an MIT student named Jane, who was studied intensively by DiSessa. Jane knew all the formalisms taught in freshman physics. She could trot out the equation $F = ma$ under appropriate textbook circumstances, she could faithfully recite Newton's laws of motion, and she could employ the principles of vector summation when asked to do so in problem sets. Yet as soon as she began the game, she adopted the same practices as the naive elementary school students, assuming that the turtle would travel in the direction of the kick. For half an hour she stuck to this inappropriate strategy. Only when she was convinced that this strategy would not work did she make the crucial observation that an object will not lose its prekick motion just because she applies a kick in a certain direction. This realization finally led to experimentation in which the velocity (or speed in a particular direction) of the dynaturtle was at last taken into account.

As the experimenter noted:

> We have already discussed the remarkable similarity of [Jane's] cluster of strategies to those exhibited by 11- and

12-year-old children. But what is equally remarkable is
the fact that she did not, indeed for a time could not, re-
late the task to all the classroom physics she had had. It
was not that she could not make the classroom analyses;
her vector addition was, by itself, faultless. It is more that
her naive physics and classroom physics stood unrelated
and in this instance, she exercised her naive physics.

But, as a battery of studies have shown, Jane's errors are fairly typical of college physics students. When asked what happens to a ball
shot out of a curved tube, students predict it will keep curving in
the same way, as if the ball somehow absorbs the curve. When asked
about the forces acting on a coin tossed into the air, 90% of engineering students say there are two: the upward force of the hand and
the downward force of gravity (in reality, there is just gravity once
the coin has left the hand). Students who have studied relativity ignore what they've learned when asked about the behavior of distant
clocks.

I could go on, but let's move to biology. Even students who have
studied biology for years continue to think that characteristics an
animal acquires in one generation can be passed down to its children (like the giraffe who stretches its neck further to reach more
distant food). They assume that all changes in animals are a result of
some change in the environment and they believe that evolution has
a particular direction rather than stumbling around randomly. They
believe that animals behave intentionally: parasites are trying to destroy their hosts, chameleons intentionally change colors to disguise
themselves. They think that plants suck up soil through their roots
and that their genetic traits are distributed in precise ratios, exactly
three to one.

You might hope that things are better in math, where there are
fewer everyday misconceptions. But even basic algebra turns out to
be a problem. When told to write an equation representing that there
are six students for every professor, most college students write: 6s =
p. But this is exactly backwards: it says the number of professors (p)
is six times the number of students (s). And this isn't simple careless-

ness; even when students are warned about this problem, they keep on making it.

This is just one example of a larger problem—students don't really seem to know what the symbols *mean*, they just know some basic operations that can be performed on them. When given a problem they're not sure how to solve, students simply start adding all numbers in sight. Asked to add two fractions, they just add the numbers on the top together and then add the numbers on the bottom. And their understanding of decimals isn't much better: they refuse to believe that .6 is bigger than .5999 yet somehow less than .6000001.

Students in computer science have an almost opposite confusion: they don't seem to understand that the computer is simply rigidly following rules and instead expect it to understand what they've written, like any human reader would. Thus, for example, they are puzzled as to why the computer doesn't simply put the largest number in the variable LARGEST, since that's so obviously what they intended.

College students who have studied economics seem to approach economic issues very similarly to those who have not. Both made claims like "The more they sell, the lower the price should be, because you can still keep the profit the same"—a statement wildly at odds with the role of profit in economic theory. College in general seems to make little dent in this kind of basic reasoning. One study found that students took pretty much the same approach to reasoning social and political issues before they went to college as they did after.

Turning to the softer subjects, a famous experiment by I. A. Richards found that when asked to summarize poems, even literary undergraduates turned out to wildly misunderstand them. Not only did they not grasp the poetic implications, they seemed incapable of following its basic meaning. As Richards wrote, "They fail to make out its sense, its plain, overt meaning, as a set of ordinary intelligible English sentences, taken quite apart from any poetic significance."

Furthermore, when asked to rate poems from which the author's name had been removed, they gave low ratings to most famous poets and instead preferred a terrible unpublished poem by an unknown poet. Why? Instead of looking at the meaning, they simply gave high ratings to poems that were positive, rhymed well, and used a sensible vocabulary.

In every case, we see the same phenomenon at work: children may be able to memorize enough formulas and facts to pass the test, but they literally have no idea what they're talking about. When asked the question in a slightly different way or with a practical application, the appearance of understanding simply collapses.

Schools do *something*. We all know that getting a degree increases your wages, even if there hadn't been "literally thousands of published estimates" of this effect.[*] But what exactly is it that schools do?

The standard theory, of course, is that schools teach. We go there, we learn things, and they make us better at our jobs, which causes employers to pay us more. But evidence for this theory turns out to be rather hard to find.

Economist Joseph Altonji tried to calculate the benefits of education by looking at the benefits of each individual high school class. He compared the wages of people who took a class with those who didn't take it to try to calculate how much more the average student made by taking that class. From that, he could work backwards to try to determine how much money a student would have lost had they taken no classes at all. The result was shocking: taking no classes has no statistically significant effect on wages; indeed, it might even increase them!

A similar study by different researchers done with different data in a completely different way came to basically the same result: students who took no classes while in school would make around $0.12 an hour *more*.

The same problems persist when we look at how well a student does in a class. "There is a long history of researchers failing to find an economically significant relationship between scores on achievement tests and wages," notes economist Andrew Weiss. Success on standard school tests of vocabulary, reading ability, math skills, and

---

*Weiss, www.jstor.org/stable/2138394.

so on have no noticeable effect on wages. Nor does getting good grades seem to be an indicator of success in the workplace. "Most students realize few benefits from studying hard while in school," complains economist John Bishop. "Performance in high school as assessed by student grades explains almost nothing about job success . . . higher grades [do] not improve the probability of getting either a job or competitive wages once one has a job."[*]

A final piece of evidence is the GED. If schools were simply about educating people, students with a GED would fare little differently from students who had graduated high school. Indeed, students with a GED are, on average, *more* educated than high school graduates—after all, most kids don't have to pass a high school achievement test to pass high school. But all this education doesn't buy them much in the labor market—students with a GED fare little differently than other high school *dropouts*.

I should note that the researchers are not happy with these results. John Bishop, for example, considers them an outrage. But despite their best efforts, they cannot make the facts go away.

So what is it schools are really doing if not educating the next generation? Well, just look at what's left over: schools are places where kids must show up every day at 8 a.m. for years on end, sit at uncomfortable desks under fluorescent lighting with a group of relative strangers, and obey arbitrary instructions from their superiors about the appropriate way to carry out repetitive intellectual assignments. Even a casual glance at a modern office will show you that these are skills very much in demand.

Ask employers what they want from their employees, and they don't say academic brilliance. Indeed, in the 1970s employers were complaining that their workers were *too* educated, causing "unrealistic job expectations." The resulting "poor worker attitudes" led to "productivity and quality problems and (in some cases) to outright sabotage."[†] Instead, employers ask for "character": "a sense of responsibility, self-discipline, pride, teamwork, and enthusiasm." In other words, employers want people they can rely on to do their

---

[*]http://digitalcommons.ilr.cornell.edu/cahrswp/400/.

[†]Capelli, 5.

work with pride and enthusiasm—and certainly not people who would engage in misbehavior and sabotage.

Looking at new hires who don't "make the cut" and get fired in their first few weeks, one can see where the problem really lies. Despite all the talk about how we need better schools to compete in a global economy, a survey of employers found that only 9% of workers were dismissed because they couldn't learn to do their jobs.

And looking at workers who are liked by their bosses finds they have basically the same traits as those students who are liked by their teachers: "consistent attender," "dependable," "identifies with job/school," a willingness to quit, and "prosocial attitudes"—I.e., a willingness to do more for the boss.*

In short, schools don't really teach kids anything because they're not about really teaching kids anything. They're about teaching kids to stay quiet, do their work, and show up on time.

This isn't an accident. This was the plan all along.

It's difficult to even imagine what America was like before the industrial revolution. Their notion of freedom was far stronger than the one we have today. For many Americans, life wasn't about showing up at a job at a specified hour, following orders all day, and returning home for a couple hours of "free time"—that would be considered slavery. A free American was one who worked on their own or with their family, worked from home, worked whatever hours they liked, and got paid based on what they accomplished.

Under the putting-out system, for example, merchants would deliver raw materials like cotton to your house. When you felt like it, you'd card, spin, and weave the raw cotton into cloth. And then the next week the merchant would come by to buy from you whatever cloth you had produced. If you wanted to make more money, you simply did more work or figured out how to work more efficiently. If you wanted to take a vacation, there was no one stopping you—you just wouldn't get paid that week.

It was far from a perfect life. It could be difficult to make ends meet and there was no protection from falling prices or market

---

*Edwards 1977.

downturns. But you were *free*. You worked as your own boss, followed your own rules. And that was not something Americans were
inclined to give up lightly.

At first the mills promised freedom too. For the daughters of these
families, they provided a chance to break away from the rule of their
fathers and strike out to work on their own—for their own wages,
in their own lives. Instead of working under the thumb of their parents, New England girls went out to mill towns—whole new cities
created along the river to staff the mills, the first real factories in the
country. Instead of women spinning cotton into cloth at home, girls
operated vast machines powered by water turbines to do the work
in the city.

And these *were* girls. Harriet Robinson went to work in the mills
of Lowell, Massachusetts, at the age of ten. "I worked first in the
spinning-room as a 'doffer,'" she recalled. "The doffers were the very
youngest girls, whose work was to doff, or take off, the full bobbins,
and replace them with the empty ones. I can see myself now, racing
down the alley, between the spinning-frames, carrying in front of
me a bobbin-box bigger than I was."[*]

> The law took no cognizance of woman as a money-
> spender. She was a ward, an appendage, a relict. . . .
> I can see them now, even after sixty years, just as they
> looked,—depressed, modest, mincing, hardly daring to
> look one in the face, so shy and sylvan had been their
> lives. But after the first pay-day came, and they felt the
> jingle of silver in their pockets, and had begun to feel
> its mercurial influence, their bowed heads were lifted,
> their necks seemed braced with steel, they looked you in
> the face, sang blithely among their looms or frames, and
> walked with elastic step to and from their work.[†]

---

[*]*Fibre & Fabric: A Record of American Textile Industries in the Cotton and Woolen Trade*,
1898, Volume 28, 170.

[†]Harriet Robinson, *Loom and Spindle*, Applewood Books, 68–70.

From a condition approaching pauperism they were at once placed above want; they could earn money, and spend it as they pleased; and could gratify their tastes and desires without restraint, and without rendering an account to anybody. At last they had found a place in the universe; they were no longer obligated to finish out their faded lives mere burden to male relatives. Even the *time* of these women was their own, on Sundays and in the evening after the day's work was done. For the first time in this country woman's labor had a money value.[*]

But while the ability to earn one's own keep was liberating, the conditions under which it was possible were not. Long before the advent of the eight-hour day, these girls worked fourteen hours, from five in the morning until seven at night—with only a half hour off for breakfast and dinner. They lived in cramped quarters with the other girls, two to a bed, four to a room, hardly any space or privacy.

Their bosses, by contrast, "lived in large houses, not too near the boarding-houses, surrounded by beautiful gardens which seemed like Paradise to some of the home-sick girls, who, as they came from their work in the noisy mill, could look with longing eyes into the sometimes open gate in the high fence, and be reminded afresh of their pleasant country homes."

The work was dull, but it allowed plenty of time to think, and despite their lack of formal education, these girls did plenty of it. And after work they read assiduously, passing books from hand to hand. And they eagerly attended the talks of visiting lecturers. "I used every winter to lecture for the Lowell Lyceum," recalled a Harvard professor. "Not amusement, but instruction, was then the lecturer's aim. . . . The Lowell Hall was always crowded, and four-fifths of the audience were factory-girls. When the lecturer entered, almost every girl had a book in her hand, and was intent upon it. When he rose, the book was laid aside, and paper and pencil taken instead; and there were very few who did not carry home full notes

---

[*]Ibid., 69.

of what they had heard. I have never seen anywhere so assiduous note-taking. No, not even in a college class."[*]

And through all that thinking and learning and discussing, they began to question the less pleasant aspects of their situation. When, in 1836, the Lowell mill owners decided to cut their employees' pay, the girls walked out. "My own recollection of this first strike (or 'turn out' as it was called) is very vivid," recalls Harriet Robinson.

> I worked in a lower room, where I had heard the proposed strike fully, if not vehemently, discussed; I had been an ardent listener to what was said against this attempt at "oppression" on the part of the corporation, and naturally I took sides with the strikers. When the day came on which the girls were to turn out, those in the upper rooms started first, and so many of them left that our mill was at once shut down. Then, when the girls in my room stood irresolute, uncertain what to do, asking each other, "Would you?" or "Shall we turn out?" and not one of them having the courage to lead off, I, who began to think they would not go out, after all their talk, became impatient and started on ahead, saying, with childish bravado, "I don't care what you do, I am going to turn out, whether anyone else does or not"; and I marched out, and was followed by the others.
>
> As I looked back at the long line that followed me, I was more proud than I have ever been since at any success I may have achieved.[†]

She was eleven years old.

What these young girls accomplished is truly amazing. They organized their own newspaper, the *Voice of Industry*, which they wrote, edited, printed, and sold themselves. Through it they organized more protests and strikes, as well as organized their own slate of candidates in the state elections to fight for better working condi-

---

[*]A.P. Peabody, "The Lowell Offering," *Atlantic Monthly*, April 1891.

[†]Robinson, *Loom and Spindle*, 84.

tions and a ten-hour day. Amazingly, their slate won. The owners, outraged, got their legislators to declare the election results invalid and hold a revote. Before the revote, large signs were posted threatening that anyone who voted for the ten-hour slate would be fired. And yet the slate won again.

Once seated, the legislators were able to pass a ten-hour bill through the state House, but as usually happens with progressive legislation, it was killed in the state Senate.

But their writing in the *Voice* shows that they wanted much more than simply better working conditions. They saw themselves as slaves—wage slaves—and concluded that the solution was not simply to demand that the bosses be nicer to them or pay them more, but to abolish the bosses entirely.

> The laborer does not yet know what terrible odds he contends with. Concentrated skill in the form of machinery and accumulated labor in the shape of capital, both directed by superior intelligence, are arrayed against him. These powerful forces, which should be on his side, should be his servants, his tools, are crushing them. . . . In the true order of things, wherever is the most wealth would be the least poverty; but now it is otherwise; the more glittering the splendor of capital; the more squalor, wretchedness, degradation obtrude near it.*

The solution was clear:

> Instead of quibbling, temporizing, and compromising with capitalists, we want to see the working classes getting daily into a position of independence through a system of cooperation and *mutual guarantees*. When they can obtain the means of *living* independent of capitalists, then and not till then, will "strikes" and "turn outs" mean something. They must consolidate and combine so as to become their own employers and do their trading

---

The Voice of Industry, April 14, 1848.

without the interference of the go-betweens and jobbers. Let them unite in themselves both the functions of laborer and capitalist. So long as we are dependent on cotton mills for employment, so long we shall be oppressed. They who work in the mills ought to own them.[*]

One is almost tempted to call this Marxist, but it was many years before Marx. "They who work in the mills ought to own them." It was just plain common sense.

The mill owners were not happy about such agitation. They fired these troublemaking (sabotaging?) workers and added their names to the blacklist shared with all the other mills. They sought out more compliant replacements. And they used their control over housing and stores to try to force their workers back to work.

But their most striking plan was also their most far-reaching: they sent the girls to school. Lowell, the home of America's industrial revolution, the home of the girls who fought back against it and concluded that "they who work in the mills ought to own them," was also the home of America's first schools.

The schools they built—the common schools—would be easily recognizable by any modern student. "The door [of each school] shall be closed precisely at the time fixed for the opening of the school, and in the morning religious exercises will be performed, for which purpose 10 minutes are allowed." (Today we just say the pledge of allegiance.) "Each teacher shall call the roll call of his or her classes . . . in the morning and afternoon, and shall keep an accurate record of all absences." The day was then divided into separate lessons, allowing "30 minutes for the study of each lesson and 10 minutes for each recitation."[†]

Instead of corporal punishment, teachers were encouraged to secure order "by the mildest possible means" to instill "a regard for right, and thus a standard of self-government in the minds of the

---

[*]*The Voice of Industry,* March 10, 1848.

[†]Reference unknown.

children themselves."* Students were tested on how much they learned and, just like today, working coordinating other students was considered "cheating" and punished. (Perhaps they were worried that if students learned to coordinate they might be more likely to foment strikes once in the mills.)

In 1855, the Lowell School Committee noted that they had some trouble with one misguided parent who believed the schools "to be a republic, where the subject may call into question the power of the ruler; whereas a school government is and must be an absolute monarchy . . . where no subject can or ought to question an order or law of the supreme head."† So much for training kids for democracy!

The curriculum was also much like that of modern schools,

> adding grammar, geography, history and physiology to the basic program of reading, writing and arithmetic. But what is striking about this extension of the curriculum is the intrinsic uselessness of the material treated . . . [these classes] were totally given over to the memorization of minute and generally trivial facts. Candidates for high school entrance in 1850, for example, were expected to know the names of the capital of Abussinia, of two lakes in the Sudan, of the river that "runs through the country of the Hottentots," and of the desert lying between the Nile and the Red Sea, as well as to locate Bombetok Bay, the Gulf of Sidra, and the Lupata Mountains. [Other subjects had] a similar approach, with all the questions given over to very specific and in most cases minute pieces of information completely unrelated to the present or future lives of the pupils being taught.

And indeed, such studies did not improve a student's performance

---

*Reference unknown.

†David Isaac Bruck, "The Schools of Lowell, 1824–1861: A Case Study in the Origins of Modern Public Education in America," honors thesis, Harvard University, 1971. http://id.lib.harvard.edu/aleph/003824609/catalog.

in the mills. Careful records kept by the mill owners allow us to compare mill workers who did and did not go to school. Just as with modern students, there is no evidence of any impact of increased education on worker productivity.*

So why did the mill owners spend so much money building and running these schools? They were quite clear about their intent. The classes were justified not for their usefulness but because memorizing them was a form of "moral education" leading to "industrious habits . . . and the consequent high moral influence which it exerts upon society at large."

As one Lowell manager explained it, "I have never considered mere knowledge, valuable as it is in itself to the laborer, as the only advantage derived from a good common-school education. I have uniformly found the better educated, as a class, possessing a higher and better state of morals, more orderly and respectful in their deportment, and more ready to comply with the wholesome and necessary regulations of an establishment."

Not only were those who went through school better at following rules, but they were less likely to stir up trouble: "In times of agitation I have always looked to the most intelligent, best educated, and the most moral for support and have seldom been disappointed. . . . But the ignorant and uneducated I have generally found the most troublesome, acting under the impulses of excited passion and jealousy."

In other words, "that class of help which has enjoyed a good common-school education are the most tractable, yielding most readily to reasonable requirements, exerting a salutary and conservative influence in times of excitement, while the most ignorant are the most refractory."† In short, "the owners of manufacturing property have a deep *pecuniary* interest in the education and morals of their help."

Another Lowell manager: "I have observed that when the demagogues have found it for their interest to persuade the *dear* people

---

*Luft.

†Letter from H. Bartlett, Esq. to Horace Mann, Lowell, Dec. 1, 1841, in Horace Mann, ed., *Common School Journal*, 1842, 366.

that are employed in the mills that their employers are exacting, over-reaching and oppressive, the minds and morals of the ignorant are usually more readily poisoned."

As the Lowell School Committee summarized their findings: "The proprietors find the training of the schools admirably adapted to prepare the children for the labors of the mills." Why? "When [their laborers] are well educated . . . controversies and *strikes* can never occur, nor can the minds of the masses be prejudiced by demagogues and controlled by temporary and factitious considerations."[*]

Students, they noted, "have to receive their first lessons of subordination and obedience in the school room. At home, they are either left wholly to their own control, or, what is almost equally bad, the discipline to which they are subjected alternates between foolish indulgence, and exasperated tyranny."[†]

Indeed, school was so important that the mill owners quickly decided to make it mandatory. "No language of ours can convey too strongly our sense of the dangers which wait us from [those who] are not and have never been members of our public schools," warned the Lowell School Committee. Universal schooling is "our surest safety against internal commotions."[‡]

The children who didn't attend school "constitute an army more to be feared than war, pestilence and famine," warned the committee. "Unsuccessful attempts, during the past year, to burn two of our school-houses . . . are an index to the evils which threaten from such sources."[§]

More accurately, such burnings were an index of public resistance to such coercion. In 1837, 300 teachers were forced to flee their classrooms by riotous and violent students.[||] In 1844, the Irish population went on strike from the schools, reducing attendance by 80%.

---

[*]Massachusetts Board of Education, *Annual Report of the Board of Education*, Vol. 23, 1860, p. 56.

[†]Lowell Mass. School Committee, *Annual Report*, 1847, Vol. 21, p. 56.

[‡]Samuel Bowles, *Schooling in Capitalist America: Educational Reform and the Contradictions of Economic Life*, Haymarket, 1976, p. 160.

[§]Ibid.

[||]David K. Cohen and Barbara Neufeld, "The Failure of High Schools and the Progress of Education," *Daedalus* I 10 (Summer 1981): 87, n. 2.

The School Committee stepped up their anti-truancy efforts to force them and others back to school.

And just as the factory model spread out from Lowell, so did the model of mandatory schooling. An analysis of census data by Alexander Field found that what led to a town getting a school was not its growth into a city nor a rise in incomes nor the introduction of expensive machinery, but instead the introduction of the factory system itself. As factories marched across the country, public schools followed.

And their justification didn't change either. As historian Merle Curti notes, "Hardly an annual meeting of the National Education Association was concluded without an appeal on the part of leading educators for the help of the teacher in quelling strikes and checking the spread of socialism and anarchism. Commissioners of education and editors of educational periodicals summoned their forces to the same end." Commissioner of education John Eaton argued that businessmen must "weigh the cost of the mob and tramp against the expense of universal and sufficient education," while NEA president James H. Smart declared that schools did more "to suppress the latent flame of communism than all other agencies combined."

"Again and again," Curti writes, "educators denounced radical doctrines and offered education as the best preventive and cure." The titans of industry agreed—business leaders like Henry Frick, John D. Rockefeller, Andrew Carnegie, and Pierre S. du Pont eagerly supported the spread of education programs. As social reformer Jane Addams put it, "The business man has, of course, not said to himself: 'I will have the public school train office boys and clerks for me, so that I may have them cheap,' but he has thought, and sometimes said, 'Teach the children to write legibly, and to figure accurately and quickly; to acquire habits of punctuality and order; to be prompt to obey, and not question why; and you will fit them to make their way in the world as I have made mine!'"*

*   *   *

---

*Merle Curti, *The Social Ideas of American Educators*, Totowa, NJ: Littlefield, Adams, 1959. An excerpt (pp. 218–220, 228, 230, 203).

And this has been their attitude ever since. Despite all the talk about educators and education priorities, the most important people in any school have always been businessmen. They constantly complain that our schools our failing, that they need to cut out modern fads and go "back to basics," that unless schools get tougher on students American business will be unable to compete.

As Richard Rothstein has shown, such claims are hardly new. Because schools have never been about actual education, businessmen have been easily collecting studies about their failure at this task since the very beginning. In 1845, only 45% of Boston's brightest students knew that water expands when it freezes. In one school, 75% knew the U.S. had imposed an embargo on British and French goods during the War of 1812, but only 5% knew what *embargo* meant. Students, the secretary of education wrote, were simply memorizing the "words of the textbook . . . without having . . . to think about the meaning of what they have learned."

In 1898, a writing exam at Berkeley found that 30 to 40% of entering freshman were not proficient in English. A Harvard report found only 4% of applicants "could write an essay, spell, or properly punctuate a sentence." But that didn't stop editorialists from complaining about how things were better in the old days. Back when they went to school, complained the editors of the *New York Sun* in 1902, children "had to do a little work . . . Spelling, writing and arithmetic were not electives, and you had to learn." Now schooling was just "a vaudeville show. The child must be kept amused and learns what he pleases." In 1909, the *Atlantic Monthly* complained that basic skills had been replaced by "every fad and fancy."

That same year, the dean of Stanford's school of education warned that in a global economy, "whether we like it or not, we are beginning to see that we are pitted against the world in a gigantic battle of brains and skill." Because of their failing schools, of course, Americans were coming up short.

In 1913, Woodrow Wilson appointed a presidential commission to study how to improve our international educational competitiveness. They found that more than half of new recruits to the Army during World War I "were not able to write a simple letter or read a newspaper with ease." In 1927, the National Association of Manufacturers complained that 40 percent of high school graduates could not perform simple arithmetic or accurately express themselves in English.

A 1938 study complained that newfangled teaching methods were forcing out basic instruction in phonics: "Teachers . . . conspire against pupils in their efforts to learn; these teachers appear to be determinedly on guard never to mention a letter by name . . . or to show how to use either letter forms or sounds in reading." A 1940 survey of business executives "found that by large margins they believed recent graduates were inferior to the previous generation in arithmetic, written English, spelling, geography, and world affairs."

A 1943 test by the *New York Times* found that only 29% of college freshmen knew that St. Louis was on the Mississippi, only 6% knew the original thirteen states of the Union, and some students even thought Lincoln was the first president. It was, the *Times* declared, a "striking ignorance of even the most elementary aspects of United States history."

In 1947, the *Times*'s education editor published a book titled *Our Children Are Cheated*. In it, businessmen lamented the poor state of American schools. One complained he had to "organize special classes to instruct [his new hires] in . . . making change . . . Only a small proportion [can] place Boston, New York . . . Chicago . . . Denver . . . in their proper sequence from east to west, or name the states in which they [are located]."

A 1951 test in L.A. found that more than half of eighth graders couldn't calculate 8% sales tax on an $8 purchase. The newspapers complained that students couldn't even tell time. In 1952, the journal *Progressive Education* complained about the "attacks on textbooks that encourage inquisitive thinking and individual reasoning, . . . mounting pressure to eliminate the 'frills and fads'—by which are meant such vital services as nurseries, classes for the handicapped, testing and guidance, programs to help youngsters understand and appreciate their neighbors of different backgrounds," what today would be called multiculturalism.

In 1958, *U.S. News and World Report* lamented that "fifty years ago a high-school diploma meant something. . . . We have simply misled our students and misled the nation by handing out high-school diplomas to those who we well know had none of the intellectual qualifications that a high-school diploma is supposed to represent—and does represent in other countries. It is this dilution of standards which has put us in our present serious plight."

A 1962 Gallup poll found "just 21 percent looked at books even casually." In 1974, *Reader's Digest* asked, "Are we becoming a nation of illiterates? [There is an] evident sag in both writing and reading . . . at a time when the complexity of our institutions calls for ever-higher literacy just to function effectively. . . . [T]here is indisputable evidence that millions of presumably educated Americans can neither read nor write at satisfactory levels."*

In 1983, Reagan's National Commission on Excellence in Education declared that our failing schools made us "a nation at risk." "If an unfriendly foreign power had attempted to impose on America the mediocre educational performance that exists today, we might well have viewed it as an act of war," it declared. In 1988, the chairman of Xerox warned that "public education has put this country at a terrible competitive disadvantage. . . . If current . . . trends continue, American business will have to hire a million new workers a year who can't read, write or count."

In 1993, the government was singing the same tune. "The vast majority of Americans do not know that they do not have the skills to earn a living in our increasingly technological society and international marketplace," lamented education secretary Richard Riley. In 1995, the chairman of IBM told state governors that our schools needed higher standards for "an era that demands improvements in skills if Americans are to succeed in the world marketplace."

Similar complaints continue right to the present day. They are always followed by calls for "education reform" and "higher standards," which in practice always translates into the same old "drill and skill" of old. And, of course, that's exactly the point.

I can hear the objections now. "That's a conspiracy theory!" they cry.

As a simple factual matter, that's badly mistaken. A conspiracy

---

*Vince Packard quoted in Richard Rothstein, *The Way We Were? The Myths and Realities of America's Student Achievement*, The Century Foundation, 1998.

theory is the notion that a small group of people have, in secret, managed to subvert the way things normally work. What I'm talking about is exactly the opposite: it's a large group of people, working in public, making sure things keep going the way they normally keep going.

So why does it seem so much like a conspiracy? I think it's because, in both instances, you're saying things don't work the way people have always believed they worked. From a young age, we're told that the society we live in may have its share of problems, but it's fundamentally sensible. Schools exist to give people an education, companies exist to make things people want, elections exist to give people a voice in how the system is run, newspapers exist to tell us what's going on. That's just how the world works.

Now, it's reasonable to believe that all of these things have flaws—that schools, for example, could do a better job of teaching students. After all, things can always be improved, sometimes quite a lot. But when you go further and say that schools are not only bad at teaching people, but that they're not about teaching people at all—well, that's when things get scary.

Because if schools aren't about teaching people, that means everything we've been told about them is a lie. And if everybody is lying to us, then, well, that does start to sound like a conspiracy theory.

But look back over our history—there's no conspiracy. A group of bold entrepreneurs find they can make cloth more efficiently by building large mills. The girls who staff them keep causing strikes and other trouble, so they require their employees go to school from a young age and learn to behave themselves.

But obviously most people won't be thrilled to go to school so that they can learn to accept lower wages without complaint. So the bosses develop a cover story: schools are about teaching people the things they need to know to survive in the world of business. It's not true, of course—there's no connection between the facts memorized in school and the skills needed on the job—but the story is convincing enough.

And so the spread of schools and factories destroys the American model of freedom. Instead of being independent farmers or self-employed manufacturers, Americans are herded into factories en masse, forced to work for someone else because they cannot earn a living any other way. But thanks to schools, this seems normal, even natural. After all, isn't that just the way the world works?

Today, it seems like everyone agrees that what we need are more rigorous schools. George W. Bush joined with Ted Kennedy to pass No Child Left Behind, which punished school districts (i.e., took away their funding) if they didn't get high enough test scores. (How failing schools were supposed to improve by having *less* money was never really explained.) Barack Obama, of course, would never support such a cruel plan. Instead, his Race to the Top program will, like Skinner, catch schools doing something right—and reward them with extra funding.

But what is being tested is never a student's "prosocial attitudes" or "consistent attendance"—instead it's how well they memorized facts and figures. Why the disconnect? Perhaps because flunking students for not being good enough quitters wouldn't play well with parents. As Peter Cappelli, director of the U.S. government's National Center on the Educational Quality of the Workforce, put it, most people are "disturb[ed]" by the suggestion "that the values, norms, and behaviors being inculcated into students through the schools appear to be in conflict with the values associated with personal growth and development."

The solution has been to fight the battle through other names. No Child Left Behind was supposed to have the effect of forcing schools to do a better job educating their students. Who could argue with that? But examining its effects on the ground finds it did something rather different. Students, of course, were not tested on how well they actually understood basic concepts but simply on how well they could answer the standard multiple-choice tests. And with so much at stake, schools converted even further from teaching kids ideas to teaching them how to perform well on tests.

Linda Perlstein spent a year at one school struggling to survive No Child Left Behind. Everything that wasn't tested had to get cut—not just art and gym, but recess, science, and social studies (yep, no science on the tests). What remains is converted entirely over to test prep—the only writing students ever do is short-answer sections

("What text feature could have been added to help a reader better understand the information?") and the stories in class are analyzed only in terms of what questions might be asked about them.

Large sections of the class have nothing to do with learning at all. Students are instead drilled on test-taking procedure: take deep breaths, work until time is called, eliminate obviously wrong answers. Every day students are taught special vocab words that will earn them extra points and reminded about how to properly phrase their answers to get the maximum score. Instead of covering the walls with students' art, they're covered with test-taking advice ("BATS: Borrow from the question, Answer the question, use Text supports, Stretch the formula").

The single-minded goal of maximizing test scores has been a blessing for the textbook market, which forces schools to buy expensive "evidence-based curricula" which have been "proven" to maximize test scores. The packages include not only textbooks and workbooks but also scripts for the teachers to read verbatim—deviating from them hasn't been proven to raise test scores, and is thus prohibited. The package also comes with trained supervisors who drop in on teachers to make sure they're actually sticking to the script.

The effect on the students is almost heartbreaking. Taught that reading is simply about searching contrived stories for particular "text features," they learn to hate reading. Taught that answering questions is simply about cycling through the multiple-choice answers to find the most plausible ones, they begin to stop thinking altogether and just spout random combinations of test buzzwords whenever they're asked a question. "The joy of finding things out" is banished from the classroom. Testing is in session.

Such drills don't teach children anything about the world, but it does teach them "skills"—skills like how to follow senseless orders and sit at your desk for hours at a time. Critics of high-stakes testing say that it isn't working as planned: teachers are teaching to the test instead of making sure kids actually learn. But maybe that is actually the plan. After all, employers seem to like it just fine.

Welcome to Unschooling

http://web.archive.org/web/20020101214543/http://www.swartzfam
.com:82/aaron/school/2001/04/05/

April 5, 2001

Age 14

What Is It?

When I first discovered Sudbury schools, I found them interesting. As I began to research them more, I found them fascinating. It
was only shortly ago that I found the missing piece of the puzzle:
unschooling.

Unschooling is a phenomenon that is still relatively small, but
steadily growing. I had heard mentions of unschooling, and local
unschooling organizations, but couldn't find much more information about it on the web and so I dismissed it as some sort of fringe
group that tried to de-brainwash schooled kids. Instead, as I recently
discovered, it is a powerful philosophy bounded by a simple principle: kids want to learn. It's based upon the writings of John Holt,
which are absolutely magnificent.

Unschooling someone is surprisingly simple. You first deal with
whatever regulations your state requires to home-school (my state,
Illinois, seems surprisingly liberal in this area), then the child simply
stays home and explores the world as he pleases. Parents and other
adults can provide him with advice and assistance on things he's interested in, but must do their best not to force the kid into things.
That's really all there is to it. Pretty simple, huh?

How Do I Do It?

I found out about unschooling through an incredible book: *Teenage Liberation Handbook* (*TLH*) by Grace Llewellyn. The book is a thick one, but is practically a step-by-step handbook to unschooling. It is divided into three major sections: why you should not go to school; how to get out of school; and what to do once you've gotten out. It's filled with quotes from *Growing Without Schooling,* a magazine for unschoolers to keep in touch and share ideas. (I'm subscribing and will report more on it soon.)

The real-life examples and experiences made it clear that this is no wacko fringe group, or simply a program for "gifted" kids. Instead, unschooling crosses nearly all boundaries—in fact, the book even recommends that adults try some of the ideas too. The book has plenty of experiences where unschooling has improved family relationships, "cured" cases of depression or "learning disabilities," and, most importantly, made kids much happier.

Various studies that the book cites show that unschooled children are perfectly successful in the "real world" and almost always do better on standardized tests than their schooled peers—even when they've never cracked a textbook or taken a conventional course. Furthermore, because they have plenty of time to take on real-life work like apprenticeship or volunteering, they are much more likely to develop skills needed to survive in the "real world."

How Will They Possibly Learn Without School?

TLH kindly provides help on how to keep up with all the basic subjects (English, history, math, science, art, etc.)—few of them recommend opening up a textbook or taking a class. Instead, unschooling focuses on the learning opportunities that surround us.

I learned English not from school, but by writing emails and this column, as well as reading heavily. When I tell this to other students, they say: "Oh, I wish I could do that, but I don't have enough time." Well, if they don't go to school, I'm sure that they'll have much more. It's quick and painless: just read interesting books and write about things that you're interested in. Keep doing it and your writing is sure to improve—no pain or struggle involved.

I've never liked history. It's always seemed like an abstract discussion of events and activities that had no relevance to my life and were just plain uninteresting. Worse, the only thing I was graded on was how well I memorized this boring stuff. Other students in my class are fascinated by history, and I've struggled to understand why. I recently figured it out: School teaches history backward. History classes always start towards the beginning of the story and move towards now. This may be a good way to tell a story, but it is awful for telling history. You start in a place I don't know, in a time I don't understand, with people I've never heard of. I'm not interested and I'll tune out. The answer is simple: start with the present and work backwards by asking the question: How did we get here? For one thing, you'll start in a world that I can easily connect to and associate with. For another, you'll ask the same question that I'm asking myself: how did we get here? Best of all, I'll develop a "sense of history" by truly seeing how everything fits in to where we are now. And I probably won't fall asleep.

Many believe that math must be learned in school, or at least through textbooks. This is simply not true, but merely shows the poor job of mathematical education done by schools today. For the most part, schools do not teach math: they teach computation, symbol manipulation, etc. These are only a small part of math and end up being the least interesting, since it can all be done by a calculator or a smart computer. Instead, math is really about the study of patterns and the development of theories. Math is a whole world of abstract beauty, full of puzzles to test your mind.

Science is not the memorization of uninteresting facts, as 12 years of science classes may lead you to believe. Science is merely a process of asking questions and searching answers, along with the combined knowledge accumulated from this search. The process is called the scientific method, and the best science teacher I ever had simply explained it to us and let us explore the world. Her room was filled with toys and puzzles to solve, and things to experiment with. She would often warn us of teachers she once had who had few hands-on activities and simply asked us to read through a textbook. Little did I know that these would be the science teachers I would have for the rest of my time at school. But now I realize that my scientific explorations need not be limited to her classroom, or any other. Instead, the world around us is an enormous classroom and we merely need the time to explore it, and the drive to ask questions and try to answer them.

Art is obviously something that can be learned outside of school. All one needs is the materials and the time to let their creativity flow. Schools often have many materials that allow you to explore different forms of art, and it may be useful to work out an arrangement with your school so that you can continue to use their supplies. If not, there are many art supply stores, and plenty of other ways to find the necessary materials. The most important ingredient of all, however, is creativity, which is something you must cultivate from inside yourself.

However, don't think that unschooling is limited to just a new way of learning the same subjects in school! Instead, it's just as important to do other things: become an apprentice or volunteer and learn how to take care of a "real job"; start your own business; lobby politicians and try to make changes in our government or society; go on an explorative trip around the world to learn about other cultures and ways of living; etc.

As *TLH* points out, adolescence is one of the most exciting and important times of transformation in a child. Other cultures mark it through strong and powerful experiences: the town coming together to perform a hallowed tribal ritual; sending the child out on a quest or journey, making him into a man when he returns; etc. Why do we go on like nothing is happening, throwing our children into a mind-numbing, spine-straightening, painfully useless ordeal?

Today (2001-04-04) I visited a museum which included a theme-park-like adventure. Like Indiana Jones, it had you climb through its mazes and passageways to find the stone statues of the spirits of Reason, Inspiration, Questions, and Perseverance. When you discovered each statue, it sang a little song where it stressed its importance. In the end, when you had found all of them, all the statues came together to do a little song-and-dance number about how the secret of knowledge was to balance all four of them. It was quite insightful and certainly true. If you have Reason, Inspiration, Questions, and Perseverance, it's hard to go wrong.

But Won't My Child Become an Unsocial Hermit?!

Interestingly, I've heard people dislike unschooling not because they are afraid that their children will not learn anything, but because they are afraid they will not develop "healthy social relationships with their peers." Nothing could be farther from the truth.

First, school is not a place to develop social relationships. In fact, it seems designed to stifle them. There is hardly time for socialization provided, and it is discouraged for the majority of the school day. Any student who does develop a true relationship with someone does it outside of school: at a local meeting place (like a park or mall); when going over to a friend's house; or after school. An unschooler can still do all of these things.

Second, who decided that meaningful relationships could only be had with other people who happen to be in roughly the same physical area at roughly the same age? If anything, this is a severely restrained peer group. I have developed my most meaningful relationships online. None of them live within driving distance. None of them are about my own age. Even among those who I would not count as "friends," I have met many people online who have simply commented on my work or are interested by what I do. Through the Internet, I've developed a strong social network—something I could never do if I had to keep my choice of peers within school grounds.

But I Don't Want the Kids at Home!

Now, I have sort of implied that unschooling only takes place at home. This is not true. As I said at the beginning, the unschooling movement considers Sudbury schools part of them, and playfully calls them the Unschooling Schools. Unfortunately, through all of my research in Sudbury schools, I had not heard them mention the unschooling movement—this would be especially appreciated for fans of the Sudbury model who do not have such a school close by.

Where Do We Go from Here?

I have strong hopes for the growth of the unschooling movement in the future. First, I think that it needs to get the word out: I never knew unschooling was a choice, or that others did it, until just recently—and I've done my best to research these things. So many people complain about the quality of our school systems today, and are ready for a change in the system. Unschooling is not only a change—it's a tidal wave knocking out all that we know and believe about the school system and providing a vastly different—and better—alternative.

Also, I hope to start a community for unschoolers on the web. If you know of any unschoolers, please point them to me. Have them send me an email. I'd love to see more sharing of experiences and collect this great knowledge that exists out there.

Finally, I end with a plea. If you have kids, or know kids, who are stuck in the monotony of school, give them an escape route: buy them a copy of *Teenage Liberation Handbook*. I'm sure they'll thank you for it. It's time for the kids to rise up and take control of our lives again. Our slavery has lasted long enough.

Large portions of this piece are based on an online discussion I've been having. I want to thank all who have participated and encourage you to join in the discussion if you haven't already.

School Rules

http://web.archive.org/web/20020101213828/http://www.swartzfam
.com:82/aaron/school/2000/12/12/

December 12, 2000

Age 14

"They" tell you to behave: to follow the rules, to do what they say, to be quiet and polite and kind. Don't listen to them. It's a scam.

It's school, right? What better place is there to experiment? School, while not exactly a playground, is supposed to be a safe place. It's somewhere that the consequences are small, but are there. Just enough to deter you, but not enough to hurt.

None of this was in my head as I hid out in the bathroom. These thoughts and justifications didn't come to mind as I slithered down the hallway. It wasn't there to console me as I was caught and dragged back down the hallway, onto the bus. The neurons didn't fire as I sat, in tears, through a bitter interrogation and reprimand by the principal. I never realized them as I scrubbed the desks and shelves during my Saturday detention. In fact, they didn't hit me with full force until several days ago—a full year or so after the event took place.

In the meantime, other kids asked me what it was that made me do it. It seemed so silly, so pointless. I wasn't the kind of kid that did these things, they said. I always apologized, or mumbled, or tried to change the subject. The truth was I really didn't know what kind of kid I was.

Now, however, I have an answer for them. It was part of my education—a more important part than science or history could ever be. They were events that did more to flesh me out as a person, and build my character than all the boring lectures put together. And that's the way it should be.

That's the kind of thing that the big folks don't understand, or at least they often pretend not to. They deliver their harsh words with all the anger they can muster, and perhaps they truly are angry. But some part of me can't help but wonder if deep inside they really understand. Somehow, perhaps, they know that it's a test. A test meant to crush the self-confidence of children, and, in doing so, have it grow back even stronger.

If that's true, I want to tell them that there are easier ways. Ones that work not through hatred and pain, but through love. Ways that bring out the inner strength of those who are weak, and cultivate it in those that are stronger. Ways that teach all of us—both the oppressor and the oppressed—that we're in this fight together. Instead of fighting each other, and sowing hatred that will last throughout our lives, why don't we work together to solve the problem, and share the love that we all want and need.

It seems like such a better solution. I'm a human, not some lab rat that needs to be rewarded and punished. I have reasons for what I do, you have reasons for what you want. Things between us can't be so different that we can't work them out eventually. You're probably thinking that this isn't just a good lesson for school, but a good lesson for life. And you'd be right. And if it's such a good lesson, how come we don't teach it through our actions? That's the way it seems to me at least. But I'm not the one who makes the rules.

The Writings of John Holt

April 29, 2001

Age 14

Whenever people talk about unschooling, one name comes up. That is the name of John Holt, the man who invented the concept. He wrote numerous books about his ideas and theories, but I think none are better than *How Children Fail* and *How Children Learn*.

John Holt, like many of the people involved in unschooling, was first a teacher. He felt he was a great educator, a man who always worked hard to make learning more enjoyable and fun for the students. He invented games, bought expensive educational toys, let the kids talk in class, and used innovative educational techniques. Yet he didn't [see] his folly.

It was only when he began to stop teaching and started sitting in on other classes that he began to see where he went wrong: He had never actually *watched* the kids—watched them carefully, that is. Throughout his year of careful observation, he wrote notes to his friends and the teacher with whom he shared the class, Bill Hull. These notes were published in the book, *How Children Fail*. Noticing that what went on in his class was not at all what he thought, he writes:

> You can't find out what a child does in class by looking at him only when he is called on. You have to watch him for long stretches of time without his knowing it. [. . .] There doesn't seem to be much a teacher can do about this [. . .].
> A teacher in class is like a man in the woods, at night

with a powerful flashlight in his hand. Wherever he turns his light, the creatures on whom it shines are aware of it, and thus to not behave as they do in the dark.

He began to realize that the students were not learning what he "taught" them, but merely pretending to. He discovered all of their fearful defense mechanisms and strategies, which they used so that they wouldn't appear stupid in front of their classmates and teacher.

One of the "innovative" things that John and Bill used in their classroom was a balance beam. The students would be given several weights and had to try and guess where on the beam to place them to make it balance. Here is what students said when they were asked to predict what would happen to the beam:

Abby: It might move a little to one side—not much.

Elaine: It might teeter a little then balance, but not really. (She is covering all the possibilities.)

Rachel: It might balance.

Pat: It will balance pretty much.

[. . .]

Gary: I think it's just going to go down—that's safer.

[. . .]

Gil: May go down a little and then come back up.

Garry: It will be about even.

Betty: I sort of think it's going to balance.

[. . .]

Betty: I'll say it will, just in case it does, so we won't get too low a score.

It's incredible how the students will do anything to get out of the spotlight, so that they wouldn't look foolish.

Later, John begins to throw away the teacher disguise and work with kids individually. Doing so, he realizes that students who supposedly know fifth-grade math are too unsure of themselves to even count by two. He works with them to rebuild their math knowledge from the beginning, but they still don't seem to remember what they're taught. After more of these experiences he gives up on teaching.

In his later book, *How Children Learn*, he decides to stop teaching and simply spend time with children. He starts with his small baby cousins, noticing that they are relentless scientists, always observing and experimenting. He documents their scientific inquiry as they begin to grow, read, talk, and play games. Soon enough, he begins visiting classrooms, bringing interesting toys with him and starting to play with them himself. Soon enough, the children go over to play with them, and begin to learn from them.

John does his best not to interfere—to let the children learn and discover on their own time. His only job is to give them very small nudges in the right direction and to provide moral support. One day he decides to bring the balance beam back and simply sets it in the back of the room, saying only that it's "just some junk I got from Bill Hull. [. . .] Nothing special; mess around with it if you want to." They began to do just that and half an hour later they all figured out how to work it.

I gave one of them one of the problems that in earlier years had given very able students so much trouble. She solved it easily and showed that she knew what she was doing. I said, "You have any trouble figuring that out?" She said, "Oh no, it was cinchy."

He explains it thus:

[The first set of children all had trouble] in spite of the fact that we—or so we thought—had done everything possible to set up a situation that would make discovery more easy. We worked with the children in small groups; we gave each child an easy problem; we encouraged the other children to say whether the solution to the problem was correct, and if not, why. We thought we had set up our class as a laboratory in miniature, and that the children would accordingly act as scientists. But we hadn't, and they didn't, for just for this reason, that it was our problem they were working on and not theirs.

Sadly, while it's clear to many that this kind of free exploration and discovery is the best way to learn, many teachers see it as a threat. They want to be, as John explains, "a tyrant [you better do this!] and a saint [you'll thank me for it later]." Worse, even well-meaning teachers have to throw away such toys so they stay on track with the curriculum—they can't be late for the next stop on the "Ivy League Express." But children don't learn that way. Instead, they hide, play dumb, forget, weasel their way out, or trick you. Worse, they begin to think that this is how to behave in every situation. But Holt gives the hope of another way.

I've only given you the smallest bit of the wealth of wisdom that is in these books. I encourage anyone who works at a school, or believes in one, to read a copy of *How Children Fail*—it has certainly taught me more about how my classmates think than I've been able to realize through years of being with them. Furthermore, it makes clear through simple stories why teaching plain doesn't work. Currently, John Holt's work is being continued by Holt Associates, which publishes his books and other materials.

Anyone with small children should really read *How Children Learn*. It describes in detail just that process, and by example, provides ways to keep your children learning their entire life, rather than hating the whole thing and quitting as soon as possible, as too many children do. For some children, it may be too late to unlearn the bad habits they learned in school, but it is certainly never too early.

Apprentice Education

http://web.archive.org/web/20020306075407/http://www.swartz
fam.com:82/aaron/school/2001/02/19/

February 19, 2001

Age 14

I was recently asked my opinion on how to best teach computer science. Being rather opinionated about such things, I prepared a rather long answer to the question. I soon realized that the plan was of general use, and that I hadn't written it up yet, so here it is.

This proposal, like most things, has its roots in history (both my own and that of my country). Starting with more general history, I remind you that education was originally practiced through a system of apprenticeship. One teacher would teach perhaps one or two pupils (generally their children) with hands-on, real-life experience in the trade. The system worked rather well.

Despite its success, as time continued on we began to move to a system of mandatory schooling. This system, while generally offering a broader choice of career options, also brought with it numerous problems. It detached students from their important one-on-one relationship with their teachers, separated what they learned from how it was used, and taught students the lessons of institutionalization instead of practicality. Now, when systems approximating apprenticeship are used, they are usually called modern or new-age educational methods.

However, despite the success of the current schoolhouse system, very little practical information was actually learned in school. The vast majority of education now takes place on the job, with a system just like the apprenticeship of history. Even more importantly perhaps, the ever-developing fields of technology, where new terms and ideas are being created every day, is next to impossible to teach in schools, and so people generally don't even try to. Many of the best programmers are self-taught, or are at least able to learn most of what they need to know on their own.

In terms of my personal history, I learned how to program myself through reading programs others had written, and asking questions about them on the web. Responses to my naive questions were generally courteous and almost always helpful. I got back responses extremely quickly—rarely longer than a day. And through this method I eventually learned to program. I took no preset course, and had no usual instruction. However, while I was able to learn to program through this method, there is no similar system to learn to program *well*, which is usually something altogether different.

So all of this leads me to my proposal on how to teach students for any given field. First, find a group of kind, older, wise, and respected people in the field and get them on the Internet. Then, take a group of brash, young, naive, and impatient kids who are interested [in the] field and have them do the same. Then, bring the two together and watch the magic happen.

The old will explain many things to the young, and the young will teach the old a few things too. The young will get an incredible opportunity to learn the most important things firsthand from the people who use them in real life; the old will get an opportunity to share the joy of their trade with bright-eyed kids eager to learn it.

While a one-on-one relationship between kid and adult should be encouraged, we don't want to cut off the rest of the community. It's important that everyone in the community have a chance to learn from each other. Soon, some of the best methods for explaining something will become well-known, and can be written up. This will provide the beginnings of a "textbook," but one written by the experts in the field, and with real-life subject matter—not the dry out-of-place examples of most textbooks.

What's important, however, is that we don't force anyone into this program. Everything must be voluntary, or else we'll lose the magic of community. Yet, if we're lucky, and everything succeeds, we'll have built an educational community that's free, enjoyable, and available to anyone worldwide. Sure seems like everyone wins to me.

Intellectual Diversity at Stanford

http://www.aaronsw.com/weblog/001588

February 26, 2005

Age 18

A shocking recent study has discovered that only 13% of Stanford professors are Republicans. The authors compare this to the 51% of 2004 voters who selected a Republican for president and argue this is "evidence of discrimination" and that "academic Republicans are being eradicated by academic Democrats."

Scary as this is, my preliminary research has discovered some even more shocking facts. I have found that only 1% of Stanford professors believe in telepathy (defined as "communication between minds without using the traditional five senses"), compared with 36% of the general population. And less than half a percent believe "people on this earth are sometimes possessed by the devil," compared with 49% of those outside the ivory tower. And while 25% of Americans believe in astrology ("the position of the stars and planets can affect people's lives"), I could only find one Stanford professor who would agree. (All numbers are from mainstream polls, as reported by Sokal.)

This dreadful lack of intellectual diversity is a serious threat to our nation's youth, who are quietly being propagandized by anti-astrology radicals instead of educated with different points of view. Were I to discover that there were no blacks on the Stanford faculty, the Politically Correct community would be all up in arms. But they have no problem squeezing out prospective faculty members whose *views* they disagree with.

Sure, some might say, but the color of a person's skin is irrelevant to their duties as a professor, while beliefs are at the core of the job.

And to these critics, one can only say: you "knowledge" elitists have ignored the devastating critique of factual knowledge put together by the postmodernists! Objective reality is unknowable; our beliefs about it are merely "local truths," cultural whims we could change at a moment's notice. The only fair way to decide what gets taught is by what is believed!

But these far-left academics just ignore these devastating critiques. They continue to pretend their job is to investigate "reality" and believe things based on "evidence," when everyone can see that these are merely absurd justifications for them to maintain their positions of power and status over society. And, as has widely been conceded, their advanced "search committees" and "hiring requirements" are just ways to prevent nonconformists from challenging their orthodoxies.

The party of McCarthy must save academic freedom. Wealthy businessmen must pool their resources to fight elitism. Racists and sexists must tout the values of diversity. Conservatives must embrace postmodernism. Hard work? No doubt. But they are bravely willing to sacrifice all credibility to protect our nation's youth. We should salute their courage.

David Horowitz on Academic Freedom

http://www.aaronsw.com/weblog/001591

February 27, 2005

Age 18

This is David Horowitz. Once a member of a militant far-left off-shoot, he has since found the light (and the cash) in renouncing his ways and joining the far right. His current project is to increase the right's domination of our country's universities. (You see, for the totalitarian right, control over all three branches of government, the state governments, the media, and the lower schools is not enough. Everything must be under their command.) Horowitz has packaged this attempt at thought control as "academic freedom" and "intellectual diversity," which presents some funny problems, not the least of which is that he opposes gender and racial diversity.

But I get ahead of myself. The talk is funded by the Stanford Hillel (I can't believe I almost considered thinking about looking at joining this disgusting far-right organization—actual talk name: "Why do Jews vote the way they do?") and Young America's Foundation (a right-wingers-on-campus group). There's very low turnout. It's in the same auditorium that hosted Amy Goodman, but instead of being standing-room-only, there are only a couple dozen people at all. I wonder how much the Stanford Hillel paid for this mess.

Horowitz has nothing to do, so he wanders through the small audience. Although I sit 2/3s of the way back, he manages to come out and sign a book for the guy behind me. "I visit FrontPageMag.com [Horowitz's website] every day," he gushes. Horowitz doesn't have a pen, so I lend him mine. (I lent Horowitz a pen!) "I tell all my friends to visit," the fan continues, "but so far all I get is epithets." I try to

hide my copy of *A People's History of the United States* as Horowitz gives
me the pen back, in order to avoid some epithets of my own.

A lady from YAF introduces Horowitz, explaining that "local phi-
lanthropists" have funded a 3-campus tour in the area. Before the
talk has even started, she already neatly refutes any pretense that
this is going to be about stifling bias or promoting diversity: she explains that she got interested in this topic because she once went to
a Stanford alumni event where a professor gave a talk on Palestinian
history. She "burned with shame" at how he (in her view) distorted
the facts, quoted out of context, pursued a "Marxist-based agenda"
which, although she could apparently discover it, remained "subter-
ranean" to everyone else. And then, to top it all off, he said he didn't
believe in objective truth! Teaching one point of view, the lady concludes, is like a pedophile giving advance warning: it's not OK.

(In reality, it's pretty obvious the guy simply gave a partway accurate description of Palestinian history and then probably echoed
Howard Zinn's comment that "any chosen emphasis supports
[whether the historian means to or not] some kind of interest." So
did she just compare all mainstream historians to pedophiles?)

An actual student follows the lady and thanks all the funding
groups: the Stanford Jewish-American Alliance, Hillel, Chabad,
Young America's Foundation. According to the bio he reads,
Horowitz was once a "civil rights activist" (this is apparently referring to Horowitz's association with the Black Panther Party) who
now runs a popular conservative website which gets 1 million readers a month.

Finally it's time for Horowitz himself. He praises Stanford for being a "civilized" institution since, unlike Berkeley and San Francisco
State University, he does not need 8 armed guards to protect his right
to speak. (Outside I notice 2 possibly armed guards, although since
nobody showed up, they don't seem to have much to do.) He says this
civility is because the university management carefully "disciplin[es]
troublemakers" to enforce decorum, so he thanks the management
for that.

Horowitz lays out his basic argument: "You can't get a good education if you only get half the story. And you're not getting a good
education." A recent study of Stanford and Berkeley found Kerry sup-

porters outnumbered 30 to 1, hardly a presence at all. Why? Because political radicals who didn't want to fight Communism got student deferments that led to graduate degrees and faculty jobs. They took over the search committees and transformed the entire culture. (Yes, Horowitz actually talks like this.)

Sure, some of it is self-selection. Leftists are by nature missionaries since, following Rousseau, they believe "man is born free, but he is everywhere in chains," while conservatives understand that the corruption is in our nature and institutions just reflect it. (I'm actually impressed with Horowitz's keen grasp of this—I don't think I've ever heard any other figure articulate the differences quite so clearly. Apparently it's from right-winger Thomas Sowell's *A Conflict of Visions*.) So leftists go into "missionary professions": journalism, teaching, politics. But we have to break up this leftist control so that students get a diversity of views.

How do they do it? They control the search committees. He's been on 250 campuses—at every one there are at most 2 or 3 professors who are sympathetic to him. One, in November 2001 in Delaware, told him that he simply wasn't allowed on the search committees. Conservatives, Horowitz says, believe in process and different points of view. But the leftists just wanted to hire another Marxist. At another university, a prospective professor says that he was about to get a job as an Asian history professor but the offer was rescinded after he let slip that he supported school vouchers. When Horowitz was a Marxist he was never singled out like that.

Professors, he says, should never reveal their political perspectives. After all, doctors don't have politics; they're professionals. But professors have the audacity to put political cartoons on their doors, scaring away timid conservatives. The administration should stop them. (Yes, he just promoted a ban on posting cartoons on your door.)

(Horowitz does a bit on Ward Churchill, which I won't go into. As an aside, Horowitz mentions that the left controls the Nobel Prizes too, because how else could Rigoberta Menchu have won?)

But all this discrimination has its benefits—conservatives have been toughened by being oppressed, they have to come up with answers to professors' questions about their beliefs, while people on the left are clueless and not familiar with the most basic conservative critiques.

(Horowitz does a bit about the war on terror; I'll omit that too, except to note that he said, "We're told the Iraq War is not about the war on terror. But all the attacks came from Arab Muslims. This is their home.")

"Campuses are, to some extent, fear societies. Kids fear they'll be denounced a racist. Or a right-winger. Campuses are less free than any other time, at least since Salem. They were *way* more free dung the McCarthy era."

Leslie Cagan of United for Peace and Justice (a Stalinist Muslim pro-terrorist North Korean Marxist-Leninist group, Horowitz says to applause) organized a teachers' strike on campus against the war, apparently. Horowitz would have fired everyone who refused to teach. Stanford may be civilized, but it still has a ways to go. (Apparently by civilized, Horowitz means uncivilized.) Lynn Stewart, the lawyer who was convicted for defending a terrorist, was a guest at the Stanford Law School. (Not so civilized.) In other news, the National Lawyers Guild is a "Soviet front," the Center for Constitutional Rights is a "Communist organization," and Lynn Stewart gave a toast to Marx, Ho, Lenin, and Mumia Abu-Jamal.

Leftist curriculum supports our enemies. Read his quotes from Todd Gitlin. "What they say about our history is the same as Hamas": the U.S. is the Great Satan. There's another way to teach history. In every "Indian war," there were the same number of Indians on the side of the settlers as on the side of the Indians, Horowitz says. (I really have a hard time believing that.) And while it's true we had slavery, they had slavery in Africa for hundreds of years—it was dead white *Christian* males in the U.S. and England who led the world in getting rid of it because it was an offense to God. (Please.)

We have to teach students this uplifting version of American history because if you're not taught to be proud of your country, you cannot defend yourself.

The talk ends and we move to Q&A. I notice Horowitz has failed to mention what we can do to fight this insidious leftist control. I get in line.

The first person asks Horowitz how to distinguish this from affirmative action. Horowitz sort of dodges the question, talking more about how conservatives are discriminated against in his view, before assuring me that he doesn't support a requirement of hiring conservatives, he just thinks the management should seek out good conservatives (he mentions Thomas Sowell as an example) and hire them.

Another student asks how liberals managed to take control of everything. "Hollywood isn't liberal," Horowitz replies. (This is pretty shocking, since Horowitz's previous job was fighting leftists in Hollywood—maybe his work is done?) Harvard is a lifetime job, but Hollywood has to reflect the culture. "Market institutions are somewhat self-correcting"—just look at talk radio, Fox, the Internet. Roger Ailes introduced the idea of two sides. But universities are still feudal. The only solution is to create a new faculty in a conservative studies department, just like women's studies, which could grow as the students vote with their feet. (I guess the economics department isn't enough for him.)

A military man says he's concerned because leftists are becoming anti-U.S. Horowitz says he's worried too. Bush-hatred, he explains, is simply a foil for America-hatred, because how could you possibly hate Bush? (Yes, he really did say that.) He's a strong leader and the leftists hate that. A girl in line responds that she doesn't like Bush (maybe she's a libertarian?) and thinks she should be able to disagree with him without hating America. Horowitz explains that Bush-*hatred* is the problem, not disagreement. "Friends disagree with me, but they don't compare me to Hitler!"

It's my turn. I say that I understand programs to ensure blacks and women aren't discriminated against, but why do conservatives deserve special treatment? Horowitz emphasizes that he's against affirmative action and says that his point is that exposure to new ideas is far more important than skin color. (The audience applauds at Horowitz's ability to evade my poorly constructed question.)

Finally, someone asks what we can do about it. Horowitz says he's started a group, StudentsForAcademicFreedom.org (200K visitors!), where conservatives can tattle on oppressive leftists. (Some samples: "I wrote about how family values in the books weve [sic] read aren't good. I know the paper was pretty much great because I spell checked it and proofred [sic] it twice. I got an D- just because the professor hates families and thinks its [sic] okay to be gay." "Talked about flags as symbols of states and argued that new Iraqi flag was not a result of a transparent and fair process . . . Claimed AS FACT that other Arab societies had red, green and black in their flags . . .") The only people opposed to his work are totalitarian professors.

He's also promoting the "Academic Bill of Rights" and while he doesn't say what it says or what it does, he assures us it's a "very liberal document." He showed it to some real liberals—Stanley Fish, Todd Gitlin (so liberal he once called for a million Mogadishus! [wrong!]), Michael Berubé (who, Horowitz says, once compared him to Hitler! Well, a propagandist for Hitler [wrong!])—and took out anything that irritated them. They approved "every jot and tittle."

Well, this didn't sound right to me—after all, Michael Berubé has some very funny posts at Horowitz's expense: Keeping conservatives out of academe, International leftist network exposed!, Clumpy v. smooth, Time to respond to Horowitz's post—and of course it turned out to be a big lie. Stanley Fish called the Bill of Rights "the Trojan horse of a dark design," Gitlin calls it "a distinctly retro, vindictive approach," and Berubé insists he "rather pointedly declined to sign it, as David asked me to, precisely because it would lead to all manner of absurd conclusions."

Anyway, Horowitz pretends the only people who oppose the bill are the American Association of University Professors, who called it a "grave threat" to academic freedom. (If you've been following along, it's pretty obvious they're leftist Stalinist Marxist terrorists.)

The bill, Horowitz explains, just says we don't know the truth and students should get the spectrum of views. Classrooms should not be used for indoctrinating, they should reflect political diversity, they shouldn't let ROTC students be called baby-killers.

Horowitz explains how he gets these bills passed. The university board really supports the bill, since it helps him get donors, but he doesn't want to fight the 50 or so extreme Marxists about it. So Horowitz goes to the legislature (controlled by Republicans) and has them pretend to pass the bill, then goes back to the university and says "You can pass this bill or we can pass it for you" and they pass it and the legislature withdraws it. Horowitz doesn't really want to regulate universities, so this is a win for him.

And time is up. The next day the *Stanford Daily* reports that "during his time on campus, Horowitz met with Jeff Wachtel, senior assistant to University President John Hennessy, to lobby for the adoption of the Academic Bill of Rights at Stanford."

Horowitz reposted the *Daily* article on his site under the heading "Horowitz Rocks Leftist Academia at Stanford," and pointing out some mistakes the paper made. (Hilariously, the paper heard "United for Peace and Justice is led by a '60s Stalinist" as "United for Peace and Justice is led by 60 Stalinists," although apparently they heard the bit about it being a "Muslim pro-terrorist" and "North Korean Marxist Leninist group" correctly.)

What It Means to Be an Intellectual

http://www.aaronsw.com/weblog/intellectuals

April 17, 2006

Age 19

A friend sent me an email this morning and at the end of it, almost as an afterthought, he responded to a quote I'd sent him from an author praising books. "He would say that," my friend replied, "he's a writer."

I want to quibble with this statement—how is it that we can dismiss someone's argument simply because of their job?—but doing so would seem bizarre. There's a social norm that how much we discuss something should be roughly proportional to its importance. Mountains of print may be spilled on the issues of international relations, but spending a couple emails discussing punctuation would seem dreadfully bizarre.

There's just one problem: I *enjoy* deep discussions of punctuation and other trivialities. I could try to justify this taste—some argument that we should think about everything we do so that we don't do everything we think about—but why bother? Do I have to justify enjoying certain television shows as well? At some point, isn't pure enjoyment just enough? After all, time isn't fungible.

But of course, the same drive that leads me to question punctuation leads me to question the drive itself, and thus this essay.

What is "this drive"? It's the tendency to not simply accept things as they are but to want to think about them, to understand them. To not be content to simply feel sad but to ask what sadness means. To not just get a bus pass but to think about the economic reasons getting a bus pass makes sense. I call this tendency the intellectual.

The word "intellectual" has a bit of a bad rap. When I think of the word I hear a man with a southern accent sneering at it. But this stain seems appropriate—*the idea* has a bad rap.

And why is that? One reason is that many people simply don't like to think about things. Perhaps it reminds them of school, which they didn't enjoy, and they don't want to go back there. Another is that they're busy people—men of action—and they don't have time to sit and think about every little detail. But mostly it's just because they think it's a waste of time. What's the point? What difference does it make what you think about punctuation? It's not going to affect anything.

This is the argument that's often used when demonizing intellectuals. As Thomas Frank summarizes the argument:

> The same bunch of sneaking intellectuals are responsible for the content of Hollywood movies and for the income tax, by which they steal from the rest of us. They do no useful work, producing nothing but movies and newspaper columns while they freeload on the labor of others.

When I think of intellectuals, though, I don't really think of Hollywood producers or politicians or even newspaper columnists. But the people I do think of seem to have something else in common. They don't just love thinking, they love language. They love its tricks and intricacies, its games, the way it gets written down, the books it gets written into, the libraries those books are in, and the typography those books use.

Upon reflection this makes perfect sense. Language is the medium of thought, and so it's no surprise that someone who spends a lot of time thinking spends a lot of time thinking about how to communicate their thoughts as well. And indeed, all the intellectuals that come to mind write, not because they have to or get paid to, but simply for its own sake. What good is thinking if you can't share?

This contrasts with how intellectuals are commonly thought of—namely as pretentious elitist snobs. But real intellectuals, at least in the sense I'm using the term, are anything but. They love nothing more than explaining their ideas so that anyone who's interested can understand them. They only seem pretentious because discussing such things is so bizarre.

This stereotype actually seems more like the caricature of the academic than the intellectual. (It's perhaps worth noting that most of the intellectuals I can think of *aren't* academics or at least have left the academy.) Far from being intellectuals, academics are encouraged to be almost the opposite. Instead of trying to explain things simply, they're rewarded for making them seem more complicated. Instead of trying to learn about everything, they're forced to focus in on their little subdiscipline. Instead of loving books, they have to love gabbing—up in front of class or at office hour with students or at professional conferences or faculty meetings.

Not that there's anything wrong with that. At the beginning I declined to justify my being an intellectual on any grounds other than pure personal enjoyment. And here, at the end, I can't think of any better justification. Certainly people should think deeply about their actions and the world's problems and other important topics. But the other ones? That's little more than personal preference.

Getting It Wrong

http://www.aaronsw.com/weblog/gettingitwrong

October 12, 2006

Age 19

Anyone who's spent any time around little kids in school, or even read books about people who have, knows that they're terrified of getting the answer wrong. Geez, you don't even need to hang around little kids. When you're out chatting with a bunch of people and you say something that shows you didn't know something, you look embarrassed. When you're playing a video game and not doing well, you try to come up with an excuse. People hate failing, so much so that they're afraid to try.

Which is a problem, because failing is most of what we do, most of the time. The only way to stretch your abilities is to try to do things a little bit beyond them, which means you're going to fail some of the time. Even weirder are the competitive situations. If I'm playing a game that relies solely on practice against someone who's practiced more than me, I'm probably going to lose, no matter how good a person I am. Yet I still feel degraded when I do.

Anyone who wants to build a decent educational environment is going to need to solve this problem. And there seem to be two ways of doing it: try and fix the people so that they don't feel embarrassed at failing, or try to fix the environment so that people don't fail. Which option to pick sometimes gets people into philopolitical debates (trying to improve kids' self-esteem means they won't be able to handle the real world! Preventing kids from experiencing failure is just childish coddling!), but for now let's just be concerned with what works.

Getting people to be OK with being wrong seems tough, if only because everybody I know has this problem to a greater or lesser degree. There are occasional exceptions—mavericks like Richard Feynman (why do *you* care what other people think?) often seem fearless, although it's hard to gauge how much of that was staged—but these just seem random, with no patterns suggesting *why*.

It seems quite likely that a lot of the fear is induced by a goal-oriented educational system, obsessed with grades for work (A, B, C) and grades for students (1st, 2nd, 3rd). And perhaps the fear of being wrong you see in older people stems from having been through such experiences in childhood. If this is the case, then simply building a decent non-coercive environment for children will solve the problem, but that seems like too much to hope for.

Perhaps the solution is in, as some suggest, building self-esteem, so that when kids are wrong on one thing, they have other things to fall back on. I certainly see this process operating in my own mind: "Pff, sure they can beat me in *Guitar Hero*, but at least I can go back to writing blog entries." But self-esteem is like a cushion: it prevents the fall from being too damaging, but it doesn't prevent the fall.

The real piece, it would seem, is finding some way to detach a student's actions from their worth. The reason failing hurts is because we think it reflects badly on us. I failed, therefore I'm a failure. But if that's not the case, then there's nothing to feel hurt about.

Detaching a self from your actions might seem like a silly thing, but lots of different pieces of psychology point to it. Richard Layard, in his survey *Happiness: Lessons from a New Science*, notes that studies consistently find that people who are detached from their surroundings—whether through Buddhist meditation, Christian belief in God, or cognitive therapy—are happier people. "All feelings of joy and even physical pain are observed to fluctuate, and we see ourselves as like a wave of the sea—where the sea is eternal and the wave is just its present form" (p. 191).

Similarly, Alfie Kohn, who looks more specifically at the studies about children, finds that it's essential for a child's mental health that parents communicate that they love their child for who they are, no matter what it is they *do*. This concept can lead to some nasty philosophical debates—what are people, if not collections of things done?—but the practical implications are clear. Children, indeed all people, need unconditional love and support to be able to survive in this world. Attachment parenting studies find that even infants are afraid to explore a room unless their mother is close by to support them, and the same findings have been found in monkeys.

The flip side is: how do we build educational institutions that discourage these ways of thinking? Obviously we'll want to get rid of competition as well as grades, but even so, as we saw with Mission Hill, kids are scared of failure.

While I'm loath to introduce *more* individualism into American schools, it seems clear that one solution is to have people do work on their own. Kids are embarrassed in front of the class, shy people get bullied in small groups, so all that really leaves is to do it on your own.

And this does seem effective. People seem more likely to ask "stupid" questions if they get to write them down on anonymous cards. When people fail in a video game, it only makes them want to try again right away so they can finally beat it. Apparently when nobody knows you're getting it wrong, it's a lot easier to handle it. Maybe because you know it can't affect the way people see you.

Schools can also work to discourage this kind of conditional seeing by making it completely unimportant. Even Mission Hill, which ensured every classroom was mixed-age, still had a notion of age and clear requirements for graduating. What if school, instead of a bunch of activities you had to march through, was a bunch of activities students could pick and choose from? When people are no longer marching, it's hard to be worried about your place in line.

But can we take the next step? Can schools not just see their students unconditionally, but actually encourage them to see themselves that way? Clearly we could teach everybody Buddhist meditation or something (which, studies apparently show, is effective), but even better would be if there was something in the structure of the school that encouraged this way of thinking.

Removing deadlines and requirements should help students live more fully in the moment. Providing basic care to every student should help them feel valued as people. Creating a safe and trusting environment should free them from having to keep track of how much they can trust everyone else. And, of course, all the same things would be positive in the larger society.

Too often, people think of schools as systems for building good people. Perhaps it's time to think of them as places to let people be good.

EPILOGUE

Legacy

http://www.aaronsw.com/weblog/legacy

June 1, 2006

Age 19

Ambitious people want to leave legacies, but what sort of legacies do they want to leave? The traditional criterion is that your importance is measured by the effect of what you do. Thus the most important lawyers are the Supreme Court justices, since their decisions affect the entire nation. And the greatest mathematicians are those that make important discoveries, since their discoveries end up being used by many who follow.

This seems quite reasonable. One's legacy depends on one's impact, and what better way to measure impact than by the effect of what you've done? But this is measuring against the wrong baseline. The real question is not what effect your work had, but what things would be like had you never done it.

The two are not at all the same. It is rather commonly accepted that there are "ideas whose time has come," and history tends to bear this out. When Newton invented the calculus, so did Leibniz. When Darwin discovered evolution through natural selection, so did Alfred Russel Wallace. When Alexander Graham Bell invented the telephone, so did Elisha Gray (before him, arguably).

In these cases the facts are plain: had Newton, Darwin, and Bell never done their work, the result would have been largely the same— we'd still have calculus, evolution, and the telephone. And yet such people are hailed as major heroes, their legacies immortalized.

Perhaps, if one only cares about such things, this is enough. (Although this seems a rather dangerous game, since the future could wake up at any moment and realize its adulation is misplaced.) But if one genuinely cares about their impact, instead of simply how their impact is perceived, more careful thought is in order.

I once spent time with a well-known academic, who had published several works widely recognized as classics even outside his field, and he offered some career advice in the sciences. (Actually, come to think of it, there are two people of whom this is true, suggesting the phenomenon has broader significance.) Such-and-such a field is very hot right now, he said, you could really make a name for yourself by getting into it. The idea being that major discoveries were sure to follow soon and that if I picked that field I could be the one to make them.

By my test, such a thing would leave a poor legacy. (For what it's worth, I don't think either person's works fall into this category; that is to say, their reputation is still deserved even by these standards.) Even worse, you'd know it. Presumably Darwin and Newton didn't begin their investigations because they thought the field was "hot." They thought through doing it they would have a significant impact, even though that turned out to be wrong. But someone who joined a field simply because they thought a major discovery would come from it soon could never enjoy such a delusion. Instead, they would know that their work would make little difference, and would have to labor under such impressions.

The same is true of other professions we misconceive of as being important. Take being a Supreme Court justice, for example. Traditionally, this is thought of as a majestic job in which one gets to make decisions of great import. In fact, it seems to me that one has little impact at all. Most of your impact was made by the politics of the president who appointed you. Had you not been around for the job, he would have found someone else who would take similar positions. The only way one could have a real impact as Supreme Court justice would be to change your politics once appointed to the bench, and the only way you could prepare for such a thing would be to spend the majority of your career doing things you thought were wrong in the hopes that one day you might get picked for the Supreme Court. That seems a rather hard lot to swallow.

So what jobs do leave a real legacy? It's hard to think of most of them, since by their very nature they require doing things that other people *aren't* trying to do, and thus include the things that people haven't thought of. But one good source of them is trying to do things that change the system instead of following it. For example, the university system encourages people to become professors who do research in certain areas (and thus many people do this); it discourages people from trying to change the nature of the university itself.

Naturally, doing things like changing the university are much harder than simply becoming yet another professor. But for those who genuinely care about their legacies, it doesn't seem like there's much choice.

CONTRIBUTOR BIOS

Aaron Swartz (1986 2013) was an American computer programmer, a writer, a political organizer, and an Internet hacktivist. He was involved in the development of RSS, Creative Commons, web.py, and Reddit. He helped launch the Progressive Change Campaign Committee in 2009 and founded the online group Demand Progress. He is survived by his parents and two brothers, who live in Chicago.

Lawrence Lessig is the director of the Edmon J. Safra Center for Ethics at Harvard University and a professor of law at the Harvard Law School. He was a founding board member of Creative Commons. He lives in Cambridge, Massachusetts.

Benjamin Mako Hill is an assistant professor in the Department of Communication at the University of Washington and a faculty affiliate at the Berkman Center for Internet and Society at Harvard. He is a participant and leader in free software and free culture communities.

Seth Schoen is senior staff technologist at the Electronic Frontier Foundation in San Francisco, where he worries about technology users' freedom and autonomy. He and Aaron were friends for over a decade; they first met at the U.S. Supreme Court in 2002.

David Auerbach is a writer and software engineer who lives in New York. He writes the "Bitwise" column for *Slate*.

David Segal is the executive director and co-founder of the activism organization Demand Progress. He previously served as a member of the Providence City Council and as a Rhode Island state representative. He ran for Congress in 2010, backed by much of the "netroots," organized labor, and the Rhode Island progressive movement. During his tenure at Demand Progress he has helped lead various grassroots efforts to protect Internet freedom, including the successful defeat of the Stop Online Piracy Act (SOPA). He co-edited and wrote much of a book about that effort, called *Hacking Politics*. His writing on public policy matters has appeared in a variety of publications. He holds a degree in mathematics from Columbia University.

Henry Farrell is associate professor of political science and international affairs at George Washington University. He works on a variety of topics, including trust, the politics of the Internet, and international and comparative political economy. He has written articles and book chapters as well as a book, *The Political Economy of Trust: Interests, Institutions and Inter-Firm Cooperation*, published by Cambridge University Press.

Cory Doctorow is a Canadian-British blogger, journalist, and science fiction author who serves as co-editor of the blog Boing Boing. He is an activist in favor of liberalizing copyright laws and a proponent of the Creative Commons organization, using some of their licenses for his books. Some common themes of his work include digital rights management, file sharing, and post-scarcity economics. His novels include *Down and Out in the Magic, Kingdom,* and *Little Brother.*

James Grimmelmann is a professor of law at the University of Maryland. He studies how laws regulating software affect freedom, wealth, and power.

Astra Taylor is a writer and documentary filmmaker. Her films include *Zizek!,* a feature documentary about the world's most outrageous philosopher, which was broadcast on the Sundance Channel, and *Examined Life,* a series of excursions with contemporary thinkers. Her writing has appeared in *The Nation, Salon, Monthly Review, The Baffler,* and other publications. Her most recent book is *The People's Platform.* She lives in New York City.

This volume was edited by **Jed Bickman**, currently an associate editor at The New Press.

PUBLISHING IN THE PUBLIC INTEREST

Thank you for reading this book published by The New Press. The New Press is a nonprofit, public interest publisher. New Press books and authors play a crucial role in sparking conversations about the key political and social issues of our day.

We hope you enjoyed this book and that you will stay in touch with The New Press. Here are a few ways to stay up to date with our books, events, and the issues we cover:

- Sign up at www.thenewpress.com/subscribe to receive updates on New Press authors and issues and to be notified about local events
- Like us on Facebook: www.facebook.com/newpressbooks
- Follow us on Twitter: www.twitter.com/thenewpress

Please consider buying New Press books for yourself; for friends and family; or to donate to schools, libraries, community centers, prison libraries, and other organizations involved with the issues our authors write about.

The New Press is a 501(c)(3) nonprofit organization. You can also support our work with a tax-deductible gift by visiting www.thenewpress.com/donate.

THE STUDS AND IDA TERKEL AWARD

On the occasion of his ninetieth birthday, Studs Terkel and his son, Dan, announced the creation of the Studs and Ida Terkel Author Fund. The Fund is devoted to supporting the work of promising authors in a range of fields who share Studs's fascination with the many dimensions of everyday life in America and who, like Studs, are committed to exploring aspects of America that are not adequately represented by the mainstream media. The Terkel Fund furnishes authors with the vital support they need to conduct their research and writing, providing a new generation of writers the freedom to experiment and innovate in the spirit of Studs's own work.

Studs and Ida Terkel Award Winners

Aaron Swartz, *The Boy Who Could Change the World: The Writings of Aaron Swartz* (awarded posthumously)

Beth Zasloff and Joshua Steckel, *Hold Fast to Dreams: A College Guidance Counselor, His Students, and the Vision of a Life Beyond Poverty*

Barbara J. Miner, *Lessons from the Heartland: A Turbulent Half-Century of Public Education in an Iconic American City*

Lynn Powell, *Framing Innocence: A Mother's Photographs, a Prosecutor's Zeal, and a Small Town's Response*

Lauri Lebo, *The Devil in Dover: An Insider's Story of Dogma v. Darwin in Small-Town America*